NEAL'S YARD

COVENT   GARDEN

REMEDIES

 Penguin
Random
House

Editor Susannah Steel
Photographers Peter Anderson,
Peter Kindersley, William Reavell

Project Editor Sarah Ruddick
Project Art Editor Kathryn Wilding
Managing Editor Dawn Henderson
Senior Managing Art Editor Marianne Markham
Senior Jacket Creative Nicola Powling
Senior Presentations Creative Caroline de Souza
Pre-Production Producer Rebecca Fallowfield
Producer Olivia Jeffries
Special Sales Creative Project Manager
Alison Donovan

DK INDIA
Editors Alicia Ingty, Chitra Subramanyam
Art Editors Neha Ahuja, Devika Dwarkadas,
Shruti Soharia Singh
Managing Editor Glenda Fernandes
Senior Designer (Lead) Navidita Thapa
Production Manager Pankaj Sharma
DTP Manager Sunil Sharma
Senior DTP Designers Dheeraj Arora,
Jagtar Singh
DTP Designers Neeraj Bhatia, Tarun Sharma

This paperback edition published in 2015
First published in Great Britain in 2011 by
Dorling Kindersley Limited
80 Strand, London WC2R 0RL

Copyright © 2011, 2015 Dorling Kindersley Limited
A Penguin Random House Company
001–178140–Sept/15

DISCLAIMER: See page 352

A CIP catalogue record for this book is available
from the British Library.
ISBN 978-0-2411-8389-2

Colour reproduction by Colourscan, Singapore
Printed and bound in China

All images © Dorling Kindersley Limited
For further information see: **www.dkimages.com**

A WORLD OF IDEAS:
SEE ALL THERE IS TO KNOW

www.dk.com

Contents

Tanacetum parthenium
Feverfew

THE AUTHORS

Susan Curtis
Susan runs a busy practice as a homeopath and naturopath and is the Director of Natural Health for Neal's Yard Remedies. She is the author of several books, including *Essential Oils*, and co-author of *Natural Healing for Women*. Susan has two children and is passionate about helping people to live a more natural and healthy lifestyle.

Louise Green
An avid supporter of the organic movement and eco-living, Louise has spent 15 years at Neal's Yard Remedies in a variety of roles ranging from buying to product development, and most recently as Head of Sustainability. Louise lives in London and is expecting her first child.

Penelope Ody MNIMH
Penelope qualified as a medical herbalist in the 1980s and practised as a consultant herbalist for 12 years. Since then she has written more than 20 books on both Western and Chinese herbalism and runs workshops on traditional uses of culinary and medicinal herbs at her home in Hampshire.

Dragana Vilinac
A fourth-generation herbalist widely respected for her vast knowledge and expertise, Dragana's passion for herbal medicine has taken her around the world, and has led her to train in disciplines including Western Herbal Medicine and Traditional Chinese Medicine. Dragana is Head Herbalist for Neal's Yard Remedies.

Introduction

According to the World Health Organization, herbal remedies are the most widespread system of medicine used in the world. In many developed countries that knowledge was almost lost, but the last couple of decades have seen a renewed interest in herbal remedies, and more and more people are recognizing the many benefits of using them to treat themselves and their family.

Used appropriately, herbs can be a satisfying part of a more holistic lifestyle, and many herbs are of course the starting point of much of the modern medicine used today. When used with common sense, herbal remedies are a safe and effective form of home help. If we can treat colds, flu, or minor injuries in the early stages we can often prevent the development of something more serious and avoid using conventional drugs with their risk of side-effects.

Learning which herbs work for us enables us to learn more about the plants that surround us, as well as our own healing processes. However, some herbs are not suitable for everyone or at every stage of life (during pregnancy, for example); if in any doubt you should always consult a medical practitioner.

We have "tried and tested" all the recipes in this book, so we can promise they are delicious as well as being good for you. We are excited to have the opportunity to introduce you to some more unusual plants and flavours so you can be more adventurous whilst trusting that your health and well-being will benefit.

Neal's Yard Remedies has over thirty years of expertise and passion in creating wonderful, natural hair- and skincare products and we are delighted to share some of our favourite ways of using herbs to heal and nurture your skin. Enjoy creating and using your own herbal remedies!

Susan Curtis, Natural Health Director, Neal's Yard Remedies

Consultant's note

Hippocrates, the father of medicine, wrote: "Let food be thy medicine, and medicine be thy food". Many herbs described in this book are used both as tasty foods and as medicines, and the delicious recipes provide new ideas for combining healthy ingredients. Although the herbal medicines have not yet all been researched by modern science, most have stood the test of time. You should always see your doctor for serious health problems, but I hope this book will help readers to treat and prevent minor illnesses, and to understand treatments prescribed by their herbalist.

Dr Merlin Willcox MRCGP MCPP

A–Z of Herbs

Discover 100 of the most useful medicinal herbs for natural health and well-being; find out how to use each herb to cure common ailments at home, as well as how to grow, forage, and harvest the herbs for yourself.

Achillea millefolium **Yarrow**

Native to Europe and western Asia, yarrow was traditionally used to treat wounds, although it was also once used in Germany and the Nordic countries as an alternative to hops in beer-making. Today it is valued for its astringent and anticatarrhal properties, and is used in remedies for colds and urinary disorders. It is widely naturalized in North America, New Zealand, and Australia.

FLOWERS
White, occasionally tinged pink, musk-scented flowers are produced from early summer to late autumn

LEAVES
The feathery leaves were once used in poultices to encourage blood clots to develop when treating battlefield wounds and severe bleeding

STEM
The tough stem and leaves can be harvested together in summer. The whole plant is highly aromatic

1m (3ft)

GROWTH HABIT
A matt-forming hardy perennial; spread 5–20cm (2–8in).

PARTS USED Leaves, flowers, essential oil
MAIN CONSTITUENTS Volatile oil, isovalerianic acid, asparagine, salicylic acid, sterols, flavonoids
ACTIONS Astringent, diaphoretic, peripheral vasodilator, digestive stimulant, restorative for menstrual system, febrifuge Essential oil: anti-inflammatory, anti-allergenic

HOW TO USE

INFUSION Take 1 cup of a standard infusion (p.342) 3 times a day to encourage sweating and reduce fevers; combines well with elderflower and peppermint for common colds. One cup stimulates the appetite.
TINCTURE Use 1–2ml (20–40 drops) 3 times daily, usually with herbs such as couchgrass or buchu, for urinary disorders.
FRESH LEAVES A single leaf inserted in the nostril will rapidly stop a nosebleed.
OINTMENT Apply to minor cuts and grazes.
MASSAGE OIL Add 10 drops of yarrow essential oil to 25ml (5 tsp) of infused St John's wort oil to make a rub for hot, inflamed joints.
STEAM INHALATION Use 1 tbsp fresh flowers in boiling water to ease hayfever symptoms. Inhale the steam for at least 2–3 minutes.

HOW TO SOURCE

GROW Prefers a well-drained position in full sun, but is tolerant of a wide range of conditions. Sow seeds in spring. Propagation by root division is best in spring or autumn. It can easily become invasive.
FORAGE Generally found in pasture, hedgerows, or among grass in meadows throughout Europe.
HARVEST Gather leaves and aerial parts in summer, and flowers when they appear.

CAUTION In rare cases yarrow can cause skin rashes, and prolonged use can increase skin photosensitivity. Avoid during pregnancy. Essential oils should not be taken internally without professional advice.

Actaea racemosa **Black cohosh**

Originally found in Canada and the eastern parts of the USA, black cohosh was a favourite remedy with Native Americans. It was used for a range of gynaecological disorders, snakebites, fevers, and rheumatism. It has been used in Europe since the 19th century, and is also known as *Cimicifuga racemosa*. Some cases of liver damage have been reported, and it is restricted in some countries.

FLOWER BUD
When in bloom in late summer, the fragrant flowers are fluffy and white, and sometimes described as being like a bottle brush

LEAVES
When fully unfurled, the elegant, divided basal leaves are as much as 90cm (36in) in length, making this plant a distinctive addition to a woodland garden

GROWTH HABIT
Erect, clump-forming woodland perennial with a spread of 60cm (24in).

2m (6ft)

PARTS USED Root and rhizome
MAIN CONSTITUENTS Cinnamic acid derivatives, chromone, isoflavones, tannins, triterpene glycosides, salicylic acid
ACTIONS Antispasmodic, anti-arthritic, anti-inflammatory, antirheumatic, mild analgesic, relaxing nervine, relaxes blood vessels, emmenagogue, diuretic, sedative, antitussive, hypotensive, hypoglycaemic

HOW TO USE

TINCTURE Take 20–40 drops in a little water 3 times daily for period pain; combine with an equal amount of motherwort tincture and take 3 times daily for hot flushes, night sweats, and emotional upsets associated with the menopause. Take 20 drops 3 times daily with an equal amount of valerian to support treatments for high blood pressure.
DECOCTION Use 15g (½oz) of the root in 900ml (1½ pints) of water simmered for 15 minutes – twice daily for rheumatic pains, lumbago, facial neuralgia, sciatica, or tendonitis.
TABLETS/CAPSULES Use for menopausal problems or rheumatic disorders; follow dosage directions on the pack. It is best not to take more than 40–80mg daily.
SYRUP Combine 300ml (10fl oz) of a decoction (made as above) with 225g (8oz) of sugar or honey, bring to the boil, and simmer gently for 5–10 minutes to make a syrup. Take in 5ml (1 tsp) doses every 2–3 hours for whooping cough and bronchitis.

HOW TO SOURCE

GROW Prefers moist, fertile soil in dappled or partial shade. Sow ripe seeds in a cold frame and transplant to 7cm (3.5in) pots; plant in final positions in late spring.
FORAGE Found in woodland areas in North America and some parts of Europe.
HARVEST Dig mature roots in autumn.

CAUTION Do not exceed recommended dosage. May rarely cause liver problems. Do not use if you have a history of liver disease; if in doubt, consult your GP. Avoid during pregnancy.

Agastache rugosa **Purple giant hyssop**

Native to eastern Asia, including parts of India, China, and Japan, purple giant hyssop is also known as Korean mint. It is one of two species that are known as *huo xiang* in Chinese medicine, and which have been used for at least 1,500 years. *Huo xiang* is largely taken for digestive problems associated with nausea, vomiting, and poor appetite.

PARTS USED Aerial parts, essential oil
MAIN CONSTITUENTS Volatile oil (incl. methyl chavicol, anethole, anisaldehyde, limonene, pinene, linalool)
ACTIONS Antibacterial, antifungal, febrifuge, carminative, diaphoretic

HOW TO USE

INFUSION Take 1 cup of a standard infusion (p.342) of the aerial parts 1–2 times a day for abdominal bloating and indigestion.
LOTION/OINTMENT Use 1 cup of infusion to bathe ringworm patches, or make into an ointment and apply 2–3 times daily. Alternatively, add 10 drops of the essential oil to 15ml (1 tbsp) of almond oil.
TINCTURE Take 10–40 drops in a little water to relieve nausea.
DECOCTION In traditional Chinese medicine it is combined in decoctions with such herbs as *huang qin* (baikal skullcap, *Scutellaria baicalensis*) and *lian qiao* (forsythia fruits, *Forsythia suspensa*) for acute diarrhoea.
PATENT REMEDIES Included in various Chinese patent formulae, such as *huo xiang zheng qi san* (powder for dispelling turbidity with giant hyssop) which is used to clear "dampness". Follow the dosage directions on the pack.

HOW TO SOURCE

GROW Prefers well-drained, fertile soil with well-rotted organic matter in full sun. Can be grown from seeds planted in 7cm (3in) pots and transplanted to their final growing position when large enough to handle.
FORAGE Unlikely to be found growing wild beyond its native habitat, although cultivated plants that then self-seed are possible. Collect leaves throughout the growing season and use in any recipe that requires mint. They can also be infused to make a refreshing tea.
HARVEST Gather aerial parts in summer before flowering.

> **CAUTION** In Chinese medicine it should be avoided in cases of fever. Avoid therapeutic doses in pregnancy.

FLOWERS
The dramatic purple to rose-violet flowers, which appear in summer, are much loved by honey bees and a favourite with flower arrangers

LEAVES
The serrated, heart-shaped leaves smell of a mixture of spearmint and liquorice and can be used to flavour meat recipes and sauces

1.2m
(4ft)

GROWTH HABIT
Hardy perennial with a spread of 60cm (24in) and large (up to 10cm/4in long) purple flowers.

Agrimonia eupatoria **Agrimony**

Widely found in Europe, western Asia, and northern Africa, agrimony has been used as a medicinal herb since ancient times. Originally used for eye problems and diarrhoea or dysentery, it later became a favourite wound herb on the battlefield, and is used today for urinary disorders and poor digestion. A related Chinese variety, *Agrimonia pilosa*, is used in similar ways in the Far East.

FLOWERS
The yellow flowers produce bristly fruits with spiny burs in autumn

The distinctive yellow flower racemes can be easily spotted in damp hedgerows and ditches in summer

LEAVES
Both the downy leaves and flowers are used for digestive or urinary problems, and as a wound herb

60cm (24in)

GROWTH HABIT
Perennial with hairy upright stems; spread 20–30cm (8–12in).

PARTS USED Aerial parts
MAIN CONSTITUENTS Tannins, coumarins, volatile oil, flavonoids, minerals (incl. silica), vitamins B and K
ACTIONS Astringent, diuretic, tissue healer, haemostatic, cholagogue, some antiviral activity reported

HOW TO USE

INFUSION Take 1 cup of standard infusion (p.342) 3 times daily to improve sluggish digestion or to help strengthen the digestive system in cases of food intolerance. Agrimony is an ideal herb for children with diarrhoea (consult a herbalist for children's dosage), and can also be taken by nursing mothers to dose babies.
LOTION Use a standard infusion to bathe cuts, grazes, skin sores, weeping eczema, and varicose ulcers. It can be applied several times daily.
GARGLE Use 1 cup of standard infusion as a gargle for hoarseness, sore throats, and laryngitis.
TINCTURE Take 1–4ml (20–80 drops) 3 times daily for cystitis, urinary infections, or incontinence. For severe or persistent urinary symptoms, seek urgent medical advice to avoid potential kidney damage.

HOW TO SOURCE

GROW Prefers damp, fertile soil, and will tolerate partial shade or full sun. Sow the seeds in a cold frame in autumn or spring and transplant them when they are large enough to handle.
FORAGE Commonly found on wasteland or in damp hedgerows. It is easily noticeable because of its tall bright yellow flower spikes. Gather the whole aerial parts in summer.
HARVEST Gather in summer while in flower.

CAUTION This astringent herb is best avoided if constipated.

Alchemilla xanthochlora **Lady's mantle**

As its name suggests, lady's mantle has a long tradition of gynaecological uses and has been a remedy for menstrual irregularities, heavy menstrual bleeding, and to ease childbirth. The plant originated in northern Europe and mountainous regions further south. In recent years it has become a popular garden plant highly valued by flower arrangers for its flower stems.

FLOWERS
Dense clusters of tiny flowers appear in late spring and early summer and can be harvested with the leaves

LEAVES
The lobed leaves were thought to resemble a traditional woman's shawl or mantle, hence the name

STEM
The tall flower stems develop from a basal rosette of leaves

GROWTH HABIT
Clump-forming perennial with a woody rootstock; spread 50cm (20in).

60cm (24in)

PARTS USED Aerial parts
MAIN CONSTITUENTS Tannins, salicylic acid, saponins, phytosterols, volatile oil, bitter principle
ACTIONS Astringent, menstrual regulator, digestive tonic, anti-inflammatory, wound herb

HOW TO USE

INFUSION Take 1 cup of a standard infusion (p.342) up to 5 times a day for acute diarrhoea or gastroenteritis, or to ease heavy menstrual bleeding or period pain.
TINCTURE Take 1–2ml (20–40 drops) 3 times daily to help regulate the menstrual cycle or, if combined with the same quantity of St John's wort, to ease period pains.
LOTION Use the standard infusion externally as a wash to bathe weeping eczema or skin sores.
GARGLE 1 cup of standard infusion can be used as a gargle for sore throats, laryngitis, or as a mouthwash for mouth ulcers.
CREAM/OINTMENT/PESSARIES Apply night and morning for vaginal discharges or itching. Insert 1 pessary at night. If symptoms do not improve in 2–3 days, seek advice from a genitourinary medicine clinic.

HOW TO SOURCE

GROW A hardy, clump-forming perennial, lady's mantle prefers moist, well-drained soil in full sun or dappled shade. The round, finely toothed leaves can have up to 11 distinct lobes. It can be grown from seed sown directly in spring or by division in spring or summer. Lady's mantle will self-seed enthusiastically.
FORAGE Found throughout northern Europe and the mountainous regions of central and southern Europe. It can also be found self-seeding outside gardens in other areas throughout the summer.
HARVEST Gather the whole aerial parts throughout the summer.

Allium sativum **Garlic**

Garlic is believed to have originated in south-west Siberia, but spread to much of Europe and Asia in ancient times. It has been used as a medicinal herb for at least 5,000 years, and is now known to reduce the risk of further heart attacks, as well as lower blood cholesterol levels. Also a strong antibiotic, garlic is used to treat colds, catarrh, and respiratory infections.

PARTS USED Bulb

MAIN CONSTITUENTS Volatile oil (incl. allicin, alliin, and ajoene), enzymes, vitamins A, B, C, and E, minerals (incl. selenium and germanium), flavonoids

ACTIONS Antibiotic, expectorant, diaphoretic, hypotensive, antithrombotic, hypolipidaemic, hypoglycaemic, antihistaminic, anthelmintic

HOW TO USE

JUICE Take up to 5ml (1 tsp) of juice in honey or water twice a day to combat infections, arteriosclerosis, or to reduce the risk of thrombosis.

FRESH CLOVES Rub the cut side of a fresh clove on acne pustules at night. Eat 2–3 cloves in cooked food each day to improve the cardiovascular system, lower cholesterol, or help prevent colds and flu.

CAPSULES Take 1 capsule before meals (check dosage on the packet) to help prevent seasonal infections.

TINCTURE Take 2–4ml (40–80 drops) in water 3 times daily for cardiovascular problems, respiratory disorders, or fungal infections.

POWDER For anyone who has suffered a heart attack, take up to 1 level teaspoon each day stirred into water or fruit juice to help prevent further attacks.

HOW TO SOURCE

GROW Prefers a warm site in deep, fertile, well-drained soil in full sun. Plant bulbs or individual cloves 5–10cm (2–4in) deep in the soil in autumn or winter.

FORAGE May be found growing wild in warm areas, but generally only likely to occur in cultivation.

HARVEST Gather the bulbs in late summer and early autumn and air-dry before storing in frost-free conditions.

> **CAUTION** Garlic oil is a skin irritant and should only be taken in capsules. Garlic can cause gastric irritation in some people.

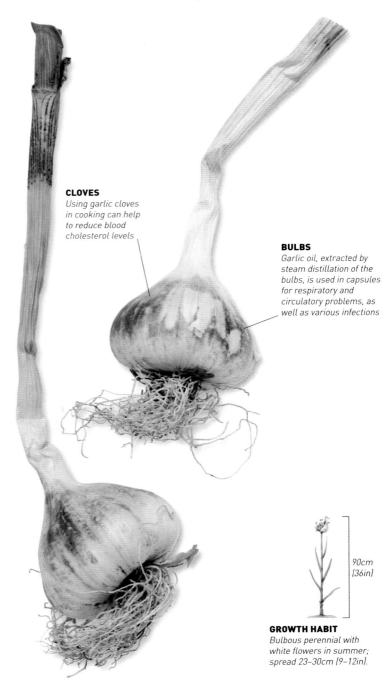

CLOVES
Using garlic cloves in cooking can help to reduce blood cholesterol levels

BULBS
Garlic oil, extracted by steam distillation of the bulbs, is used in capsules for respiratory and circulatory problems, as well as various infections

90cm (36in)

GROWTH HABIT
Bulbous perennial with white flowers in summer; spread 23–30cm (9–12in).

Aloe vera **Aloe vera**

Native to tropical Africa, where it has been used as an antidote to poison arrow wounds, aloe vera reached Europe in ancient times and was well known to the Greeks and Romans as a wound herb. The sap is cooling and healing and for centuries has been used to treat burns, inflammation, and skin ulcers, while the whole leaf is purgative. Internal use is restricted in some countries.

LEAVES
The leaves are thick, spiky, and grey-green in colour; red spots sometimes appear on young leaves

The gel contained in the fleshy leaves is antibacterial to both Staphylococcus aureus *and several species of* Streptococcus

GROWTH HABIT
Frost-tender, evergreen perennial with an indefinite spread.

60cm (24in)

PARTS USED Leaves, gel
MAIN CONSTITUENTS Anthraquinone glycosides (incl. aloin and aloe-emodin), resins, polysaccharides, sterols, saponins, chromones
ACTIONS Purgative, cholagogue, wound healer, tonic, demulcent, antibacterial, antifungal, styptic, sedative, anthelmintic

HOW TO USE

FRESH GEL Split open a leaf and use the gel directly, or scrape it out with a blunt knife. Apply directly to burns, sunburn, dry skin, wounds, fungal infections, nappy rash, shingles, ringworm, insect bites, allergic rashes, eczema, or any itchy skin condition.
TINCTURE Made from the whole pulped leaf. Take 5ml (1 tsp) 3 times daily for constipation or take 0.5–3ml (10–60 drops) 3 times daily for poor appetite or to stimulate bile flow in sluggish digestion.
CAPSULES Commercially made from powdered leaf. Use in 100–500mg doses for constipation.
HAIR RINSE Combine 10ml (2 tsp) of gel with 120ml (4fl oz) of standard chamomile infusion (p.342) and use as a conditioner.

HOW TO SOURCE

GROW Prefers well-drained sandy soil in full sun with a moderate summer water supply and dry winters. Usually propagated by breaking off and replanting the small offsets that appear on mature plants, but can be grown from seeds sown in spring or early summer at 21°C (70°F). Grown as a houseplant in temperate areas; benefits from being kept outside in warm summers.
FORAGE Likely to be found growing wild in tropical regions only. Easily confused with many related, generally larger, species that grow outside in warmer regions.
HARVEST Collect the gel and leaves from plants as required throughout the year.

CAUTION Do not take aloe vera internally during pregnancy.

Aloysia triphylla **Lemon verbena**

Originally found growing in rocky areas of Chile and Argentina, lemon verbena is now cultivated worldwide both as a highly aromatic garden ornamental and for use in perfumery. It is also used in pot pourri or in cooking to give a strong lemony taste to desserts, marinades, and fruit drinks. It is traditionally regarded as both soothing and uplifting, so is used in restorative teas.

FLOWERS
Tiny white or pale lilac flowers appear in summer, which is generally when the leaves are harvested

LEAVES
The leaves are steam-distilled to make an essential oil, which is used in aromatherapy for digestive and nervous problems

STEM
The woody parts of the plant need protection in winter if grown outside in cold areas

GROWTH HABIT
Half-hardy deciduous shrub with a spread of 3m (10ft).

3m (10ft)

PARTS USED Leaves, essential oil
MAIN CONSTITUENTS Volatile oil (incl. citral, nerol, and geraniol)
ACTIONS Sedative, carminative, antispasmodic, febrifuge, stimulates liver and gall bladder function, some antifungal activity (to *Candida albicans*) reported

HOW TO USE

INFUSION Use ½ tsp dried leaves per cup (p.342) after meals for flatulence or at night for insomnia. Combine with dandelion leaves and drink 3 times daily to improve liver function. Can be used to ease feverish conditions in children; consult a herbalist for advice on dosage.
BATHS Add 1 cup of a standard infusion to bathwater to ease stress and tension.
MASSAGE OIL True lemon verbena oil is difficult to obtain, as it is often adulterated with other lemon-scented oils. Use 5 drops in 15ml (1 tbsp) of almond oil as a massage for cramps, indigestion, anxiety, insomnia, or other stress-related conditions.

HOW TO SOURCE

GROW Prefers full sun and moist but well-drained soil. Usually propagated by heeled softwood cuttings in summer; it also self-seeds if it sets fruit after a hot summer. It is not frost-hardy, so in colder areas is best grown in containers and over-wintered under glass. Alternatively, cut back to the wood, keep dry, and protect with fleece or straw lagging in winter (it should survive temperatures as low as -15°C/5°F).
FORAGE Unlikely to be found growing wild outside South America, although self-seeding in warmer areas is possible.
HARVEST Collect the leaves in summer.

CAUTION Prolonged use or large internal doses can cause gastric irritation. The oil can irritate sensitive skin and is photosensitizing, so avoid bright sunlight if using it externally.

Althaea officinalis **Marshmallow**

Originally found in coastal areas of Europe, marshmallow is now widely naturalized. The plant's botanical name comes from the Greek verb, *altho* (to heal), and it has been valued for its soothing and healing action, both internally and externally, for at least 3,500 years. As well as being used medicinally, both the root and leaves can be eaten as vegetables.

PARTS USED Root, leaves, flowers
MAIN CONSTITUENTS Root: asparagine, mucilage, polysaccharides, pectin, tannins
Leaves: mucilage, flavonoids, coumarin, salicylic, and other phenolic acids
ACTIONS Root: demulcent, expectorant, diuretic, wound herb
Leaves: expectorant, diuretic, demulcent
Flowers: expectorant

HOW TO USE

MACERATION Soak 30g (1oz) of root in 600ml (1 pint) of cold water overnight and strain: the result can often be very thick and mucilaginous and may need further dilution. Take ½–1 cup 3 times daily for acid reflux, gastric ulceration, cystitis, and dry coughs.
POULTICE Make a paste from 1 tsp of powdered root mixed with a little water and use on boils, abscesses, ulcers, or poorly healing infected wounds.
OINTMENT Use to draw pus, splinters, or thorns.
INFUSION Take 1 cup of a standard leaf infusion (p.342) 3 times daily for bronchitis, bronchial asthma, catarrh, or pleurisy.
SYRUP Make a syrup by combining 600ml (1 pint) of a standard infusion of fresh flowers with 450g (1lb) of honey or syrup; bring to the boil and simmer gently for 10–15 minutes. Take 5ml (1 tsp) doses as required.

HOW TO SOURCE

GROW Prefers fertile, moist, well-drained soil in full sun; tolerates other conditions. Sow seed in trays of compost in midsummer and transplant to 7.5cm (3in) pots when large enough to handle. Plant out the following spring. Alternatively, divide plants in autumn. Can self-seed enthusiastically in ideal conditions.
FORAGE Likely to be found in ditches, riversides, tidal zones, and pond margins, especially in coastal areas. Gather the flowers in summer to make a cough syrup, or the leaves during the growing period. The root can be boiled as a vegetable.
HARVEST Dig the root in autumn. Cut the aerial parts as the plant starts to flower.

FLOWERS
The pale pink flowers bloom in summer: a traditional French recipe combines them with the flowers of corn poppy (Papaver rhoeas), sweet violet (Viola odorata), and mullein in a tisane des quatre fleurs

LEAVES
The leaves can be cooked and eaten like cabbage, or the leaf tips eaten in salads

1.8m
(6ft)

GROWTH HABIT
Upright perennial with a spread of 60–90cm (24–36in).

Angelica archangelica **Angelica**

Native to northern Europe, angelica is a statuesque plant with striking flowerheads in summer. It reputedly takes its medieval Latin name (*herba angelica*) from a belief that it protects against evil spirits, and has been used for a wide range of ailments for centuries. The stems are also used in cooking, and the essential oil is used as a food flavouring.

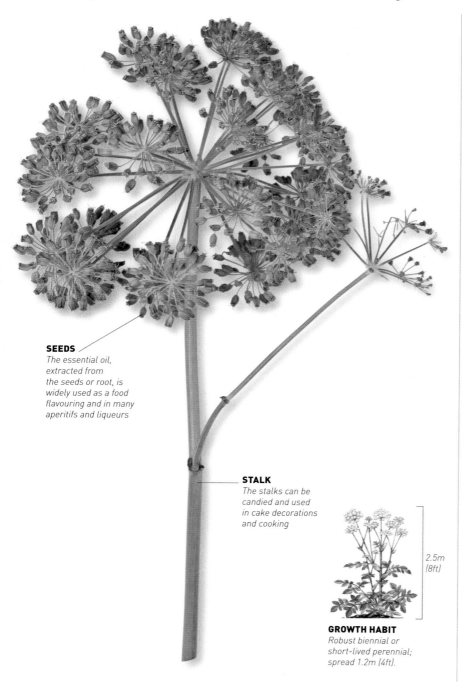

SEEDS
The essential oil, extracted from the seeds or root, is widely used as a food flavouring and in many aperitifs and liqueurs

STALK
The stalks can be candied and used in cake decorations and cooking

2.5m (8ft)

GROWTH HABIT
Robust biennial or short-lived perennial; spread 1.2m (4ft).

PARTS USED Leaves, root, essential oil
MAIN CONSTITUENTS Volatile oil (incl. phellandrene, pinene, borneol, linalol, and limonene), iridoids, resin, coumarins (incl. bergapten and angelicin), valerianic acid, tannins
ACTIONS Antispasmodic, diaphoretic, anti-inflammatory, expectorant, carminative, diuretic, antibacterial, digestive stimulant

HOW TO USE

INFUSION Take 1 cup of a standard infusion (p.342) of leaves after meals for indigestion.
DECOCTION Take ½–1 cup of a root decoction, made by simmering 15g (½oz) of root in 600ml (1 pint) of water for 5 minutes, for any cold condition where increased body heat is required, including arthritic and rheumatic problems in the elderly, poor circulation, or weak digestion.
TINCTURE Take 3ml (60 drops) 3 times daily of the leaf tincture for bronchitis or flatulent digestion. Take 1–2ml (20–40 drops) of the root tincture 3 times daily for bronchial catarrh, chesty coughs, digestive disorders including chronic indigestion and loss of appetite, or as a liver stimulant.
MASSAGE OIL Use 5 drops in 15ml (1 tbsp) of almond oil as a chest rub for bronchitis and coughs or to massage arthritic joints.

HOW TO SOURCE

GROW Prefers deep, fertile, moist soil in sun or partial shade. Surface-sow seeds when ripe or in spring. Thin out seedlings as required when they are large enough to handle. Self-seeds in the right conditions.
FORAGE Found in damp grassy places in northern and eastern Europe and into Asia.
HARVEST Gather leaves and stems in early summer, year-old roots in autumn, and seeds as they ripen.

CAUTION Avoid during pregnancy. Do not take therapeutic doses if diabetic, unless under professional guidance. Avoid exposure to sun if using externally (phototoxic).

Apium graveolens **Wild celery**

Native to Europe, the Mediterranean region, and western Asia, celery has long been cultivated as a vegetable and cooked or used raw in dishes such as Waldorf salad (celery, walnuts, and apple). Medicinally, the seeds and essential oil of celery are used mainly for urinary and arthritic disorders, and also to help clear uric acid from joints affected by gout.

LEAVES
Also known as smallage, wild celery is a more leafy plant than cultivated varieties, with divided, wedge-shaped leaves

STEM
The fleshy stems can be juiced as a detoxifying remedy

GROWTH HABIT
Biennial with a bulbous root; spread 15–30cm (6–12in).

50cm (20in)

PARTS USED Seeds, stalks, essential oil

MAIN CONSTITUENTS Volatile oil (incl. limonene, apiol, selinene, and phthalides), coumarins, furanocoumarins, flavonoids, minerals (incl. iron, phosphorus, and potassium)

ACTIONS Antirheumatic, sedative, urinary antiseptic, diuretic, carminative, hypotensive, antispasmodic, galactagogue, anti-inflammatory, encourages elimination of uric acid, antifungal activity reported

HOW TO USE

DECOCTION Use 15g (½oz) of seeds to 600ml (1 pint) of water, simmer for 10 minutes and take in ½–1 cup doses 3 times daily for rheumatic disorders, gout, rheumatoid arthritis, and urinary tract inflammations.

MASSAGE OIL Use 1ml (20 drops) oil in 60ml (2fl oz) of almond oil and massage into the abdomen for indigestion, flatulence, and liver congestion. Use also for sciatica, rheumatism, and arthritis.

FOOTBATH Add 1ml (20 drops) oil to a bowl of warm water to soak feet or toe joints with very painful gout.

JUICE Liquidize the stalks and leaves and drink in wine-glass doses as a remedy for debility and nervous exhaustion.

HOW TO SOURCE

GROW Prefers moist, well-drained soil in full sun. Plant the seeds in seed trays in spring, cover with a thin layer of compost, and place in a heated propagator or on a warm window sill. Pot on to 7.5cm (3in) pots, and when 10cm (4in) tall plant in final growing positions 30cm (12in) apart.

FORAGE Grows wild in coastal areas.

HARVEST Pick the cultivated variety as a vegetable in the first year; collect the seeds when ripe in the second summer.

> **CAUTION** Do not use seeds if pregnant. Do not use cultivated seeds medicinally, as they are often treated with fungicides. Do not take the essential oil internally unless under professional supervision.

Aralia racemosa **American spikenard**

Used by many Native Americans for a range of ailments including rheumatism, coughs, indigestion, asthma, and blood poisoning, American spikenard is found in many parts of the United States, from the Midwest to the eastern seaboard. The herb is known to encourage sweating and is detoxifying, but has otherwise been poorly researched.

PARTS USED Root
MAIN CONSTITUENTS Volatile oil, tannins, glycosides, diterpenes
ACTIONS Expectorant, diaphoretic, warming stimulant, detoxifying

HOW TO USE

DECOCTION Take ½ cup of a decoction made from 15g (½oz) dried root in 600ml (1pint) of water 3 times daily for rheumatic disorders.
SYRUP Combine 300ml (10fl oz) of strained decoction with 225g (8oz) of sugar or honey, bring to the boil, and simmer gently for 5–10 minutes to make a syrup. Take in 5ml (1 tsp) doses every 2–3 hours for coughs including bronchitis and whooping coughs.
LIQUID EXTRACT Take 1.5–3ml (30–60 drops) 3 times daily in a little water for rheumatic disorders, lumbago, and similar aches and pains.
POULTICE Mix 15g (½oz) of powdered root into a paste with a little water, spread on gauze, and use as a poultice for skin conditions including eczema.

HOW TO SOURCE

GROW Prefers partial shade, but tolerates sun. Sow the seeds where you want to grow them in autumn or in winter in a cold frame or unheated greenhouse; transplant into final positions the following spring.
FORAGE Largely found in woodland areas in the Midwest and eastern US; unlikely to occur growing wild in other areas. As well as their medicinal applications, the roots can be used in teas or to flavour beer.
HARVEST Dig up the roots in summer or autumn.

CAUTION Avoid during pregnancy.

FLOWERS
When fully in bloom in summer, the flowers are tiny, white-green, and carried in umbels

STEM
The stem is herbaceous, erect, and green to purple

LEAVES
The large, heart-shaped leaves, which can grow up to 20cm (8in) in length, are purple at the nodes

1.5m (5ft)

GROWTH HABIT
Herbaceous perennial with tiny flowers in summer and a spread of 60cm–2m (2–6ft).

Arctium lappa **Burdock**

Native to Europe and Asia, burdock is largely regarded as a cleansing remedy that helps to rid the body of toxins, including heavy metals, and is generally used for skin problems, arthritic conditions, and infections. The root and leaves are traditionally used in Europe, while the seeds are preferred in Chinese medicine and are often included in remedies for common colds.

FLOWERS
When in full bloom in summer, the thistle-like flowers have long purple spines

LEAVES
The leaves, which are oval and up to 30cm (12in) in diameter, were traditionally used in poultices for skin inflammations including acne

GROWTH HABIT
Vigorous, tap-rooted biennial; spread of up to 1m (3ft).

1.5m (5ft)

PARTS USED Root, leaves, seeds
MAIN CONSTITUENTS Leaf/root: bitter glycosides (incl. arctiopictrin), flavonoids (incl. arctin), tannins, volatile oil, antibiotic polyacetylenes, resin, mucilage, inulin, alkaloids, sesquiterpenes
Seeds: essential fatty acids, vitamins A, B2
ACTIONS Root: cleansing, mild laxative, diuretic, diaphoretic, anti-rheumatic, antiseptic, antibiotic
Leaves: mild laxative, diuretic
Seeds: febrifuge, anti-inflammatory, anti-bacterial, hypoglycaemic

HOW TO USE

ROOT DECOCTION Take ½–1 cup of a standard decoction (p.342) of the root 3 times daily for skin disorders, including persistent boils, sores, and dry eczema. Use a cup of the mix as a wash for acne and fungal skin infections including athlete's foot or ringworm.
INFUSION Take 1 wineglass of a standard leaf infusion (p.342) before meals as a mild digestive stimulant to combat indigestion.
SEED DECOCTION Take 1 cup of a standard decoction of the seeds up to 3 times daily for feverish colds and infections with sore throat and cough; it is often combined with honeysuckle flowers or forsythia berries.
TINCTURE Take 5–10ml (1–2 tsp) root tincture 3 times daily to detoxify the system in arthritic conditions, for urinary stones and gravel, or to stimulate digestion. Usually used in combination with other herbs.
POULTICE Use a root poultice for skin sores and leg ulcers.

HOW TO SOURCE

GROW Prefers moist, neutral to alkaline soil in full sun to partial shade. Sow the seeds where you want to grow them in spring. Self-seeds prolifically and can be invasive. Harvest the plant before the fruits are ripe to reduce the spread.
FORAGE Easily spotted in hedgerows and waste areas in Europe and western Asia.
HARVEST The root is generally collected in late summer and the leaves when the plant is just starting to flower; the seeds should be gathered when ripe in autumn.

Arctostaphylos uva-ursi **Bearberry**

Native to moorland in Europe, Asia, and North America, this plant's fruits are a favourite food for bears – hence its common name, bearberry or uva-ursi (in Latin literally, "grape-bear"). It is highly regarded by herbalists as a urinary antiseptic largely due to the presence of chemicals called hydroquinones, which help to disinfect the urinary tract.

LEAVES
The small leaves need to be gathered and dried individually for use in remedies for cystitis and other urinary problems

FLOWERS
The bell-shaped flowers have 5 white or pink petals that curl in around the narrow centre of the flower. They appear in late spring/early summer

GROWTH HABIT
Creeping, mat-forming, evergreen shrub with bell-shaped flowers; spread 90cm (36in) or more.

15cm
(6in)

PARTS USED Leaves, berries
MAIN CONSTITUENTS Hydroquinones (incl. arbutin), ursolic acid, tannic acid, gallic acid, phenolic glycosides, flavonoids, volatile oil, resin, tannins
ACTIONS Astringent, antibacterial, urinary antiseptic, possibly diuretic, haemostatic, oxytocic

HOW TO USE

INFUSION Take 1 cup of a standard infusion (p.342) of leaves 3 times daily for temporary cystitis, urethritis, or burning pain when urinating. It is often combined with couch grass or cleavers. For any severe or persistent urinary symptoms, you should seek urgent medical advice to avoid any potential damage to the kidneys.
TINCTURE Take 2–4ml (40–80 drops) 3 times daily for urinary problems or leucorrhoea (a white or yellow vaginal discharge).
TABLETS Available commercially, often in combination with dandelion, as a remedy for fluid retention. Follow the directions on the pack.

HOW TO SOURCE

GROW A moorland plant, it prefers moist, fertile, acid soil in partial or dappled shade, and makes good ground cover in the right conditions. Requires lime-free (ericaceous) soil. Sow seeds in a cold frame in autumn and pot on as soon as the seedlings are large enough to handle.
FORAGE Found in moorland areas. The leaves can be harvested in summer. The berries are edible and can be gathered in autumn and made into jellies and jams.
HARVEST The leaves are mainly collected in spring or summer, and the berries are collected in autumn.

CAUTION Do not take in pregnancy, while breast-feeding, or if suffering from kidney disease. It should not be taken for more than 10 consecutive days without professional advice. Large doses may cause nausea and vomiting.

Artemisia absinthium **Wormwood**

An extremely bitter herb, wormwood is largely used today as a digestive stimulant. Native to Europe, it was once a popular remedy for treating parasitic worms, as its name implies, and is still occasionally used in this way today. Its botanical name highlights a link to the French drink, absinthe, a favourite with the 19th-century avant garde that was highly addictive.

PARTS USED Leaves, flowering tops
MAIN CONSTITUENTS Volatile oil (incl. sesquiterpene lactones, thujone, and azulenes), bitter principle, flavonoids, tannins, lignan, silica, antibiotic polyacetylenes, inulin, hydroxycoumarins
ACTIONS Bitter digestive tonic, anthelmintic, uterine stimulant, cholagogue, choleretic, carminative, anti-inflammatory, immune stimulant

HOW TO USE

NB: Use only under medical supervision.
TINCTURE Take 1 drop on the tongue to stimulate the digestion and combat any late-afternoon chocolate cravings.
MACERATION Add ½ level tsp of dried herb to 1 cup of cold water, steep overnight, strain, and drink in the morning for poor appetite, hepatitis, sluggish digestion, and stagnant liver syndromes.
COMPRESS Soak in a strained maceration and apply to bruises and insect bites.
WASH Use 1 cup of strained maceration as a wash for scabies or other parasitic skin infections.
FLUID EXTRACT Take 2ml (40 drops) well diluted with water on an empty stomach for parasitic worms; repeat fortnightly.

HOW TO SOURCE

GROW Prefers well-drained, fertile soil in full sun, but tolerates poor, dry soil. Sow seeds in a cold frame in autumn or spring and transplant to their final positions when large enough to handle. Alternatively, divide clumps in spring or take heeled semi-ripe cuttings in midsummer.
FORAGE Found in hedgerows and waste areas in Europe, central Asia, and parts of the US; gather the leaves in summer.
HARVEST Cut aerial parts while flowering.

CAUTION Avoid if pregnant or if blood pressure is high. Do not take for more than four to five weeks at a time. Take only under professional supervision and do not exceed stated dosages.

FLOWERS
The pale yellow tubular flowers are clustered in spherical heads and appear in the summer

AERIAL PARTS
The aerial parts are generally harvested in mid- to late summer while the plant is flowering

LEAVES
The deeply divided leaves are strongly aromatic and can make a dramatic addition to a herbaceous border

90cm
(36in)

GROWTH HABIT
Woody-based perennial sub-shrub with a spread of 60–90cm (24–36in).

Astragalus membranaceus **Astragalus**

One of China's most important medicinal herbs, astragalus – the English name is milk vetch – is generally used as a tonic for younger people (whereas ginseng is the preferred stimulant for older people). It is particularly effective at strengthening the immune system and boosting energy levels, and is also used to clear abscesses and ulcers.

LEAVES
The leaves are green and divided into 12–18 pairs of oval leaflets on each stem

GROWTH HABIT
Perennial member of the pea family with a spread of 30–40cm (12–16in).

1m
(3ft)

PARTS USED Root parts
MAIN CONSTITUENTS Flavonoids (mainly isoflavones), saponins (incl. astragalosides), polysaccharides (astragalans), asparagine, sterols
ACTIONS Antispasmodic, adaptogenic, diuretic, cholagogue, antibacterial, hypoglycaemic, nervous stimulant, hypotensive, immune stimulant

HOW TO USE

DECOCTION Generally used in combination with other herbs rather than by itself: typically 9–15g (1/3–1/2oz) is added to Chinese *tang* ("soup"), a therapeutic decoction generally taken once or twice a day. It is used with ginseng *(Panax ginseng)* for general debility and fatigue, or with Chinese angelica *(Angelica sinensis)* for low energy, blood loss, or some types of pain.
TINCTURE Take 2–4ml (40–80 drops) up to 3 times daily as a general tonic, to boost the immune system if suffering from fatigue with recurrent infections, or for conditions involving excess sweating.
CAPSULES Widely available in commercial products that are generally marketed as energy tonics. Follow the dosage directions on the pack.

HOW TO SOURCE

GROW Prefers full sun. Scarify seeds before planting 1cm (1/2in) deep and about 10cm (4in) apart in late winter/early spring in a prepared seed bed that contains sharp sand and is alkaline (above pH7). Thin to 30cm (12in) apart and only water when the soil dries out, as astragalus does not like wet ground.
FORAGE Only likely to be found growing wild in north-west China, Mongolia, or Manchuria.
HARVEST Dig the roots of four-year-old plants in autumn.

CAUTION Avoid in conditions involving excess heat and in acute stages of infections; may interfere with immune-suppressant or blood-thinning drugs.

Avena sativa **Oats**

Native to northern Europe, oats are cultivated worldwide as a cereal crop. Both oatmeal and oatbran are readily available and used in savoury dishes, oatcakes, porridge, or added to breakfast cereals. The whole plant is restorative for the nervous system, and can help to reduce blood cholesterol levels. Traditionally the green, newly harvested whole plant was used medicinally.

PARTS USED Seeds, bran, oatstraw (whole plant)

MAIN CONSTITUENTS Saponins, flavonoids, many minerals (incl. calcium), alkaloids, sterols, vitamins B1, B2, D, and E, carotene, silicic acid, protein (gluten), starch, fat

ACTIONS Antidepressant, restorative nerve tonic, diaphoretic, nutritive, reduces cholesterol levels

HOW TO USE

TINCTURE This should ideally be made from the fresh green whole plant. Take 1–5ml (20 drops–1 tsp) 3 times daily for nervous exhaustion, tension, anxiety, debility following illness, or depression. It combines well with vervain, wood betony, or valerian.

INFUSION Take 1 cup of a standard infusion (p.342) of oatstraw as required as a restorative for the nervous system.

FACIAL SCRUB For dull, greasy skin or a tendency for acne, mix ½ cup of fine oatmeal with water to make a paste. Apply to the face and leave for 10 minutes before rinsing.

BATH Strain 600ml (1 pint) of a standard decoction of the oatstraw or whole grains into the bath to ease itching and eczema.

HOW TO SOURCE

GROW Prefers neutral or slightly acidic soil and cool, damp conditions, but will tolerate dry spells. Winter oats are sown in autumn for a late summer harvest, or in spring as an early autumn crop.

FORAGE Do not trespass in a farmer's crop, but self-seeding plants are often found in hedgerows or field margins. Forage for dried stalks if they are not used for fodder. Wild oats are preferred by many herbalists as a more effective treatment.

HARVEST Harvest in late summer or early autumn as the grains turn to pale cream.

CAUTION For those sensitive to gluten, decoctions or tinctures should be allowed to settle and then the clear liquid only decanted for use.

SEEDS
Oats are harvested in late summer or early autumn when turning from green to cream, and are then threshed to separate the grains from the straw

1m (3ft)

GROWTH HABIT
An erect annual grass with flat rough leaves; spread 15–23cm (6–9in).

Borago officinalis **Borage**

A native of Mediterranean regions and western Asia, borage has long been noted for its uplifting effects, and was called "the plant that cheers" (*euphrosynum*) by the Romans. This effect is in part due to its stimulant action on the adrenal glands to produce the "fight or flight" hormone, adrenaline. The seed oil is also produced commercially.

FLOWERS
The bright blue flowers, appearing in summer, are a popular addition to drinks and salads and give their name to "starflower oil" – a seed extract produced commercially

LEAVES
The coarse hairy leaves have a cucumber-like flavour and can be shredded and added to summer salads

After flowering, the seeds that are produced are a rich source of gamma-linolenic acid

60cm
(24in)

GROWTH HABIT
Vigorous annual with upright, hollow stems; spread 15–30cm (6–12in).

PARTS USED Leaves, flowers, seeds
MAIN CONSTITUENTS Aerial parts/leaves: saponins, mucilage, tannins, vitamin C, calcium, potassium.
Seeds: cis-linoleic and gamma-linolenic acids
ACTIONS Adrenal stimulant, galactagogue, diuretic, diaphoretic, expectorant, antidepressant, anti-inflammatory

HOW TO USE

TINCTURE Use 2–5ml (40 drops–1 tsp) 3 times daily for 2–3 weeks only, to help combat the effects of stress, or following steroidal treatment.
LOTION Add an equal amount of water to the fresh juice and use to bathe itching skin or nervous rashes.
INFUSION Take 1 cup of a standard infusion (p.342) 3 times daily, combined with peppermint and elderflower for feverish colds.
CAPSULES The seed oil is widely available in capsules, which can be taken to help treat eczema, rheumatoid arthritis, menstrual irregularities, or irritable bowel syndrome.
SYRUP Make a standard infusion using either flowers or whole aerial parts and sweeten with honey or sugar (450g/1lb to every 600ml/1 pint of infusion) for coughs.

HOW TO SOURCE

GROW Prefers any type of well-drained soil, in dappled shade or sun. Plant the seeds in late summer, then thin to about 30cm (12in) apart when the seedlings are established. It self-seeds enthusiastically.
FORAGE Originally found growing in rocky places in Mediterranean regions, it now self-seeds in other areas.
HARVEST Gather aerial parts in summer.

> **CAUTION** Avoid during pregnancy. Restricted in Australia and New Zealand, as it is related to comfrey, which is banned in these countries. Not recommended for prolonged treatment (2–3 weeks maximum).

Calendula officinalis **Calendula or marigold**

Traditionally said to lift the spirits and encourage cheerfulness, calendula or marigold is one of the most popular and versatile medicinal herbs in current use. It is widely available in commercial calendula ointments and creams, and is also used internally for digestive and gynaecological problems or as a cleansing remedy in skin and rheumatic disorders.

FLOWERS
The flowers, which appear from spring to autumn, are used in many commercially available "calendula" creams and ointments

FLOWERHEADS
For medicinal use, dry the whole flowerheads on trays in a warm place, and then pull off petals for storage

LEAVES
The bright green lance-shaped leaves were once used in poultices and compresses for gout and other hot swellings

70cm
(28in)

GROWTH HABIT
Upright, bushy aromatic annual; spread 50–70cm (20–28in).

PARTS USED Flowerheads, essential oil
MAIN CONSTITUENTS Flavonoids, mucilage, triterpenes, volatile oil, bitter glycosides, resin, sterols, carotenes
ACTIONS Astringent, antibacterial, antifungal, anti-inflammatory, wound herb, mildly oestrogenic, antispasmodic, menstrual regulator

HOW TO USE

Do not confuse with preparations made from French marigold (*Tagetes patula*).
INFUSION Take 1 cup of a standard infusion (p.342) 3 times daily for inflammatory digestive disorders. It also makes a suitable douche for vaginal thrush, or a mouthwash for gum disease and mouth ulcers.
CREAM/OINTMENT Use for minor cuts and grazes, and any inflamed or dry skin: eczema, chapped hands, chilblains, sore nipples in breast-feeding, acne, minor burns and scalds, sunburn, etc. It is also helpful for fungal infections such as ringworm, thrush, and athlete's foot.
MACERATED OIL Use as a cream or ointment on piles or broken capillaries; add up to 20% lavender oil for sunburn.
TINCTURE Take 2–5ml (40 drops–1 tsp) 3 times a day for menstrual problems, (irregular, heavy, or painful periods).

HOW TO SOURCE

GROW Prefers well-drained soil in a sunny site, but will tolerate partial shade. Sow seeds in autumn or spring, and thin or transplant seedlings when large enough to handle. Can also be grown in containers. It flowers throughout the summer and self-seeds enthusiastically, so gather flowers regularly to avoid excessive seeding.
FORAGE Most likely to be found naturalized in Mediterranean areas in rocky places or cultivated sites and on wasteland; elsewhere, self-seeded plants outside gardens are possible, but less common.
HARVEST Collect flowers in summer.

CAUTION Avoid internal use of calendula during pregnancy.

Capsicum annuum **Cayenne or chilli pepper**

Originally found in tropical America, cayenne was first described in 1493 by the physician accompanying the Portuguese explorer, Christopher Columbus. The plant was introduced into India and Africa by the Portuguese and reached Europe by the mid-16th century. It soon became an established culinary seasoning and medicinal herb. Today it is widely used as a warming remedy.

FLOWERS
The plant has small, solitary, white to purple flowers (depending on the variety) that appear in spring and summer

FRUITS
Chilli fruits are heating and stimulating, increasing blood flow and sweating and stimulating digestion. Related varieties of Capsicum may be in different shapes

GROWTH HABIT
Bushy perennial shrub; spread 50cm–2m (20in–6ft).

1.5m (5ft)

PARTS USED Fruit
MAIN CONSTITUENTS Capsaicin, carotenoids, fatty acids, flavonoids, vitamins A, B1, and C, volatile oil, sugars
ACTIONS Circulatory stimulant, diaphoretic, gastric stimulant, carminative, antiseptic, antibacterial
Topically: counter-irritant, rubefacient

HOW TO USE

MACERATED OIL Heat 30g (1oz) of the powder, or 3–4 chopped fresh chillies, in 600ml (1 pint) of sunflower oil in a bowl over a saucepan of simmering water (bain-marie) for 2 hours. Use as a massage for rheumatism, lumbago, arthritis, and so on, or to relieve pain from shingles.
TINCTURE Take 1ml (20 drops) in a cup of warm water as a circulatory stimulant for cold hands and feet.
GARGLE Use ¼–½ml (5–10 drops) of tincture or a pinch (⅛ tsp) of cayenne powder to half a tumbler of warm water for sore throats or laryngitis.

HOW TO SOURCE

GROW Sow 2–3 seeds in each 7.5cm (3in) pot using good-quality compost. Plant out when the soil temperature reaches 15°C (59°F) or, in temperate regions, pot on into large containers and keep in a greenhouse.
FORAGE Unlikely to be found growing wild outside its native region, but self-seeded plants that grow outside gardens are possible; grown throughout the tropics in America, Africa, and India.
HARVEST Gather the fruits when ripe in summer and dry immediately in the shade.

CAUTION Do not exceed the stated dose: excess can lead to gastric irritation. Avoid touching the eyes or any cuts after handling chillies, as it can sting. Compresses left on the skin for long periods can cause blistering.

Carum carvi **Caraway**

Native to Mediterranean regions, caraway is now naturalized in parts of Asia and North America. Cultivated commercially, the oil is used in pharmaceuticals and toiletries such as toothpastes and mouthwashes, and as a food flavouring. Like its relatives anise and fennel, caraway is used for digestive and respiratory disorders, and is popular for treating colic in infants.

PARTS USED Seeds, essential oil
MAIN CONSTITUENTS Volatile oil (mainly carvone and limonene), flavonoids, polysaccharides
ACTIONS Antispasmodic, carminative, antimicrobial, expectorant, galactogogue, emmenagogue, diuretic, tonic

HOW TO USE

INFUSION Use a weak infusion (p.342) of the seeds 3 times daily for wind and colic in children. Reduce the dosage according to age. For children aged 1–2, use 10ml (2 tsp) of a standard infusion diluted with 100ml (3½fl oz) of warm water per dose; for children aged 3–4, use 20ml (4 tsp) of a standard infusion similarly diluted. Take a standard infusion 3 times daily for menstrual cramps or colic in adults, or drink 1 cup a day to improve milk flow when breastfeeding.
TINCTURE Take 3–5ml (60 drops–1 tsp) of a tincture of the seeds 3 times daily for poor appetite or flatulence.
ESSENTIAL OIL Add 5 drops of essential oil to 5ml (1 tsp) of almond oil and use as a chest rub for bronchitis and productive coughs (a cough that produces phlegm, rather than a dry cough).

HOW TO SOURCE

GROW Prefers deep, fertile, well-drained soil and full sun. Sow seeds where you want them to grow in spring, and thin out seedlings to 7.5–10cm (3–4in) if required. The plant is biennial, flowering in its second year. Caraway requires a long, hot growing season to set seed, so it may not produce as many seeds in cooler areas.
FORAGE Found in grassy areas or wastelands. In warmer zones it will set seed in late summer; in cooler areas seeds are likely only if the summer has been hot.
HARVEST Collect ripe seeds in late summer.

CAUTION The essential oil can cause skin irritation.

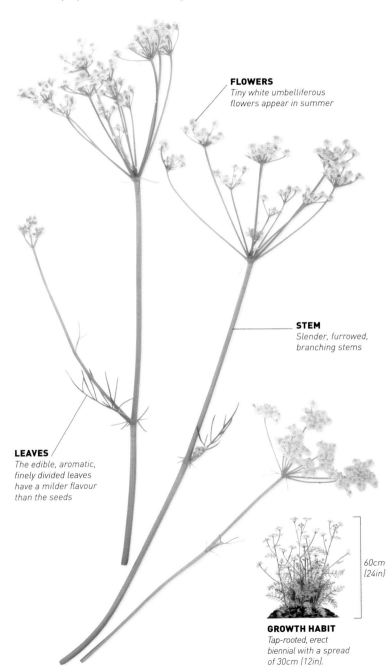

FLOWERS
Tiny white umbelliferous flowers appear in summer

STEM
Slender, furrowed, branching stems

LEAVES
The edible, aromatic, finely divided leaves have a milder flavour than the seeds

60cm (24in)

GROWTH HABIT
Tap-rooted, erect biennial with a spread of 30cm (12in).

Centella asiatica **Gotu kola**

Native to India, south-east Asia, and parts of northern Australia, gotu kola – a Sri Lankan name, which translates as "conical leaf" – is used as a fodder crop, green vegetable, or salad herb, and medicinal plant. In Ayurveda it is generally known as *brahmi* and used as a tonic remedy to improve longevity, memory, and intelligence. It is a restricted herb in some countries.

LEAVES
The round, almost coin-shaped leaves are smooth and nearly hairless

FLOWERS
Small pink or red flowers grow in bunches near the surface of the soil

STOLONS
The plant spreads by creeping stolons, or runners, that root at leaf nodes

GROWTH HABIT
Creeping perennial or annual rooting at nodes with clusters of kidney-shaped leaves; indefinite spread.

20cm (8in)

PARTS USED Whole plant
MAIN CONSTITUENTS Alkaloids (incl. hydrocotyline), terpenoid saponins, flavonoids, bitter principle, volatile oil
ACTIONS Tonic, antirheumatic, cleansing, adaptogen, relaxant, diuretic, laxative

HOW TO USE

INFUSION Use ½ tsp of the dried herb per cup of boiling water and take 1 cup daily for skin problems, rheumatism, or as a restorative for tiredness and depression.
TINCTURE Take 5ml (1 tsp) in water daily for poor memory, inability to concentrate, or general exhaustion.
LOTION/OINTMENT Use on poorly healing wounds or skin ulcers.
FRESH LEAVES Traditionally given to Indian children to combat dysentery, or included in salads as a restorative tonic.
FLUID EXTRACT Take 20 drops in water up to 3 times daily for rheumatic disorders and poor venous circulation.
POWDER Used in Ayurvedic medicine to make a paste (mixed with a little water) and applied to eczema and skin sores.

HOW TO SOURCE

GROW Generally gathered in the wild, but can be grown in warmer areas from seeds sown directly in the spring. It prefers marshy ditches and riverbanks, so is best grown in partial shade in moist soil. It has an indefinite spread, so can make useful ground cover with the right growing conditions, but can become invasive.
FORAGE The whole plant can be gathered at any time where it is naturalized (parts of southern Africa, South America, the southern United States, and its native Asia).
HARVEST The whole plant matures in three months and is gathered – including the roots – throughout the year.

CAUTION Can occasionally cause photosensitivity. Do not take for more than six weeks without a break.

Cichorium intybus **Chicory**

Native to Mediterranean regions, chicory is now naturalized in many parts of Europe, North America, and Australia. It is cultivated as a vegetable – usually by producing chicons in complete darkness – and is also grown as a coffee substitute. The plant is extremely bitter, so it makes an excellent digestive stimulant and tonic, and is also a gentle laxative.

FLOWERHEADS
The flowerheads, which bloom throughout the summer, are 2-4 cm (¾-1½ in) wide with two rows of involucral bracts: the outer are short and spreading while the inner are longer and erect

FLOWERS
The bright sky-blue flowers can be added to the leaves to make a tea that aids digestion

LEAVES
The bitter leaves can be blanched and then sautéed with garlic and red peppers or anchovies and served with pasta

1.5m
(5ft)

GROWTH HABIT
Tap-rooted, clump-forming perennial with a spread of 45–60cm (18–24in).

PARTS USED Root, leaves, flowers
MAIN CONSTITUENTS Inulin (in the root), sesquiterpene lactones (lactucin and lactucopicrin), oligosaccharides, glycosides, vitamins, minerals
ACTIONS Laxative, diuretic, mild sedative, liver, and digestive tonic

HOW TO USE

DECOCTION Take ½–1 cup of a standard decoction (p.342) of chicory root 3 times daily as a stimulating tonic for the liver and digestive system. Use ½–1 cup of a quarter- to half-strength or less decoction 1–2 times a day for constipation. Chicory also contains oligosaccharides, which are probiotic and help to maintain healthy gastrointestinal flora.
INFUSION Combine the leaves and flowers in a standard infusion (p.342) and take 1 cup 3 times daily to improve digestion.
TINCTURE Take 1–2ml (20–40 drops) of the root tincture 3 times daily as an appetite stimulant.
FLUID EXTRACT Extracts have been successfully used for parasitic worm infections in sheep and cattle, although there is little research as to the effect on human parasites.

HOW TO SOURCE

GROW Prefers fertile, moist but well-drained, neutral to alkaline soil in full sun. Sow seeds in a cold frame in autumn or spring and when the seedlings are established transplant them to final positions in rows at least 60cm (24in) apart. Dead-head the flowers regularly, as the plant can be a prolific self-seeder.
FORAGE Sometimes found in hedgerows and field borders, especially in southern Europe. The leaves can be collected during summer. They have a bitter taste and can be boiled to improve their flavour.
HARVEST Lift the roots in early spring in the second year.

Crataegus laevigata **Hawthorn**

Thorny shrubs and trees from various species of hawthorn are found throughout northern temperate zones. *Crataegus laevigata* is the European species, but *Crataegus pinnatifida* is native to northern China, and is also used as a medicinal herb. The berries are traditionally made into a savoury jelly to eat with cheese, game, and cold meats.

FLOWERS
The flowering tops are especially good for stimulating circulation. Flowers appear in late spring

STEM
Hawthorn's spiky stems have made it a popular field boundary plant, and offers a safe haven for nesting birds

GROWTH HABIT
Deciduous shrub or small tree; spread 5–8m (15–25ft).

6m (20ft)

PARTS USED Flowering tops, berries
MAIN CONSTITUENTS Bioflavonoid glycosides (incl. rutin and quercetin), triterpenoids, procyanidins, polyphenols, saponins, tannins, coumarins, minerals
ACTIONS Peripheral vasodilator, cardiac tonic, astringent, relaxant, antioxidant

HOW TO USE

INFUSION Take 1 cup of a standard infusion (p.342) of the flowering tops 3 times daily to improve peripheral circulation or to support treatments for high blood pressure.
DECOCTION Make a standard decoction of the berries and drink ½ cup up to 6 times daily for acute diarrhoea and digestive upsets. The same mixture can be used as a general tonic for the heart: take 2 cups daily.
TINCTURE Take 1–2ml (20–40 drops) of a standard tincture of either the berries or the flowering tops for high blood pressure; best combined with other herbs as appropriate.
JUICE Pulp the berries in a food processor, squeeze out the juice, and take in 10ml (2 tsp) doses twice daily for sluggish digestion and diarrhoea.

HOW TO SOURCE

GROW It can be grown from seed if planted in the autumn and allowed to over-winter in a cold frame, but is more often propagated from cuttings in spring. Plant heeled cuttings in a small pot and, once rooted, pot on into 20cm (8in) pots until sufficiently established to plant out. Will self-seed.
FORAGE A common hedgerow shrub found on field borders and roadsides. It is best to gather from shrubs within fields rather than those adjacent to roads. The flowering tops can be gathered in late spring/early summer for use in teas, and the berries in late autumn to make into jelly.
HARVEST Gather flowering tops in spring, and the red berries in autumn when ripe.

CAUTION Seek professional advice before self-medicating with hawthorn for heart disorders, or if using prescribed medication.

Curcuma longa **Turmeric**

Familiar to many people as a key ingredient in curry powder, turmeric, which originates in southern Asia, has a long history of use in both Ayurveda and traditional Chinese medicine. It is largely used for digestive and liver disorders, although modern research also suggests that it has potent antioxidant properties and can reduce cholesterol levels.

PARTS USED Rhizome
MAIN CONSTITUENTS Volatile oil, curcumin (yellow pigment), resin, vitamins, minerals, bitter principle
ACTIONS Carminative, cholagogue, antioxidant, choleretic, detoxifier, antibacterial, anti-inflammatory, antitumour activity, hypolipidaemic

HOW TO USE

DECOCTION Take ½ cup of a standard decoction (p.342) up to 3 times daily for digestive problems including nausea, gastritis, excessive stomach acid, indigestion, and liver or gall bladder disorders. Can also be combined with remedies for arthritis such as angelica or devil's claw and taken 3 times daily.
TINCTURE Take 2–4ml (40–80 drops) in a little water 3 times daily to help reduce blood cholesterol levels, or take 5ml (1 tsp) up to 3 times daily for period pain.
POWDER Take 1–2g (½–1 level tsp) stirred into a cup of water, fruit juice, or milk for arthritic problems or eczema.
OINTMENT Apply 2–3 times daily for athlete's foot, psoriasis, or ringworm.

HOW TO SOURCE

GROW Prefers moist, fertile soil with high humidity and partial shade. Will only grow in warm regions (minimum temperature 15–18°C/59–64°F), but can be cultivated under glass elsewhere. Sow seeds at 21°C (70°F) in autumn. Alternatively, propagate by root division while the plant is dormant in winter or by root cuttings in autumn.
FORAGE Unlikely to be found growing wild outside dry forest areas in India and some other parts of southern Asia.
HARVEST The rhizome is dug in autumn and is boiled and steamed before drying.

CAUTION May occasionally cause skin rashes or increase photosensitivity. Avoid therapeutic doses in pregnancy, but culinary quantities are perfectly safe. Seek professional advice if you suffer from gallstones.

LEAVES
The green, pointed, oblong leaves can grow up to 60cm (24in) in length

The leaves are used in India, Indonesia, and other parts of south-east Asia to flavour curries or wrap up food ready to be cooked

90cm (3ft)

GROWTH HABIT
Aromatic perennial with shiny pointed leaves and an indefinite spread.

Cymbopogon citratus **Lemon grass**

Originally native to grasslands in south-east Asia, lemon grass is now cultivated in many tropical regions, including Guatamala, the West Indies, and the Philippines, both as a culinary herb and for its essential oil. The herb is a popular digestive remedy in parts of Asia, and is used as a flavouring in perfumery and the food industry.

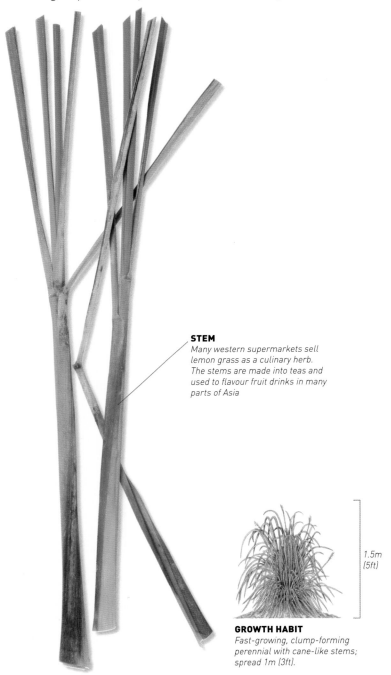

STEM
Many western supermarkets sell lemon grass as a culinary herb. The stems are made into teas and used to flavour fruit drinks in many parts of Asia

GROWTH HABIT
Fast-growing, clump-forming perennial with cane-like stems; spread 1m (3ft).

1.5m (5ft)

PARTS USED Leaves and stems, essential oil

MAIN CONSTITUENTS Volatile oil mostly citral (65–85%) as well as nerol, geraniol, citronellol, myrcene, and borneol

ACTIONS Antispasmodic, carminative, febrifuge, analgesic, antidepressant, antiseptic, astringent, antibacterial, antifungal, sedative, tonic

HOW TO USE

LOTION Dilute 30 drops of essential oil in 1 tbsp vodka, then add to 120ml (4fl oz) water and use in a spray bottle as an insect repellant (fleas, ticks, and lice), or as a deodorant and antiperspirant.

MASSAGE RUB Dilute 20 drops of essential oil in 60ml (2fl oz) of almond oil and massage into aching muscles, or use on the abdomen for stomach cramps.

INFUSION Take 1 cup of a standard infusion (p.342) 3 times daily for wind, flatulence, indigestion, or stomach cramps.

POULTICE Simmer a handful of chopped fresh lemon grass for 1–2 minutes in olive oil and use on arthritic or painful joints.

HOW TO SOURCE

GROW Grow in containers in cooler areas and over-winter in a conservatory or heated greenhouse, as not frost hardy (minimum temperature 7°C/45°F). In frost-free areas plant in fertile, moist, well-drained soil in full sun, keeping 60cm (24in) between plants. Sow seeds (at 18°C/64°F) in early spring in seed trays and transplant to 7cm (3.5in) pots when large enough. Alternatively, propogate by root division in late spring.

FORAGE Unlikely to be found growing wild other than in its native area of grassland in south-east Asia.

HARVEST Gather stems through the year.

CAUTION Do not take the essential oil internally without professional advice. Avoid therapeutic doses in pregnancy, but culinary quantities are safe.

Cynara cardunculus Scolymus Group **Globe artichoke**

Originating in the Mediterranean region, the globe artichoke was probably developed from *Cynara cardunculus* in ancient times. The ball-like flowerheads, which are picked before they open, are valued as a vegetable, while the hearts can be used in salads. Medicinally, the plant is used as a liver remedy that helps to protect against toxins and infection and improve function.

FLOWERHEADS
The flowerheads are harvested before opening, boiled as a vegetable, and generally served with melted butter

Artichoke hearts, found at the centre of the flowerheads, can be added to salads

PARTS USED Flowerheads, leaves, root
MAIN CONSTITUENTS Sesquiterpene lactone (cynaropicrin), cynarin, inulin
ACTIONS Cholagogue, choleretic, liver restorative, hypoglycaemic, diuretic, hypolipidaemic

HOW TO USE

JUICE Mix an equal amount of juice from the leaves and flowerheads with water and drink 1 cup daily as a liver tonic.
INFUSION Take 1 cup of a standard infusion (p.342) of the leaves 3 times daily for liver and gall bladder disorders, including liver damage or jaundice, or for indigestion, nausea, or abdominal bloating. Also helps to reduce blood cholesterol levels and can be useful in the control of late-onset diabetes where treatment is focused on diet rather than medication.
DIET Eating artichoke hearts regularly can be helpful in the management of late-onset diabetes.
CAPSULES Take 3 x 250mg capsules containing powdered leaf before meals morning and evening to improve liver function.

HOW TO SOURCE

GROW Prefers an open but sheltered site in full sun in well-drained soil; add well-rotted manure to the soil before planting. Sow seeds in a cold frame in spring and transplant to their final growing positions when large enough to handle. Alternatively, propagate from suckers in spring or take root cuttings in winter.
FORAGE Unknown in the wild.
HARVEST Cut the leaves before flowering. Gather the flowerheads before the bracts open from the second year onwards to eat as a vegetable.

1.8m (6ft)

GROWTH HABIT
Large perennial with a spread of 1.2m (4ft) and thistle-like flowers.

Dioscorea villosa **Wild yam**

Perhaps best known as the herb that gave rise to the first oral contraceptive pill, wild yam is native to the south and east USA and central America, although it is now naturalized in many semi-tropical areas worldwide. The chemical from the yam, diosgenin, was identified in the 1930s, and by 1960 was being used to manufacture the hormone progesterone.

PARTS USED Root and tuber
MAIN CONSTITUENTS Alkaloids, steroidal saponins (mainly dioscin, which breaks down to diosgenin), tannins, phytosterols, starch
ACTIONS Relaxant for smooth muscle, antispasmodic, cholagogue, anti-inflammatory, diaphoretic, antirheumatic, diuretic

HOW TO USE

DECOCTION Take ½–1 cup 3 times daily of a decoction made by simmering 10g (¼oz) in 600ml (1 pint) of water for 20 minutes for colicky pains associated with IBS or diverticulosis. Drink ½ cup every 3–4 hours for period pains, or sip cups constantly during labour to relieve pain.
TINCTURE Take 2–3ml (40–60 drops) 3 times daily for menopausal problems.
FLUID EXTRACT Take 1–2ml (20–40 drops) in a little water 3 times daily for arthritis: usually combined with other herbs such as black cohosh, cramp bark, meadowsweet, or white willow for rheumatoid arthritis. Also useful to stimulate liver function.

HOW TO SOURCE

GROW Prefers light to medium (sandy to loamy) soil that is moist but well drained, and requires partial shade. Usually grown from root cuttings, or from pea-sized tubers found growing in the leaf axils in late summer that can be collected and planted immediately. The plants are dioecious (have separate sexes), so both male and female plants are needed to set seeds, which can be sown in a cold frame in early spring and transplanted when large enough to handle.
FORAGE Generally found in damp woods, swamps, thickets, and hedgerows in central and southern USA and parts of central America.
HARVEST Dig tubers and roots in autumn, and wash and dry them.

> **CAUTION** Saponin content may cause nausea in sensitive individuals.

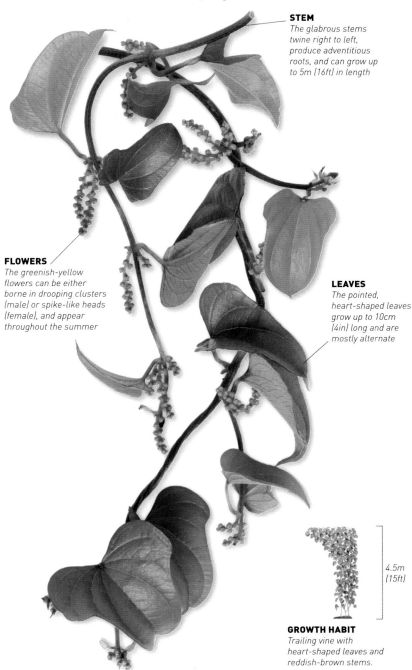

STEM
The glabrous stems twine right to left, produce adventitious roots, and can grow up to 5m (16ft) in length

FLOWERS
The greenish-yellow flowers can be either borne in drooping clusters (male) or spike-like heads (female), and appear throughout the summer

LEAVES
The pointed, heart-shaped leaves grow up to 10cm (4in) long and are mostly alternate

4.5m (15ft)

GROWTH HABIT
Trailing vine with heart-shaped leaves and reddish-brown stems.

Echinacea purpurea **Echinacea**

Native to the eastern states of the USA, echinacea was once known as "Missouri snakeroot" and was traditionally used by Native Americans for fevers and poorly healing wounds. It was introduced into Europe in the 19th century and has been extensively researched since, largely as an antibiotic remedy for treating a broad range of infections.

FLOWERS
The brightly coloured purple flowers, which appear in late summer, are a favourite with bees and butterflies, and were once used for treating minor colds and chills

LEAVES
German research suggests that the long, oval leaves can be just as effective in combating infections as the root

GROWTH HABIT
Upright, rhizomatous perennial with daisy-like flowers; spread 35cm (18in).

1.2m (4ft)

PARTS USED Root, leaves
MAIN CONSTITUENTS Volatile oil (incl. humulene), glycosides, alkamides, inulin, polysaccharides, antibiotic polyacetylenes
ACTIONS Immune stimulant, anti-allergenic, lymphatic tonic, antimicrobial, anti-inflammatory

HOW TO USE

INFUSION Take 1 cup of a standard infusion (p.342) of fresh leaves 3 times daily for common colds, chills, or influenza.
DECOCTION Take 10ml (2 tsp) of a standard decoction of the root every 2–4 hours for acute stages of infections. Combines well with hemp agrimony.
GARGLE/MOUTHWASH Use 1 cup of the root decoction or 10ml (2 tsp) of tincture in a cup of warm water 2–3 times daily for sore throats, mouth ulcers, and tonsillitis.
TINCTURE Take 5ml (1tsp) of tincture 3 times daily for urinary infections; combine with an equal amount of cleavers tincture for enlarged lymphatic nodes or glandular fever. For colds and influenza, take 10ml (2 tsp) of tincture as symptoms occur and repeat up to 4 times daily for 48 hours.
CREAM/OINTMENT Use on infected cuts, boils, acne, and skin sores.

HOW TO SOURCE

GROW Prefers fertile, moist, well-drained soil in full sun. Sow seeds in containers in spring and pot on; when well established, plant in permanent positions. Alternatively, divide established plants in autumn or spring or take root cuttings in late autumn or early winter.
FORAGE Unlikely to be found growing wild outside the USA. Over-cropping has caused it to become rare, so avoid foraging for the plant in its native habitat.
HARVEST The leaves can be gathered throughout the growing season, and the roots of four-year-old plants are lifted in autumn after flowering is over.

CAUTION High doses can occasionally cause nausea and dizziness.

Equisetum arvense **Horsetail**

Native to Europe, Asia, and North America, horsetail is a survivor from prehistoric times. This early plant has been unchanged for millennia and once formed the vegetation that decomposed to produce coal seams. It encourages the healing of connective tissue, and has been used as a wound herb to stop bleeding since ancient times.

LEAVES AND STEM
Both the leaves and the stem are healing for connective tissue and damaged lungs

The silica content in the stem and leaves means that the whole plant is highly abrasive: it was once used for scouring pans, hence its common name, bottlebrush

GROWTH HABIT
Upright branched perennial with an indefinite spread.

80cm (32in)

PARTS USED Aerial parts
MAIN CONSTITUENTS Silicic acid and silicates, alkaloids (incl. nicotine), tannins, saponins, flavonoids, bitter principles, other minerals (incl. potassium, manganese, magnesium), phytosterols
ACTIONS Astringent, haemostatic, diuretic, anti-inflammatory, tissue healer, increases coagulation

HOW TO USE

DECOCTION Take ½–1 cup of a decoction (p.342) made from 15g (½oz) of the herb to 600ml (1 pint) water 3 times daily for excessive menstruation, inflammation of the urinary tract, prostate problems, or chronic lung disorders.
JUICE Take 5–10ml (1–2 tsp) 3 times daily for damaged lungs or urinary disorders.
BATH Add 300ml (10fl oz) of the decoction to bath water for sprains, fractures, or irritable skin conditions including eczema.
POULTICE Use 1 tsp of powder made into a paste with a little water, or a handful of the fresh aerial parts sweated in a bowl over a saucepan of simmering water (bain marie); spread on gauze and use for leg ulcers, wounds, sores, or chilblains.
MOUTHWASH/GARGLE Use ½ cup of a decoction with an equal amount of water for mouth or gum infections or sore throats.

HOW TO SOURCE

GROW Prefers moist soil in full sun or partial shade. Usually propagated by root division in early spring. Under statutory control as an invasive weed in some countries.
FORAGE Found in meadows, field borders, hedgerows and waste ground. Don't confuse with marsh horsetail (*Equisetum palustre*), a larger plant that contains toxic alkaloids.
HARVEST Cut stems in the growing season.

CAUTION Seek professional guidance in all cases of blood in the urine, or for sudden changes in menstrual flow leading to heavy bleeding. Do not use for more than four weeks continuously without professional guidance.

Eucalyptus globulus **Eucalyptus**

Native to Australia and Tasmania, the eucalyptus, or "blue gum", tree is now cultivated worldwide both as a commercial crop and for its ability to absorb water and dry up marshes. It is an important remedy among the Australian Aboriginals, although in medicine the essential oil is more commonly used, largely as an antiseptic.

PARTS USED Leaves, essential oil
MAIN CONSTITUENTS Volatile oil (incl. cineole), tannins, aldehydes, bitter resin
ACTIONS Antiseptic, decongestant, antibiotic, antispasmodic, stimulant, febrifuge, hypoglycaemic, anthelmintic

HOW TO USE

DECOCTION Simmer 3–4 leaves per cup of water for 10 minutes in a covered pan and take ½–1 cup 3 times daily for the early stages of colds, chills, nasal catarrh, influenza, asthma, sinusitis, sore throats, and other respiratory disorders.
CHEST RUB Use ½ml (10 drops) of eucalyptus oil in 30ml (1fl oz) of almond oil as a chest rub for colds, bronchitis, asthma, and respiratory problems.
STEAM INHALATION Use ½ml (10 drops) of essential oil or 6 leaves in a bowl of boiling water as a steam inhalation for colds and chest infections.
COMPRESS Soak a pad in a mixture of 10 drops of essential oil and 60ml (2fl oz) of water and apply to inflammations, painful joints, or minor burns.

HOW TO SOURCE

GROW Prefers moisture-retentive soil that is neutral-to-slightly acid in a sunny site that is also sheltered from cold, dry winds. Sow the seeds at 21°C (70°F) in spring and grow on until large enough to transplant into final positions, although buying young trees from a nursery is a quicker process. As the plant absorbs so much water, it can deplete the soil over a significant area.
FORAGE Now found – often in commercial plantations – in many tropical, sub-tropical, and temperate areas worldwide, although it can also be found growing wild in marshy areas. Collect the leaves as required.
HARVEST Gather the leaves as required throughout the year.

> **CAUTION** Do not take the essential oil internally; fatalities have been reported from comparatively low doses.

LEAVES
The leaves are used in Aboriginal medicine as poultices for wounds, or internally for fevers and infections

50m
(164ft)

GROWTH HABIT
Large, evergreen tree with pale blue leaves that turn green as they mature; spread 25m (80ft).

Eupatorium cannabinum **Hemp agrimony**

Native to Europe, hemp agrimony was traditionally used for feverish colds or as a poultice for skin sores. A bitter compound called eupatoriopicrin has now been identified in the plant and is believed to have an antitumour action. The plant also appears to be immunostimulant – increasing resistance in viral infections. However, it also contains toxic alkaloids, so must be used with caution.

LEAVES
The leaves can be pulped and the juice extracted to use as an insect repellent to rub into the coats of dogs and horses

FLOWERHEADS
The pink flowerheads, which appear from summer to early autumn, are a favourite with butterflies and bees

The leaves were traditionally used to wrap up bread to prevent it going mouldy

GROWTH HABIT
Herbaceous perennial with cannabis-like leaves; spread 1.2m (4ft).

1.5m (5ft)

PARTS USED Aerial parts, root
MAIN CONSTITUENTS Volatile oil (incl. thymol, azulenes, alpha-terpinene), flavonoids, sesquiterpene lactones (incl. eupatoriopicrin), pyrrolizidine alkaloids
ACTIONS Febrifuge, diuretic, antiscorbutic, laxative, cholagogue, expectorant, immune stimulant, antirheumatic, diaphoretic, tonic

HOW TO USE

NB: Take for short periods and only under professional guidance.
INFUSION Traditionally used in the treatment of certain skin conditions, rheumatism, and arthritis, but use only under guidance from a qualified herbalist.
POULTICE Pulp a handful of fresh leaves in a blender, spread on gauze, and use on suppurating skin sores or ulcers.

HOW TO SOURCE

GROW Tolerates a range of soil conditions and grows in sun or partial shade, although prefers moist soil. Sow seeds in a cold frame in early spring and lightly cover with compost. Transplant to 7cm (3.5in) pots and plant out in early summer or when well established; allow 60cm (24in) between plants. Alternatively, sow seeds where you want them to grow in spring or autumn.
FORAGE Found in damp woods, ditches, waste ground, or marshy areas. Naturalized in parts of western Asia and North Africa.
HARVEST Cut flowering aerial parts in late summer/early autumn. Dig roots in autumn.

CAUTION Contains pyrrolizidine alkaloids, which are carcinogenic, so only use under professional guidance. High doses may cause nausea and vomiting. Avoid during pregnancy.

Eupatorium purpureum **Gravel root**

Originally found in damp thickets in the eastern USA, gravel root is grown as a statuesque garden ornamental in many parts of the world. Its other common name, Joe Pye weed, is reputedly named after a Native American medicine man who used it to cure typhus. The herb is used for clearing gravel and kidney stones and for other problems affecting the urinary tract.

PARTS USED Rhizome and root
MAIN CONSTITUENTS Eupatorin, volatile oil, flavonoids, resin
ACTIONS Soothing diuretic, antirheumatic, astringent

HOW TO USE

DECOCTION Take ½ cup of a decoction made of 1 tsp dried root to 1 cup water and simmered for 20 minutes for kidney stones, gravel, or painful urination. This mixture was traditionally used to ease the pain of childbirth. Gravel root is believed to enhance the removal of waste products by the kidneys, so the decoction is also useful in rheumatism and gout to improve the excretion of uric acid.
TINCTURE Use 2–4 ml (40–80 drops) 3 times daily for urinary disorders including cystitis and gravel, or discharges associated with infection. It combines well with white dead-nettle (*Lamium album*) for prostate problems and with parsley piert (*Aphanes arvensis*), pellitory-of-the-wall (*Parietaria judaica*), or hydrangea (*Hydrangea* spp.) for kidney stones.

HOW TO SOURCE

GROW Prefers moist, fertile soil in sun or partial shade. Sow seeds in spring in a cold frame and when the seedlings are large enough to handle transplant them to final positions. Allow at least 90cm (36in) between plants. It is best grown at the back of a border, but is popular in planting schemes as it flowers late in the season.
FORAGE Unlikely to be found growing wild beyond the eastern states of the USA, although it might occur as a garden escape. As the root is used, it is best not to collect from the wild. In Europe the related species *Eupatorium cannabinum* (hemp agrimony, p.54) is more likely to be found growing as a hedgerow plant.
HARVEST The roots of two-year-old, or older, plants are dug in autumn.

> **CAUTION** Avoid during pregnancy.

FLOWER BUD
When open, the striking cream to purple flowerheads make gravel root a popular addition to a herbaceous border

LEAVES
The lance-shaped leaves can be large and rather coarse

STEMS
Hollow stems are produced from the fibrous rootstock and are marked with purple where the leaves attach

2.2m (7ft)

GROWTH HABIT
Robust, clump-forming perennial with erect stems; spread 1m (3ft).

Filipendula ulmaria **Meadowsweet**

Growing in damp ditches throughout Europe and western Asia, meadowsweet takes its name from is original use of flavouring mead, or honey wine. Today it is highly regarded as an antacid herb, helping both to combat excess stomach acid leading to indigestion and gastritis and to reduce the body's acidity generally, so helping with arthritic conditions.

FLOWER
The fluffy flowerheads appear in summer and smell slightly of aspirin

LEAVES
The leaves and flowerheads are generally harvested together and used in teas and tinctures

90cm
(36in)

GROWTH HABIT
Clump-forming perennial; spread 60cm (24ft).

PARTS USED Aerial parts, flowers
MAIN CONSTITUENTS Salicylates, flavonoids (incl. rutin and hyperin), volatile oil (incl. salicylaldehyde), citric acid, mucilage, tannins
ACTIONS Antacid, anti-inflammatory, antirheumatic, soothing digestive remedy, diuretic, diaphoretic, anticoagulant

HOW TO USE

INFUSION Take 1 cup of a standard infusion (p.342) of leaves and flowers 3 times daily for feverish colds or mild rheumatic pains. Take ½ cup every 2 hours for acid reflux or indigestion. Can be given to children for stomach upsets; consult a herbalist for advice on dosage.
FLUID EXTRACT Take 2–5ml (40 drops– 1 tsp) 3 times daily for gastritis, gastric ulceration, or chronic rheumatism. Combine with angelica, bogbean (*Menyanthes trifoliata*), or willow for arthritis.
COMPRESS Soak a pad in dilute tincture and apply to painful arthritic joints or for rheumatism or neuralgia.

HOW TO SOURCE

GROW Prefers fertile, non-acid, moist-to-boggy soil in a sunny or lightly shaded position. Sow seeds in autumn in a cold frame and transplant the following spring when the seedlings are established. Allow 60cm (24in) between plants. Alternatively, propagate by division in autumn or spring, or by root cuttings in winter.
FORAGE Found in damp meadows and hedgerow ditches throughout Europe and western Asia. The aerial parts can be collected as flowering begins, or the flowers harvested separately when in full bloom.
HARVEST Collect in summer just before, or at, flowering.

CAUTION Avoid meadowsweet during pregnancy. Avoid in cases of salicylate (or aspirin) sensitivity.

Foeniculum vulgare **Fennel**

Cultivated as both a herb and a vegetable since Roman times, fennel originated in Mediterranean areas, but by the 8th century AD had spread to northern Europe. It is widely available as an after-dinner herbal drink in teabags to improve the digestion, and has been used as a culinary herb with fish for centuries.

PARTS USED Seeds, root, leaves, essential oil

MAIN CONSTITUENTS Volatile oil (incl. estragole, anethole), essential fatty acids, flavonoids (incl. rutin), vitamins, minerals

ACTIONS Carminative, circulatory stimulant, anti-inflammatory, encourages milk flow, mild expectorant, diuretic

HOW TO USE

INFUSION ½–1 tsp of seeds to 1 cup of boiling water as an after-dinner tea to combat wind and indigestion. A standard infusion (p.342) taken 3 times daily can increase milk flow when breast-feeding.

MOUTHWASH/GARGLE Use 1 cup of a standard infusion of seeds as a wash for gum disorders or a gargle for sore throats.

TINCTURE ¼–½ml (5–10 drops) as a remedy for constipation to combat griping pains.

DECOCTION Take 1 cup of a standard decoction of the root 3 times daily for disorders linked to high uric acid levels.

CHEST RUB Add ¼–½ml (5–10 drops) each of fennel, thyme, and eucalyptus essential oil to 20ml (4 tsp) of almond oil and massage into the chest for coughs and bronchitis.

HOW TO SOURCE

GROW Sow fennel seeds where you want them to grow in spring and thin to 30cm (12in), or transplant self-sown seedlings. Generally fairly hardy, but may suffer in severe winters. Can be treated as a biennial. The *dulce* variety is grown as a vegetable.

FORAGE Generally grows on waste ground and in coastal areas, but self-seeded plants growing outside gardens can be found in many places. Gather the leaves in summer for culinary use and the seeds in autumn for teas and medicinal use.

HARVEST Collect the leaves in summer and the seeds in autumn. Lift the root, if using, once the leaves have died down.

CAUTION Essential oils should not be taken internally except under professional advice.

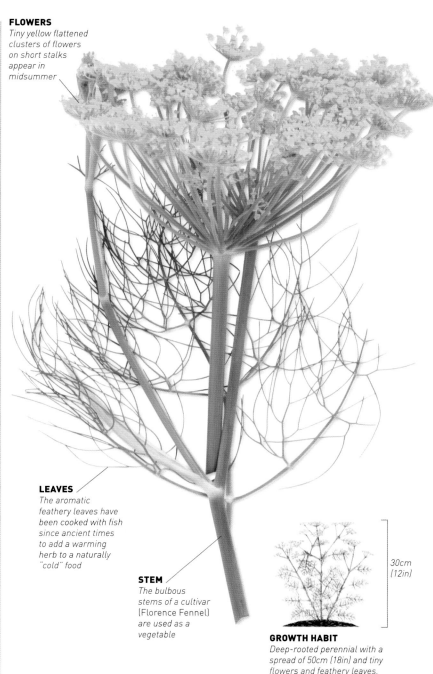

FLOWERS
Tiny yellow flattened clusters of flowers on short stalks appear in midsummer

LEAVES
The aromatic feathery leaves have been cooked with fish since ancient times to add a warming herb to a naturally "cold" food

STEM
The bulbous stems of a cultivar (Florence Fennel) are used as a vegetable

30cm (12in)

GROWTH HABIT
Deep-rooted perennial with a spread of 50cm (18in) and tiny flowers and feathery leaves.

Fragaria vesca **Wild strawberry**

Alpine strawberries, now grown worldwide, originated from this wild strawberry and have smaller, more aromatic fruits than "cultivated" strawberries (which were developed in the 18th century from an American hybrid). Wild strawberry is found in woodlands and grassy areas of Europe, western Asia, and North America. Its leaves and fruits are used medicinally – mainly in astringent teas.

FRUITS
The sweet fruits can be eaten fresh or cooked in preserves, syrups, and drinks

FLOWERS
White five-petalled flowers are borne in early summer, followed by edible fruits

LEAVES
The leaves form in basal clumps and can be collected and dried during the summer to use in astringent teas for diarrhoea and digestive upsets

GROWTH HABIT
Low-growing perennial with edible fruits in summer, that spreads by stolons; indefinite spread.

30cm (12in)

PARTS USED Leaves, fruit
MAIN CONSTITUENTS
Leaf: Volatile oil, flavonoids tannins
Fruit: Fruit acids, salicylates, sugar, vitamins B, C, and E
ACTIONS Astringent, wound herb, diuretic, laxative, liver tonic, cleansing

HOW TO USE

INFUSION Take 1 cup of a standard infusion (p.342) of the leaves 3 times daily for diarrhoea.
MOUTHWASH/GARGLE Use 1 cup of the standard infusion of the leaves for sore throats and gum disease.
LOTION Use the standard infusion of the leaves as a lotion to bathe minor burns, cuts, and grazes.
FRESH BERRIES Traditionally regarded as cooling, strawberries have, in the past, been prescribed for gout, arthritis, rheumatism, and tuberculosis. They can also be soothing for gastritis and in convalescence.
JUICE Juice some fresh berries and take in 10ml (2 tsp) doses 3 times daily to combat infections and as a mild, cleansing laxative in constipation and arthritic disorders.
POULTICE The crushed fresh berries can be used as a poultice to soothe sunburn and skin inflammations.

HOW TO SOURCE

GROW Prefers moist but well-drained fertile soil, which is rich in organic matter, in sun or partial shade. Propagate by sowing seeds in trays in spring or autumn and lightly covering them with soil. Keep moist and transplant to 7.5cm (3in) pots when large enough to handle. Alternatively, grow from rooted stolons (horizontal shoots) separated from the mother plant in late summer. It can be grown as an edging plant in a herb garden.
FORAGE Can be found in hedgerows, woodlands, and grassy areas in many parts of the world. Gather the berries when ripe and the leaves throughout the summer.
HARVEST Collect the fruit as it ripens in the summer and gather the leaves throughout the growing period.

Galium aparine **Cleavers**

A familiar garden weed, cleavers is found throughout Europe and northern and western Asia. In China the whole plant is sometimes eaten as a vegetable. It has been used in cancer treatments since ancient times, although its efficacy has not been confirmed by modern research. It is, however, highly regarded as a cleanser for the lymphatic system.

SEEDS
In times of shortage, the bristly seeds have been roasted as a coffee substitute

STEM
The stem is rough and hairy

LEAVES
The leaves form in whorls around the stem, with tiny white flowers in spring giving rise to bristly fruits in autumn

1.2m (4ft)

GROWTH HABIT
Scrambling annual that climbs by hooked bristles; spread to 3m (10ft).

PARTS USED Whole plant
MAIN CONSTITUENTS Flavonoids, anthraquinone derivatives (in the root), iridoids, coumarins, tannins, polyphenolic acids
ACTIONS Diuretic, lymphatic cleanser and detoxifier, astringent tonic, anti-inflammatory

HOW TO USE

JUICE Take 10ml (2 tsp) of freshly made juice up to 3 times daily as a lymphatic cleanser and diuretic for conditions such as glandular fever, tonsillitis, and prostate disorders.
CREAM Use frequently for psoriasis; it is most effective if treatment begins early when the skin patches are still small.
INFUSION Take 1 cup of a standard infusion (p.342) of the fresh herb 3 times daily for urinary problems, such as cystitis and stones in the urinary tract. Usually combined with other urinary remedies, such as yarrow, couchgrass (*Elymus repens*), marshmallow, or buchu (*Agathosma* spp.).
TINCTURE Take up to 5ml (1 tsp) 3 times daily as a lymphatic cleanser and detoxifier for any enlargement of the lymph nodes.
COMPRESS Apply a pad soaked in a standard infusion to grazes, skin ulcers, and inflammations.

HOW TO SOURCE

GROW Regarded by most gardeners as an irritating annual weed, cleavers climbs by means of hooked bristles through shrubs to reach heights of 1.2m (4ft), and spreads to 3m (10ft). It is not a plant many would choose to cultivate, as it usually grows anywhere and everywhere, but the bristly fruits that appear in autumn can be collected and immediately scattered where the plant is to grow the following year.
FORAGE From spring to autumn, cleavers can be found scrambling through banks, hedgerows, and garden borders. The whole plant can be gathered, and is best used fresh.
HARVEST The whole plant is best gathered in the spring just before flowering.

Ginkgo biloba **Ginkgo**

A survivor of the fossil age, the ginkgo or maidenhair tree is the sole member of its genus and dates back at least 200 million years. The trees are either male or female and only flower when in close proximity. The edible seeds are used in traditional Chinese medicine for some types of asthma, while the leaves have become popular in the West for circulatory disorders.

PARTS USED Leaves, seeds

MAIN CONSTITUENTS Leaves: flavone glycosides, bioflavones, beta-sitosterol, lactones, anthocyanin
Seeds: fatty acids, minerals, bioflavones

ACTIONS Leaves: vasodilator, circulatory stimulant
Seeds: astringent, antifungal, antibacterial

HOW TO USE

FLUID EXTRACT Take 1–3ml (20–60 drops) up to 3 times daily for diseases involving the peripheral circulation, or for cerebral arteriosclerosis in the elderly.

TINCTURE Take 3–5ml (60 drops–1 tsp) 3 times daily for cardiovascular system disorders. It is generally combined with periwinkle (*Vinca* spp.) and lime flowers for circulatory problems, or melilot for venous disorders.

DECOCTION Take 1 cup of a decoction of the seeds, made from 3–4 seeds to 600ml (1 pint) of water, 3 times daily for wheeziness, persistent coughs, or asthmatic conditions. This can be combined with an infusion of coltsfoot and mulberry leaves (*Morus* spp.).

TABLETS Widely available and generally recommended for poor circulation, varicose veins, or memory loss.

HOW TO SOURCE

GROW Most commercially available trees are grown from cuttings from male trees; so female trees can be hard to find. Prefers fertile, moist, but well-drained soil in full sun. Grow from ripe seeds collected from a female tree in autumn and plant in a cold frame, or take semi-ripe cuttings in summer. Avoid pruning.

FORAGE Rarely found in the wild, but widely cultivated as a specimen tree in parks and gardens.

HARVEST Collect leaves and fruits in autumn.

> **CAUTION** Avoid if taking aspirin or warfarin. High doses of the seeds can lead to skin disorders and headaches. Restricted in some countries.

LEAVES
The distinctive leaves give the plant its common name – maidenhair tree, after the fern

40m (130ft)

GROWTH HABIT
Upright, tall, spreading deciduous tree; spread 20m (65ft).

Glycyrrhiza glabra **Liquorice**

A native of the Mediterranean region and south-west Asia, liquorice has been valued for its sweet taste since ancient times. The Romans also used it as a remedy for asthma and coughs. Its cultivation spread to northern Europe in the 15th century. A related Asian species (*Glycyrrhiza uralensis*) is known as "the grandfather of herbs", and is widely used in Chinese medicine.

LEAVES
The pinnate leaves are arranged in pairs and are 7.5–15cm (3–6in) long

FLOWERS
A member of the pea family, liquorice produces small, pea-like, cream to pale lilac flowers in spring

GROWTH HABIT
Tap-rooted perennial with oblong pods; spread 1m (3ft).

2m (6ft)

PARTS USED Root

MAIN CONSTITUENTS Saponins, glycyrrhizin, oestrogenous substances, coumarins, flavonoids, sterols, asparagine

ACTIONS Anti-inflammatory, demulcent, tonic stimulant for adrenal cortex, mild laxative, expectorant, lowers cholesterol levels, soothing for gastric mucosa

HOW TO USE

TINCTURE Take 2–5ml (40 drops–1 tsp) 3 times daily for gastritis, peptic ulceration, mouth ulcers, or excessive stomach acid. Add a similar amount to cough syrups.

FLUID EXTRACT Take 1–2ml (20–40 drops) 3 times a day to strengthen the adrenal glands, especially after steroidal therapy, or as a digestive tonic.

DECOCTION Take 1 cup of a standard decoction (p.342) up to 3 times daily to reduce stomach acid and ease any inflammation or ulceration. Take 1 cup last thing at night for mild constipation.

SYRUP Combine the decoction with an equal amount of honey to make a cough syrup. Combines well with thyme, hyssop, or elecampane for chest problems including bronchitis, asthma, and chest infections.

WASH Add 5ml (1 tsp) of tincture to 50ml (1¾fl oz) of warm water to bathe skin inflammations and irritant skin rashes.

HOW TO SOURCE

GROW Prefers deep, neutral to alkaline, well-drained soil in full sun. Sow seeds in autumn or spring and transplant into 7.5cm (3in) pots when large enough. Grow on in containers until sturdy enough to plant out.

FORAGE Grows wild in southern Europe. Collecting wild roots is not recommended. Gather the seed pods to cultivate at home.

HARVEST Gather the roots of three- or four-year-old plants in autumn.

CAUTION Do not take therapeutic doses if pregnant. Avoid if you have high blood pressure or take digoxin-based drugs. Do not take for prolonged periods except under professional advice.

Hamamelis virginiana **Witch hazel**

Used by Native Americans for traumatic injuries and aching muscles, Virginian witch hazel was originally found in North America's moist woodland areas, from Nova Scotia to Florida. Today it is widely cultivated for its medicinal properties, and as an attractive garden ornamental with heavily scented autumn flowers. Distilled Virginian witch hazel is a familiar first aid remedy.

PARTS USED Leaves, twigs

MAIN CONSTITUENTS Tannins, flavonoids (incl. kaempferol and quercetin), saponins, bitters, volatile oil (incl. eugenol and safrole), choline, gallic acid

ACTIONS Astringent, stops internal and external bleeding, anti-inflammatory

HOW TO USE

DISTILLATE/HYDROSOL The leaves and twigs are distilled commercially to produce a mixture of water and essential oil (sometimes preserved with alcohol). It can be used to stop bleeding from cuts, grazes, or nosebleeds, to bathe varicose veins and irritant skin rashes, and in compresses for sprains or sore eyes.

INFUSION Take 1 cup of a standard infusion (p.342) of leaves up to 3 times daily for diarrhoea, bleeding piles, or capillary fragility.

MOUTHWASH/GARGLE Use 1 cup of a standard infusion of the leaves for sore throats, mouth ulcers, tonsillitis, pharyngitis, and spongy or bleeding gums.

TINCTURE Add 5ml (1 tsp) of the bark tincture to 50ml (1¾fl oz) of water and use as an alternative to distilled witch hazel.

CREAM/OINTMENT Use the bark for minor cuts, grazes, bruises, piles, or varicose veins.

HOW TO SOURCE

GROW Prefers fertile, well-drained, slightly acidic soil in sun or dappled shade, but will tolerate deep soil over chalk. Sow ripe seeds in a cold frame in autumn. The seeds can be slow to germinate, but grow on in larger pots until the young tree is large enough to plant out. Alternatively, take softwood cuttings in summer or hardwood cuttings in autumn.

FORAGE Virginian witch hazel may be found growing wild in woodlands on the eastern side of North America. Gathering bark from wild trees is not recommended, as it can damage the tree, although leaves and a few twigs can be harvested in summer and early autumn before flowering.

HARVEST The leaves are gathered in summer and the bark in autumn. The twigs can be cropped when the tree is dormant.

TWIGS
A decoction of the twigs can be used in exactly the same way as a leaf infusion if you have access to a suitable tree

4m
(12ft)

GROWTH HABIT
A small deciduous single- or multi-stemmed tree or shrub with a spread of 4m (12ft).

Houttuynia cordata **Dokudami**

This plant was once used as an antidote to poisons and its common name, dokudami, translates as "poison blocking" in Japanese. Its Chinese name, *yu xing cao*, means "fish-smelling plant", and houttuynia is a common addition to savoury dishes. One of the most popular medicinal herbs in Japan, dokudami is used widely as a cleanser and detoxifier.

FLOWERS
Tiny yellow flowers appear on white bracts in early summer, and once they fall off in midsummer the leaves and root can be harvested

LEAVES
The leaves can be eaten in salads, or cooked for tempura

The aromatic, heart-shaped leaves are an ingredient of dokudami cha (houttuynia tea) in Japan

30cm (12in)

GROWTH HABIT
Vigorous spreading rhizomatous perennial; spread indefinite.

PARTS USED Leaves, root

MAIN CONSTITUENTS Flavonoids (incl. quercetin and hyperin), terpenes (incl. limonene and camphene), linalool, sitosterols, potassium salts, volatile oil (incl. decanol-acetaldehyde)

ACTIONS Astringent, diuretic, antibacterial, laxative, urinary antiseptic, anti-inflammatory, antitussive, wound herb

HOW TO USE

TINCTURE Take up to 10ml (2 tsp) 3 times daily for urinary infections or pain on urination. For severe or persistent urinary symptoms, seek urgent medical advice to avoid any potential kidney damage.

INFUSION Make a standard infusion (p.342), using the fresh herb when available, and take 1–2 cups on 1 day each month as a general detoxifier.

SYRUP Add 450g (1lb) of honey to 600ml (1 pint) of a standard infusion containing equal amounts of dokudami and Chinese balloon flower and take in 5ml (1 tsp) doses 4–5 times daily for coughs with thick, yellow-green sputum.

DECOCTION Make a standard decoction of the whole plant and take 1–2 cups daily for boils and abscesses, although abscesses will not improve unless drained.

LOTION/OINTMENT Use on cuts, grazes, acne, boils, athlete's foot, or insect bites.

HOW TO SOURCE

GROW Prefers damp, fertile soil in full sun or dappled shade, but will grow in dry conditions, and may require protection in cold areas in winter. Sow seeds in trays in the summer, pot on, and transplant to their final growing positions in spring when well established. Can be invasive.

FORAGE Native to marginal aquatic and marshy areas in China, Japan, Laos, and Vietnam. It is classified as an alien invasive species in North America and Australia.

HARVEST Cut after flowering in summer.

CAUTION A cooling herb, so avoid in cold syndromes.

Humulus lupulus **Hops**

The strobiles, or female flowers, of the hop plant have been used since the 11th century for brewing beer, while the Romans used the leaves as a salad herb. The plant, which is native to Europe, is sedative and bitter, so it is used medicinally both for nervous disorders and digestive problems. It is also oestrogenic, leading to a loss of libido in men who regularly drink large amounts of beer.

FLOWERS
Male and female flowers occur on separate plants. The male flowers are tiny, green, and produced in branched clusters while the larger female flowers are the familiar strobiles under soft green bracts

LEAVES
The leaves are divided into three or five coarsely toothed lobes

An infusion of the female flowers was once mixed with bread to keep the dough light and improve its rising qualities

7m
(22ft)

GROWTH HABIT
A vigorous, deciduous perennial climber with bristly stems.

PARTS USED Strobiles (female flowers)
MAIN CONSTITUENTS Bitter principles (incl. humulon and valerianic acid), tannins, volatile oil (incl. humulene), oestrogenic substances, asparagine, flavonoids
ACTIONS Sedative, anaphrodisiac, restoring tonic for the nervous system, bitter digestive stimulant, diuretic, soporific, astringent

HOW TO USE

TINCTURE Take 1–2ml (20–40 drops) in water 3 times a day as a sedative for nervous tension and anxiety, to stimulate the digestion in poor appetite, and to ease gut spasms and colic.
INFUSION For insomnia, use 2–4 fresh strobiles per cup of boiling water, infuse for 5 minutes, and drink 30 minutes before bedtime. Freshly dried hops can also be used (older plant material is less effective).
WASH Use a standard infusion of fresh or freshly dried hops (above) as a wash for chronic ulcers, skin eruptions, or wounds.
COMPRESS Add 10ml (2 tsp) of tincture to 120ml (4fl oz) of water, soak a pad in the mixture, and use as a compress on varicose ulcers.

HOW TO SOURCE

GROW Prefers fertile, well-drained soil in sun or partial shade, and must be supported on canes or trellises. Sow the seeds in spring in trays in a propagator at 15°C (59°F) and transplant to their final growing positions when established. Alternatively, propagate by softwood cuttings in spring or early summer. Cut down old growth in winter.
FORAGE Likely to be found in hedgerows or waste ground, especially if plants have self-seeded outside commercial hop-growing areas. Collect the female flowers.
HARVEST Collect the strobiles in summer.

CAUTION Do not take if suffering from depression. The growing plant can cause contact dermatitis. Harvesting large amounts can disrupt a menstrual cycle.

Hydrastis canadensis **Goldenseal**

Used by Native Americans for a wide range of ailments, including whooping cough, liver disorders, and heart problems, goldenseal originated in mountain woodlands in North America, and today is used mainly for ulceration and inflammations affecting the mucous membranes. By the 20th century over-harvesting caused the plant to become endangered.

PARTS USED Rhizome
MAIN CONSTITUENTS Alkaloids (incl. hydrastine, canadine, and berberine), volatile oil, resin
ACTIONS Astringent, tonic, digestive, bile stimulant, anti-inflammatory, antibacterial, anticatarrhal, laxative, healing to gastric mucosa, uterine stimulant, stops internal bleeding

HOW TO USE

TINCTURE Take 0.5–2ml (10–40 drops) 3 times a day for catarrhal conditions, mucous colitis, gastroenteritis, or vaginal discharge, as a liver tonic for sluggish digestion, or to help control heavy menstrual and postpartum bleeding.
MOUTHWASH/GARGLE Use 2–3ml (40–60 drops) of tincture in 100ml (3½fl oz) of warm water for mouth ulcers, gum disease, sore throats, and catarrhal conditions.
CAPSULES Use 1 x 300mg capsule 3 times daily for catarrh, infections, or with powdered eyebright to relieve hay fever symptoms.

HOW TO SOURCE

GROW Prefers moist, well-drained slightly acid to neutral soil in shade. Plant seeds in a cold frame in small pots when ripe. Pot on and plant out when large enough, or propagate by root division in autumn.
FORAGE The plant is on the CITES list of endangered species and should not be harvested from the wild.
HARVEST Roots of mature plants are lifted in the autumn and dried.

CAUTION A uterine stimulant, so avoid during pregnancy and lactation.
Avoid if you have high blood pressure.
Prolonged use can reduce absorption of B vitamins.

LEAF
The leaves are carried in pairs, and are each up to 10cm (4in) across

FRUIT
The flowers and fruits form singly at the top of the leaf stalk, with the flowers appearing as the leaves unfurl in the spring

30cm (12in)

GROWTH HABIT
A rhizomatous, deciduous perennial; spread 15–30cm (6–12in) or more.

Hypericum perforatum **St John's wort**

Native to temperate zones in Europe and Asia, St John's wort has been used as a wound herb since the Crusades, and was widely regarded as a cure-all in earlier centuries. It was also used for treating hysteria and mental illness. Today it is widely prescribed in parts of Europe for depression; the quality of commercial preparations, readily available to purchase, can vary.

FLOWERS
The flowering tops should be harvested in summer, when the star-shaped flowers are fully open

LEAVES
When held up to the light, the tiny leaves appear covered with pinpricks – actually oil sacs – that give the plant its botanical name

1m
(3ft)

GROWTH HABIT
Compact, erect perennial with a spread of 1m (3ft).

PARTS USED Aerial parts, flowering tops
MAIN CONSTITUENTS Hypericin, pseudohypericin, flavonoids (incl. rutin), volatile oil, tannins, resins
ACTIONS Astringent, analgesic, antiviral, anti-inflammatory, sedative, restoring tonic for the nervous system

HOW TO USE

INFUSION Take 1 cup of a standard infusion (p.342) of the aerial parts 3 times daily for anxiety, nervous tension, irritability, or emotional upsets associated with menopause or PMS.
TINCTURE Take 2–5ml (40 drops–1 tsp) 3 times daily for nervous tension leading to exhaustion and depression. 5–10 drops of tincture at night can be useful for childhood bed-wetting.
WASH Use 1 cup of a standard infusion to bathe wounds, skin sores, and bruises.
MACERATED OIL Apply a little oil 2–3 times daily to minor burns, sunburn, cuts, or grazes. Massage gently to relieve inflamed joints and tendonitis, and to ease nerve pains. Up to 10 drops of lavender or yarrow essential oil with 5ml (1 tsp) of the oil increases efficacy.

HOW TO SOURCE

GROW Prefers a sunny position and well-drained, alkaline soil. Sow seeds in seed trays in autumn or spring and pot up when large enough to handle. Harden off before planting in final positions.
FORAGE Found growing wild, often in hedgerows, in many parts of the world. A number of closely related species can be easily mistaken for *Hypericum perforatum*.
HARVEST Gather the whole plant just before flowering, or just the flowering tops in midsummer.

CAUTION Avoid during pregnancy. May cause gastrointestinal disturbances and allergic reactions. Interacts with many prescription medicines, including the contraceptive pill. Photosensitive: do not apply topically before sun exposure.

Hyssopus officinalis **Hyssop**

Originally found in rocky areas around the Mediterranean, hyssop is now cultivated in many parts of the world and is often grown as low edging in knot gardens or as a companion plant to keep butterflies from brassicas. It can be used both as a culinary herb to flavour stews and in remedies for coughs and feverish chills.

FLOWERS
The flowers, which bloom in midsummer, were once collected separately and used – often with fresh marshmallow and mullein flowers – for syrups

LEAVES
Sprigs of the leaves can be added to casseroles and stews or tied with thyme and rosemary to make a strongly flavoured bouquet garni

GROWTH HABIT
A semi-evergreen shrub with whorled flower spikes and a spread of 60–90cm (24–36in).

60cm (24in)

PARTS USED Aerial parts, flowers, essential oil

MAIN CONSTITUENTS Volatile oil (incl. camphor and pinocamphone), flavonoids, terpenes (incl. marrubiin), hyssopin, tannins

ACTIONS Expectorant, carminative, diaphoretic, anticatarrhal, antispasmodic, hypertensive, emmenagogue, some antiviral action reported (to *Herpes simplex*)

HOW TO USE

INFUSION Drink ½ cup of a hot standard infusion (p.342) every 2 hours to encourage sweating in the early stages of colds or flu.

TINCTURE Take 2–4ml (40–80 drops) 3 times daily for wind, indigestion, bloating, or colic, especially if anxious.

SYRUP Combine 600ml (1 pint) of an infusion of the whole herb (or the flowers only, if you have them) with 450g (1lb) honey to make a syrup for productive coughs and catarrh. Take in 5ml (1 tsp) doses as required. Combines well with coltsfoot, thyme, or mullein flowers.

CHEST RUB Combine 15ml (1 tbsp) macerated oil of hyssop with 2 drops (1ml) each of essential oils of thyme and eucalyptus as a chest rub for bronchitis and chesty colds.

HOW TO SOURCE

GROW Prefers fertile, neutral to alkaline soil, and full sun. Grow from seed in trays in autumn or spring and transplant to final positions when established; allow up to 90cm (36in) between plants. Alternatively, take softwood cuttings in summer. Prune lightly after flowering, and harder in spring.

FORAGE Unlikely to be found growing in the wild beyond the Mediterranean region.

HARVEST Gather leaves and flower buds in summer and sprigs in the growing season.

CAUTION In high doses the essential oil can trigger epileptic seizures; use only under professional guidance. Avoid during pregnancy.

Inula helenium **Elecampane**

Native to woods and grassy areas across Europe and western Asia, elecampane is largely used today as a cough remedy and respiratory tonic. In earlier ages it was regarded much more as a cure-all: the Romans prescribed the herb for digestive upsets and sciatica; while the Anglo-Saxons used it for skin diseases, leprosy, and for sudden onset disorders or "elf-shot".

PARTS USED Root and rhizome

MAIN CONSTITUENTS Inulin, helenin, volatile oil (incl. azulenes and sesquiterpene lactones), sterols, possible alkaloids, mucilage

ACTIONS Tonic, stimulating expectorant, diaphoretic, antibacterial, antifungal, antiparasitic

HOW TO USE

DECOCTION Take 1 cup of a standard decoction (p.342), best made with fresh root, 3 times daily for bronchitis, asthma, and upper respiratory catarrh. The same mixture can also ease hay fever symptoms, and is valuable as a respiratory tonic. The decoction has a distinctive taste, so sweeten with 1 teaspoon of honey if desired.

TINCTURE Take 3–5ml (60 drops–1 tsp) 3 times daily for chronic respiratory complaints such as bronchitis.

SYRUP Combine 300ml (10fl oz) of a decoction (ideally from fresh root) with 225g (8oz) of honey to make a cough syrup and take in 5ml (1 tsp) doses as required for productive coughs or to ease hay fever symptoms.

HOW TO SOURCE

GROW Prefers moist but well-drained soil in a sunny position. Sow the seeds in a cold frame in autumn and transplant to their final position when established; allow 90cm (36in) between plants. Alternatively, propagate by division in spring or autumn. The plant has a deep-rooted rhizome and, once established, can be difficult to eradicate. Flowers appear in summer.

FORAGE The root is generally used, which can make foraging difficult, although the plant is commonly found in hedgerows and grassy places. The flowers can be easily harvested in summer and used to make a mild cough syrup.

HARVEST The root is dug in autumn, chopped, and dried quickly at a high heat.

> **CAUTION** Avoid during pregnancy and if breast-feeding.

FLOWER
The flowers of a related species (Inula japonica) are used in cough remedies in China

LEAVES
The large bright green leaves can be up to 70cm (28in) in length and have a soft, downy underside

2m (6ft)

GROWTH HABIT
Tall, upright, rhizomatous perennial; spread 1.5m (5ft).

Jasminum officinale **Jasmine**

Native to Himalayan regions, India, Pakistan, and parts of China, jasmine is widely grown as a garden ornamental and is also extensively cultivated for its essential oil, which is used mainly as a sedative and antidepressant. Its close relation, *Jasminum grandiflorum*, is known as *jati* in India and is considered an important spiritual tonic to emphasize love and compassion.

Jasmine oil, produced from the flowers, is extremely expensive owing to its complex and lengthy production

FLOWERS
The flowers, which appear from summer to early autumn, are rarely available commercially, as they are used to produce oil, but can be gathered from garden plants and used in infusions to relieve stress and tension

STEM
The stems, with their small, bright-green leaves, can grow to 12m (40ft)

12m (40ft)

GROWTH HABIT
Woody stemmed deciduous climber with fragrant white star-shaped flowers.

PARTS USED Flowers, essential oil
MAIN CONSTITUENTS Alkaloids (incl. jasminine), volatile oil (incl. benzyl alcohol, linalool, and linyl acetate), salicylic acid
ACTIONS Aphrodisiac, astringent, bitter, relaxing nervine, sedative, mild analgesic, galactagogue, antidepressant, antiseptic, antispasmodic, uterine tonic, encourages parturition

HOW TO USE

INFUSION Use 4–6 fresh flowers in 1 cup of boiling water, infuse for 5 minutes, and drink 2–3 times a day to relieve stress and tension, or for mild depression.
MASSAGE OIL Add 1–2 drops of essential oil to 5ml (1tsp) of almond oil for massage rubs to relieve anxiety, insomnia, or depression. Use 20 drops of essential oil in 30ml (1fl oz) of almond oil to massage the abdomen during the first stages of labour. The same mixture can be used for period pains.
DIFFUSER Use 2–3 drops of essential oil in a diffuser to scent a bedroom for problems with impotence or frigidity; a mutual massage between partners using 1–2 drops of jasmine oil in 5ml (1 tsp) of almond oil before lovemaking can help.

HOW TO SOURCE

GROW Prefers fertile, well-drained soil in a sun or partial shade. Prune after flowering if necessary. Usually grown from semi-ripe cuttings in summer, although established plants will frequently self-seed.
FORAGE Rarely found in the wild outside its native area, although cultivated commercially worldwide.
HARVEST The flowers are traditionally gathered in the evening when their scent is greatest while in full bloom.

Juniperus communis **Juniper**

Native to Europe, North America, and many parts of Asia, juniper has long been associated with ritual cleansing and has been burned in various temples throughout history. Today the herb is mainly used as remedy for urinary disorders, while its essential oil is included in various massage rubs for muscle and joint pains.

PARTS USED Fruits, essential oil, cade oil
MAIN CONSTITUENTS Volatile oil (incl. myrcene and cineole), flavonoids, sugars, glycosides, tannins, vitamin C
ACTIONS Urinary antiseptic, diuretic, carminative, digestive tonic, emmenagogue, antirheumatic

HOW TO USE

TINCTURE Take 1–2ml (20–40 drops) in a little water 3 times daily for urinary tract problems including cystitis, or to stimulate the digestion and ease flatulence.
INFUSION Infuse 15g (1/2oz) of crushed berries in 600ml (1 pint) of boiling water for 30 minutes and take 1/2–1 cup 3 times daily for gastric upsets, stomach chills, or period pains. The infusion can also be sipped during the first stages of labour.
MASSAGE OIL Use 10 drops of juniper essential oil in 5ml (2 tsp) of almond oil as a massage for arthritic pains.
HAIR RINSE Use 10 drops of cade oil in 1 tbsp almond oil, add to 600ml (1 pint) of hot water, mix well, and apply for psoriasis affecting the scalp. Leave for 15 minutes or longer, and rinse thoroughly.

HOW TO SOURCE

GROW Tolerates almost all conditions including both acid and alkaline soils, sun and partial shade or exposed positions, but dislikes water-logged soil. Usually grown from seed sown in a propagator in autumn or spring or by heeled cuttings in autumn. Grow on until the plants are well established and can be moved to their final positions.
FORAGE Found on moors, heaths, conifer woods, and scrubland in temperate regions throughout the northern hemisphere.
HARVEST Collect the "berries" – actually small cones –by shaking the branches over a groundsheet to dislodge them.

CAUTION Avoid during pregnancy. May irritate the kidneys after long-term use, so do not take for more than six weeks internally without a break or if there is already kidney damage.

LEAVES
The juvenile juniper leaves are needle-like, while the mature leaves are awl-shaped (narrowly triangular with a tapering point) and arranged in whorls

STEMS
The stems and branches are covered in red-brown papery bark

CADE OIL
Cade oil is made by dry distillation of the heartwood, and is used for psoriasis

GROWTH HABIT
An upright shrub with a spread of 1.5m (5ft). Its fruits take two years to ripen.

4m (13ft)

Lavandula angustifolia **Lavender**

Lavender takes it name from the Latin *lavare* (to wash), and has been used to scent bath oils and soaps for centuries. It originates in Mediterranean regions and is still closely associated with the perfume industry in southern France. The flowers are valued for their soothing and sedating properties, and the essential oil is used for muscle aches and respiratory problems.

FLOWERS
The dense spikes of flowers are steam-distilled to produce an essential oil that can be used for easing muscle pains and headaches

GROWTH HABIT
Compact, bushy, evergreen shrub with a spread of 90cm (36in).

90cm (36in)

PARTS USED Flowers, essential oil
MAIN CONSTITUENTS Volatile oil (mostly linalyl acetate and cineole), tannins, coumarins, flavonoids, triterpenoids
ACTIONS Relaxant, antispasmodic, tonic for the nervous system, circulatory stimulant, antibacterial, analgesic, carminative, cholagogue, antidepressant

HOW TO USE

INFUSION Take 1 cup of a standard infusion (p342) of the flowers up to 3 times daily for nervous exhaustion tension headaches. A cup before bedtime can also help with insomnia, or after meals with indigestion.
TINCTURE Take up to 5ml (1 tsp) twice a day for headaches, depression, or nervous tension. Can also help ease asthma, especially where attacks are triggered by nervousness or stress.
MASSAGE OIL Dilute 2ml (40 drops) of essential oil in 10ml (2 tsp) carrier oil. Use for muscular pains, or rub into the temples and the nape of the neck for tension headaches or at the first sign of a migraine.
HAIR RINSE Dilute 1ml (20 drops) of essential oil in a jug of water as a final hair rinse for head lice, and use a few drops of neat oil on a fine-toothed comb run through the hair to remove both lice and nits.
ESSENTIAL OIL Use neat on insect bites or stings, or add 10 drops to 50ml (1¾fl oz) of water to use as a lotion for sunburn. Add 3–4 drops to a tissue and place on the pillow to aid sleep.

HOW TO SOURCE

GROW Prefers well-drained, moderately fertile soil in full sun. Germination from seed can be erratic; alternatively, take semi-ripe cuttings in summer.
FORAGE Native to dry, rocky regions in the Mediterranean and south-west Asia; may grow wild in other areas.
HARVEST Flowers are usually harvested in the mornings on sunny days in summer.

Leonurus cardiaca **Motherwort**

As its name suggests, motherwort has a long tradition as a woman's herb and was used both to calm the mother in childbirth and encourage contractions. Native to much of Europe, the plant has striking foliage and is sometimes grown as a garden ornamental. It is also used in treating heart conditions and it is commonly given for palpitations and to improve heart function.

LEAVES
The distinctive leaves were thought to resemble a lion's mane, hence the plant's botanical name, Leonurus

STEM
A member of the mint family, motherwort has its group's characteristic square stem

GROWTH HABIT
Upright perennial with purple stems; spread 60cm (24in).

1.2m (4ft)

PARTS USED Aerial parts
MAIN CONSTITUENTS Alkaloids (incl. stachydrine), iridoid (leonurine), flavonoids, diterpenes, volatile oil, tannins, vitamin A
ACTIONS Uterine stimulant, relaxant, cardiac tonic, carminative, antispasmodic, hypotensive, diaphoretic

HOW TO USE

INFUSION Take ½ cup of a standard infusion (p.342) 3 times daily for anxiety, menopausal problems, or heart weakness. Sip the tea flavoured with cloves (*Syzygium aromaticum*) during labour, and after childbirth to help restore the womb and reduce the risk of bleeding. Combine with lemon balm and lime flowers and use 2–4 tsp per cup to relieve symptoms of angina pectoris.
TINCTURE Take 5ml (1 tsp) 3 times daily for palpitations, menopausal problems such as hot flushes and emotional ability, rapid heartbeat, or PMS.
CAPSULES/POWDER Use as an alternative to the bitter infusion. Blend 1 level tsp of powdered herb with 1 tsp of honey, or take 2 x 500mg capsules, 2–3 times daily.

HOW TO SOURCE

GROW Prefers moist but well-drained soil in sun or partial shade. Sow seeds in a cold frame in spring and transplant to their final position when the seedlings are well-established; allow 45cm (18in) between plants. Alternatively, propagate by division in spring or autumn. It can self-seed enthusiastically and become invasive.
FORAGE May be found growing on waste ground, at woodland edges, or by roadsides across Europe. Avoid plants from busy roadsides to minimize pollutants.
HARVEST Gather in summer while the plant is flowering.

CAUTION A uterine stimulant, so avoid in pregnancy (except during labour) and heavy menstruation. Seek professional advice for all heart conditions.

Levisticum officinale **Lovage**

Traditionally associated with love potions and aphrodisiacs, lovage was originally called *luveshe* (Old French) or "loveache". It originates in the eastern Mediterranean, although it is now widely naturalized. A culinary herb used in stock cubes, lovage is also used for treating various digestive, respiratory, and urinary problems, and is generally warming for the circulation.

PARTS USED Root, leaves, seeds
MAIN CONSTITUENTS Volatile oil (mostly phthalides), coumarins (incl. bergapten), beta-sitosterol, resins, and gums
ACTIONS Mild antibiotic, anticatarrhal, antispasmodic, diaphoretic, expectorant, sedative, carminative, mild diuretic, emmenagogue

HOW TO USE

DECOCTION Add 15g (½oz) of the root to 900ml (1½ pints) of water and simmer to reduce the volume by one third. Take ½–1 cup up to 3 times daily for indigestion, cystitis, rheumatism, gout, poor appetite, or painful menstruation. Combines well with an equal amount of agrimony infusion for indigestion.
TINCTURE Take 1–3ml (20–60 drops) of the root tincture in warm water 3 times daily for indigestion, poor appetite, urinary tract problems, or period pain. Take every 2 hours for colic.
GARGLE Use 1 cup of the root decoction as a mouthwash for mouth ulcers or as a gargle for tonsillitis.
SEEDS Chew 2–3 seeds to relieve flatulence and indigestion.
FRESH LEAVES AND STEMS Chop and add to casseroles to flavour the stock.

HOW TO SOURCE

GROW Prefers fertile, moist, well-drained soil in full sun and an open position; tolerates other conditions. Sow seeds when ripe in early autumn and transplant into position when large enough, or propagate by dividing established plants in spring.
FORAGE Sometimes found growing wild; harvest the leaves and seeds to use in cooking throughout the growing period. Lovage shoots appear early in the year, so can be useful when little else is available.
HARVEST Gather leaves through spring and early summer, seeds in late summer or autumn, and the root in late autumn.

CAUTION Avoid during pregnancy. The foliage can irritate skin.

FLOWERS
The tiny yellow-green flowers, which are borne in umbels, appear in midsummer

STEM
The thick stems have a celery-like flavour and can be chopped fresh and added to stews and casseroles

2m
(6ft)

GROWTH HABIT
Perennial with triangular divided leaves and tiny yellow flowers; spread 90cm (36in).

Linum perenne **Perennial flax**

Perennial flax is very similar to a related species, common flax or linseed *(Linum usitatissimum)*, which is the more commonly cultivated form. Both are native to Europe, although linseed also grows from the Mediterranean to India. The seeds of perennial flax are used much like linseed, although – unlike common flax – the fresh aerial parts are also a traditional remedy.

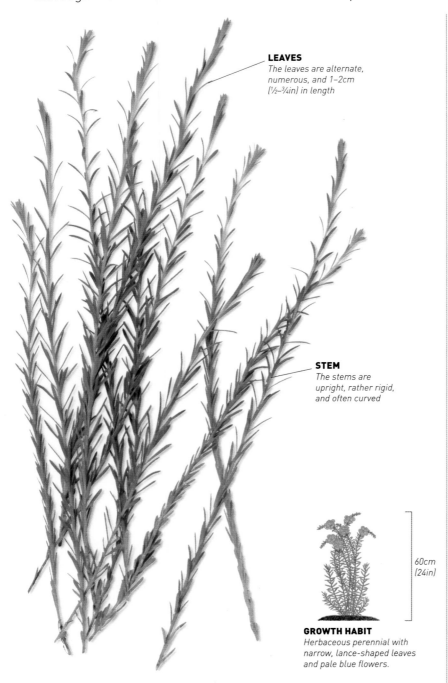

LEAVES
The leaves are alternate, numerous, and 1–2cm (½–¾in) in length

STEM
The stems are upright, rather rigid, and often curved

60cm (24in)

GROWTH HABIT
Herbaceous perennial with narrow, lance-shaped leaves and pale blue flowers.

PARTS USED Aerial parts, seeds, seed oil
MAIN CONSTITUENTS Mucilage, linoleic acid, cyanogenic glycosides, bitter principle, fixed oil incl. linolenic acid, vitamins A, B, D, and E, minerals, and amino acids
ACTIONS Antirheumatic, diuretic, anti-inflammatory, demulcent, soothing antitussive, antiseptic, laxative

HOW TO USE

INFUSION Add 60g (2oz) of fresh chopped aerial parts to 600ml (1 pint) of boiling water and take 1 cup 3 times daily for colds.
POULTICE The seeds can be used as linseeds: crush or pulp in a blender or food processor, spread on gauze, and apply to boils, abscesses, or skin ulcers.
CRUSHED SEEDS Crush 30g (1oz) in a pestle and mortar or food processor and mix with yoghurt as a dietary supplement providing essential fatty acids to support treatments for eczema, menstrual disorders, rheumatoid arthritis, or atherosclerosis.
SEEDS For constipation, mix 1–2 tsp of dried seeds with muesli, porridge, or yoghurt and eat at breakfast. Then drink 300ml (10fl oz) of water or fruit juice.

HOW TO SOURCE

GROW Prefers well-drained light or sandy soil in full sun. Sow seeds in trays in early spring in a cold frame and transplant out after the last frosts; alternatively, sow seeds directly in spring after all danger of frost is past, or in late summer, and cover with a light dusting of compost. Transplant out, leaving 25cm (10in) between plants.
FORAGE Commonly found at higher altitudes (eg, the Alps) and northern regions. Only collect seeds from sustainable populations. Collect the aerial parts while flowering in summer for use in infusions.
HARVEST Gather seeds in summer and aerial parts through the growing season.

CAUTION The seeds contain traces of prussic acid (which are potentially toxic in large quantities). Do not exceed stated dosages.

Lycium barbarum **Goji**

Native to China and Tibet, goji – variously known as wolfberry, matrimony vine, or Chinese boxthorn – is used as a hedging shrub. Both the root bark and berries have been used in China for more than 2,000 years as remedies for various problems associated with weakened liver or kidney energy, including impotence and eye disorders.

PARTS USED Fruit

MAIN CONSTITUENTS Fruit: vitamins, minerals, amino acids, essential fatty acids Bark: alkaloids, saponins, tannins

ACTIONS Hypotensive, hypoglycaemic, hypolipidaemic, immune stimulant, liver tonic and restorative

HOW TO USE

FRESH BERRIES Add up to 30g (1oz) to breakfast cereal or yoghurt to increase vitamin and mineral intake, enhance energy and well-being, or stimulate the immune system.

DRIED BERRIES Add up to 30g (1oz) to soups and stews, or add to cakes and desserts as alternatives to blueberries.

TINCTURE Take 1–2ml (20–40 drops) up to 3 times daily as a general energy tonic.

PATENT CHINESE REMEDIES Various products such as *qi ju di huang wan* (pills that include lycium and chrysanthemum) are used as a tonic for blood and *yin* energy, but are best prescribed by professional practitioners.

HOW TO SOURCE

GROW Prefers average soil in a sunny position and is drought tolerant. Sow fresh seeds 1cm (½in) deep in compost. Keep in a warm place until germinated, and pot on when the leaves develop. Pinch out the tops when 10cm (4in) high to ensure bushy growth. Will produce fruit from the second year.

FORAGE Introduced into Europe in the 18th century, it can sometimes be found naturalized in hedgerows.

HARVEST Gather berries in autumn. They discolour if touched by hand, so shake them into a cloth.

> **CAUTION** Avoid therapeutic doses in pregnancy – small doses in cooking are perfectly safe. Avoid during colds or flu, if suffering from diarrhoea and/or if digestion is poor. Ensure that your supplies are of good quality.

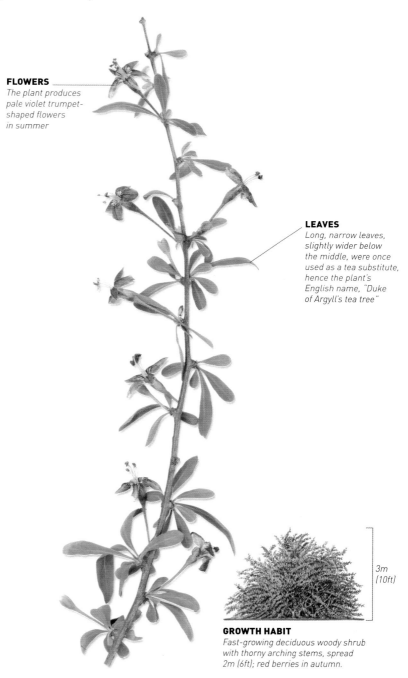

FLOWERS
The plant produces pale violet trumpet-shaped flowers in summer

LEAVES
Long, narrow leaves, slightly wider below the middle, were once used as a tea substitute, hence the plant's English name, "Duke of Argyll's tea tree"

3m (10ft)

GROWTH HABIT
Fast-growing deciduous woody shrub with thorny arching stems, spread 2m (6ft); red berries in autumn.

Matricaria recutita **German chamomile**

Also known as scented mayweed, German chamomile's apple-scented fragrance is familiar to herbal tea drinkers, and is used both for digestive disorders and nervous problems and as an ingredient in anti-inflammatory creams and ointments. Its close relation, Roman chamomile (*Chamaemelum nobile*), is used in similar ways. It is native to Europe, western Asia, and India.

FLOWERS
Single daisy-like flowers appear from early summer to autumn; double flowers are found in some varieties of Roman chamomile

LEAVES
The fine aromatic feathery leaves gave rise to one of the plant's common names, "scented mayweed"

GROWTH HABIT
Upright annual or biennial; spread 10–38cm (4–15in).

60cm (24in)

PARTS USED Flowers, essential oil
MAIN CONSTITUENTS Volatile oil (incl. proazulenes), flavonoids (incl. rutin), valerianic acid, coumarins, tannins, salicylates, cyanogenic glycosides
ACTIONS Anti-inflammatory, antispasmodic, bitter, sedative, anti-emetic, carminative, anti-allergenic

HOW TO USE

INFUSION Take 1 cup of standard infusion (p.342) of the flowers for mild digestive problems or insomnia. German chamomile is a gentle herb that is suitable for children at reduced doses.
STEAM INHALATION Add 10ml (2 tsp) of flowers or 5 drops of essential oil to a basin of boiling water for hay fever or mild asthma.
TINCTURE Take 10ml (2 tsp) of the flower tincture 3 times daily for irritable bowel syndrome or nervous tension.
BATHS Add 4–5 drops of essential oil to the bath to heal wounds or soothe the skin. Add 1 cup of strained infusion to a baby's bath at night to encourage sleep.
CREAM/OINTMENT/LOTION Use on insect bites, wounds, or eczema.
MOUTHWASH/GARGLE Use 10ml (2 tsp) of tincture in a glass of warm water, or 1 cup of standard infusion for gum disease and mouth inflammations or as a gargle for sore throats.

HOW TO SOURCE

GROW Prefers well-drained, neutral to slightly acid soil, and a sunny site. Sow seeds where you want them to grow in autumn or spring. It self-seeds freely.
FORAGE Found growing in Europe, western Asia, and India. Easily confused with other daisies, so be familiar with its distinctive smell before gathering.
HARVEST Gather flowers in summer.

CAUTION Can cause contact dermatitis. Avoid if you are allergic to the Compositae family.

Melilotus officinalis **Melilot**

Also known as king's clover, melilot is native to Europe, north Africa, and temperate regions of Asia, and is widely cultivated as a fodder crop for silage. Today it is largely used for problems associated with venous circulation, including thrombosis and varicose veins, although in the past it was a popular remedy for indigestion, bronchitis, and insomnia in children.

FLOWERS
The fragrant yellow, pea-like flower spikes blossom in summer

The whole plant, including the stems, needs to be dried quickly or used fresh immediately, as toxins develop as it rots

LEAVES
The three-lobed leaves are smooth and green with oval leaflets

GROWTH HABIT
Upright or spreading slender biennial; spread 20–90cm (8in–36in).

1.2m (4ft)

PARTS USED Aerial parts
MAIN CONSTITUENTS Flavonoids, coumarins, resin, tannins, volatile oil; dicoumarol (an anti-coagulant) is produced as the plant ages and rots
ACTIONS Antispasmodic, anti-inflammatory, diuretic, expectorant, sedative, styptic, mild analgesic

HOW TO USE

INFUSION Take ½–1 cup of a standard infusion (p.342) of the aerial parts up to 3 times daily for varicose veins, lymphatic swellings, piles, anxiety, menopausal disorders, insomnia, or to reduce the risk of thrombosis. Can be used for insomnia in children; consult a herbalist for advice on dosage.
CREAM Combine with an equal amount of calendula cream and apply 3–4 times daily for varicose eczema.
OINTMENT Use several times daily for piles (haemorrhoids).
COMPRESS Apply a pad soaked in 1 cup of infusion for facial or intercostal neuralgia.
EYEBATH Simmer 1 cup of well-strained standard infusion gently for 2–3 minutes to sterilize the mix; allow to cool thoroughly and used as an eyebath for conjunctivitis.

HOW TO SOURCE

GROW Prefers sun and well-drained neutral to alkaline soil; tolerates other conditions. Sow seeds in spring or summer where you want to grow them, then thin out to 60cm (24in) apart. Self-seeds in ideal conditions.
FORAGE Found in meadow borders, dry waste ground, and hedgerows. Collect the whole plant in late spring or early summer and use fresh, or dry immediately while still flowering. Collect the flowers separately to use in cold macerated oils.
HARVEST Gather while flowering in late spring or early summer.

CAUTION Do not take if on anti-coagulant medication (such as warfarin or heparin); can be emetic in large doses.

Melissa officinalis **Lemon balm**

A European native, also known as "bee balm", this herb takes its botanical name from the Greek word for "honey bee" as it was regarded as being as healing and curative as honey. Both relaxing and tonifying for the nervous system, lemon balm is largely used today for anxiety, depression, nervous tension, and related digestive disorders.

PARTS USED Aerial parts, essential oil
MAIN CONSTITUENTS Volatile oil (incl. citronellal, linalool, and citral), polyphenols, tannins, bitter principle, flavonoids, rosmarinic acid
ACTIONS Sedative, antidepressant, digestive stimulant, peripheral vasodilator, diaphoretic, relaxing restorative for nervous system, carminative, antiviral, antibacterial

HOW TO USE

INFUSION Take 1 standard infusion (p.342) of fresh or dried leaves 3 times daily for depression, nervous exhaustion, indigestion or nausea; use a dilute infusion for children suffering from chicken pox.
CREAM/OINTMENT Use on sores, cold sores, poorly healing wounds, or insect bites.
LOTION Add 1ml (20 drops) of essential oil to 100ml (3½fl oz) of water in a spray bottle and spray on skin to repel biting insects.
TINCTURE Take 10–20 drops in water 3–5 times daily for depression, tension headaches, and anxiety. Best made from fresh leaves.
MASSAGE OIL Add 5–6 drops of essential oil to 15ml (1 tbsp) of almond oil and use as a massage for depression, tension, asthma, and bronchitis, or dab on cold sores at the first sign of symptoms.

HOW TO SOURCE

GROW Prefers moist, well-drained soil, but thrives in poor soil and tolerates full sun or shade. Sow seeds in a cold frame in spring and transplant when well established, or divide roots in spring when growth starts to appear in autumn. Self-seeds, and can be invasive. Less vigorous variegated or golden cultivars are an alternative option.
FORAGE Grows in scrubby, partially shaded areas across Europe, or as cultivated plants that have self-seeded elsewhere.
HARVEST Gather the aerial parts just before the flowers open in summer, and the leaves throughout the growing period.

LEAVES
The leaves are easily confused with other members of the mint family, but their dominant lemon aroma makes them easy to distinguish

FLOWERS
The flowers, which bloom in summer, are much loved by bees, and it is said that rubbing the hive with the herb will prevent honey bees from swarming

1.2m (4ft)

GROWTH HABIT
Dense, bushy upright perennial spreading to 45cm (18in), with aromatic lemon-scented leaves.

Mentha x piperita **Peppermint**

There are more than 25 different types of mint, many of which cross-pollinate readily to produce variable hybrids. Peppermint, which originates in Europe, was the result of one such cross, possibly in ancient times, and is now naturalized worldwide. It is widely cultivated for its oil, which is used in flavourings and to scent perfumes and toiletries.

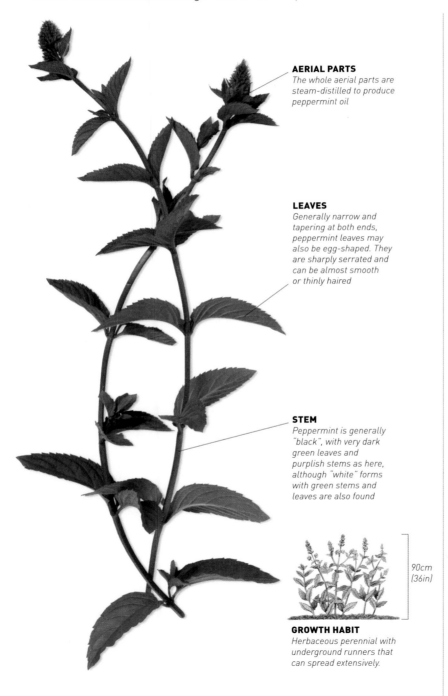

AERIAL PARTS
The whole aerial parts are steam-distilled to produce peppermint oil

LEAVES
Generally narrow and tapering at both ends, peppermint leaves may also be egg-shaped. They are sharply serrated and can be almost smooth or thinly haired

STEM
Peppermint is generally "black", with very dark green leaves and purplish stems as here, although "white" forms with green stems and leaves are also found

90cm
(36in)

GROWTH HABIT
Herbaceous perennial with underground runners that can spread extensively.

PARTS USED Aerial parts, essential oil
MAIN CONSTITUENTS Volatile oil (mainly menthol), tannins, flavonoids (incl. luteolin), tocopherols, choline, bitter principle, triterpenes
ACTIONS Antispasmodic, digestive tonic, anti-emetic, carminative, peripheral vasodilator, diaphoretic, cholagogue, analgesic, antiseptic

HOW TO USE

TEA Add 2–3 fresh leaves to 1 cup of boiling water and infuse for 5 minutes for everyday drinking; especially suitable after meals.
STEAM INHALATION Add a few fresh sprigs to a basin of boiling water and use as an inhalant to ease nasal congestion.
INFUSION Use 15g (½oz) to 600ml (1pint) of boiling water and take ½–1 cup 2–3 times daily for nausea, indigestion, flatulence, or colic, or with other herbs for colds or catarrh.
LOTION Add 30 drops of essential oil to 120ml (4fl oz) vegetable oil and massage into aching muscles and joints, or use for scabies or ringworm. Use in a spray bottle as a mosquito repellent or foot deodorant.

HOW TO SOURCE

GROW Prefers fertile, moist soil in full sun or partial shade. Can be invasive if growing conditions are ideal. Propagated by division in spring or autumn or by tip cuttings in spring or summer; easy to root if the sprigs are kept standing in water for a few days. As a hybrid, it is sterile and produces no seeds. In general, mints should not be grown from seed, as they cross-pollinate readily and may not come true.
FORAGE Generally found in moist areas. Native to Europe and the Mediterranean area; classified as invasive in parts of North America. Collect the leaves for tea throughout the growing season.
HARVEST Cut aerial parts before flowering.

CAUTION Do not use peppermint oil for children under the age of five.

Nepeta cataria **Catnip**

Also known as catmint, catnip – as the name implies – is much loved by cats, who will roll ecstatically in the young plants. Native to Europe and Mediterranean regions, but now naturalized in many parts of the world, the herb is used for digestive disorders or feverish chills. As a gentle remedy, it is also safe to use for many childhood disorders.

PARTS USED Aerial parts
MAIN CONSTITUENTS Volatile oil (incl. citronellol, geraniol, and nepetalactone), glycosides
ACTIONS Antispasmodic, antidiarrhoeal, emmenagogue, diaphoretic, carminative, nerve relaxant

HOW TO USE

INFUSION Take ¹/₂–1 cup of a standard infusion (p.342) 3 times a day for colds, flu, stomach upsets, and indigestion. Reduce the dose, depending on age, for children and use for childhood illnesses, colic, or emotional upsets.
TINCTURE Take up to 5ml (1 tsp) 3 times daily with the infusion for headaches associated with digestive disturbances. Use 5–10ml (1–2 tsp) neat externally as a friction rub for rheumatism and arthritis.
ENEMA Use up to 1 litre (1³/₄ pints) of a well-strained standard infusion to clear toxic wastes from the colon.
OINTMENT Apply 2–3 times daily for piles (haemorrhoids).

HOW TO SOURCE

GROW Prefers moist but well-drained soil in full sun. Sow the seeds in autumn in trays of compost in a cold fame and transplant to 7.5cm (3in) pots when large enough to handle. Plant out in early summer in their final growing positions. Alternatively, propagate by root division in autumn or spring or take cuttings in spring or early summer. Self-seeds in favourable conditions, especially in gardens where there are no cats. Said to repel aphids, cucumber beetles, and other pests in companion planting.
FORAGE Found in scrubby, waste ground and wayside places in many parts of Europe and Asia, and now naturalized in North America. Collect the aerial parts in summer.
HARVEST Cut the aerial parts just as the plant is starting to flower.

> **CAUTION** Avoid during pregnancy.

FLOWERS
The tubular, two-lipped flowers, which appear in whorls from summer to mid autumn, are spotted white with purple patches

LEAVES
The dried leaves are used in teas, which can be soothing for many childhood ailments including fevers, colic, and hyperactivity

STEM
Like all members of the mint family, catnip has a square stem

GROWTH HABIT
Pungent, hairy perennial with grey-green oval leaves and a spread of 23–60cm (9–24in).

90cm (36in)

Oenothera biennis **Evening primrose**

Native to North America, evening primrose is now grown worldwide both as a garden ornamental and as a commercial crop to supply a global trade in its seed oil, which is rich in essential fatty acids. The oil is marketed as a food supplement and remedy for a variety of ailments, including skin, arthritic, and menstrual disorders.

PARTS USED Seed oil, leaves, stems, flowers

MAIN CONSTITUENTS Seeds: rich in essential fatty acids, including gamma-linolenic acid – a precursor of prostaglandin E1

ACTIONS Whole plant: astringent, sedative. Seed oil: hypotensive, anticoagulant, hypolipidaemic

HOW TO USE

INFUSION Make a standard infusion (p.342) of the leaves and stems and take 1 cup 3 times daily for digestive upsets including poor appetite and diarrhoea.

SYRUP Combine 450g (1lb) of sugar or honey with 600ml (1 pint) of a strained standard infusion of the leaves and stems, bring to the boil, and simmer gently for 10 minutes; take in 5–10ml (1–2 tsp) doses as required for whooping cough.

CAPSULES Commercial capsules often contain vitamin E as a preservative; take 500mg daily or follow the directions on the pack. Generally used for menopausal problems, skin disorders including psoriasis and eczema, and rheumatoid arthritis. The oil is also combined with fish oils as an anti-ageing remedy. Follow the directions on the pack.

CREAM/SEED OIL Use 2–3 times daily on dry, scaling skin.

HOW TO SOURCE

GROW Prefers poor to moderately fertile, light, well-drained soil in full sun; tolerates dry periods. Sow seeds in a cold frame in late spring and transplant when established in summer, or sow directly in late summer to autumn.

FORAGE Naturalized in many parts of the world and often found in dry, stony, waste areas. Collect the leaves and stems in the second year when the flower stem appears.

HARVEST Collect the seeds when ripe.

CAUTION Do not take the oil if suffering from epilepsy.

FLOWERS
The fragrant, bell-shaped yellow flowers, which bloom in summer, open fully in the evenings

LEAVES
The leaves, stems, and flowers can be made into teas for syrups for whooping cough and asthmatic problems

1m (3ft)

GROWTH HABIT
Upright annual or biennial with a spread of 22–30cm (9–12in).

Panax japonicus **Japanese ginseng**

Found in mountainous woodland areas of Japan, Japanese ginseng is one of several related species used medicinally, and is largely used for coughs. The most popular is Korean ginseng (*Panax ginseng*) which, like American ginseng (*Panax quinquefolius*), is an important energy tonic. San qi ginseng (*Panax pseudo-ginseng*) is used to control bleeding.

FRUITS
Umbels of green-yellow flowers appear in spring and are followed by fruits, which are initially green and ripen to red

LEAVES
The whorls of five divided leaves grow on upright stems

GROWTH HABIT
Perennial with aromatic rootstock and divided bright green leaves.

60cm
(2ft)

PARTS USED Root
MAIN CONSTITUENTS Saponins, steroidal glycosides, sterols, volatile oil
ACTIONS Expectorant, tonic, febrifuge

HOW TO USE

TABLETS/CAPSULES Available in Japan. Can be used as a substitute for Korean ginseng, although the tonic effect is significantly reduced. Take 600mg daily.
DECOCTION Recent research suggests that Japanese ginseng may have a mild stimulatory effect on the immune system. Take ½–1 cup of a decoction, made by heating 10g (¼oz) of root in 600ml (1 pint) of water for 20 minutes, 2–3 times daily for recurrent infections or as a general immune tonic. The decoction is used in Japanese folk medicine for non-insulin dependent diabetes and to combat obesity.
SYRUP Add 450g (1lb) of sugar to 600ml (1 pint) of a standard decoction, bring to the boil, and simmer for 5–10 minutes. Take in 5ml (1 tsp) doses for productive coughs.

HOW TO SOURCE

GROW Sow seeds in a shaded area in a cold frame as soon as they are ripe. Germination can be slow and erratic. Transplant to 7.5cm (3in) pots as soon as the seedlings are large enough to handle, and continue growing in a shady position in the greenhouse for at least the first winter. Plant into a permanent position in moist but well-drained soil in shade in late summer. Alternatively, propagate by root division in spring.
FORAGE Unlikely to be found outside its native habitat.
HARVEST The roots of plants that are at least four years old are dug in autumn.

CAUTION Avoid in pregnancy. Do not take with drinks containing caffeine. Japanese ginseng has been little researched and can be of poor quality.

Passiflora incarnata **Passionflower**

Native to woodlands in the eastern United States, passionflower, a species of which is shown below, is known locally as "maypop" and was used by many Native American people for swellings, fungal infections, and as a blood tonic. Today it is generally regarded as a sedative and used for problems ranging from hyperactivity in children to the tremors of Parkinson's disease.

PARTS USED Leaves and stems
MAIN CONSTITUENTS Flavonoids (incl. rutin and apigenin), cyanogenic glycosides, alkaloids, sapanarin
ACTIONS Analgesic, antispasmodic, bitter, cooling, hypotensive, sedative, heart tonic, relaxes blood vessels

HOW TO USE

INFUSION Take 1 cup of a standard infusion (p.342) made from equal amounts of passionflower and raspberry leaf 3 times daily for period pain. For insomnia, take ¹/₂–1 cup of an infusion made from ¹/₂ tsp of dried passionflower to 1 cup of boiling water infused for 15 minutes, at night. For period pain or tension headaches take 3 times daily; reduced doses are suitable for hyperactivity in children.
TINCTURE Take 2–4ml (40–80 drops) in water 3 times daily for nervous tension, high blood pressure associated with nervous stress, or to reduce the severity of attacks in Ménière's disease.
FLUID EXTRACT Take up to 2ml (40 drops) in water twice a day to ease the pain associated with shingles and toothache.
TABLETS/CAPSULES Take 1–2 x 200mg tablets or capsules night and morning for anxiety, tension, and nervous headaches.

HOW TO SOURCE

GROW Prefers poor, sandy soil that is slightly acid. Sow the seeds at 18–21°C (64–70°F) in trays in spring and transplant to 7.5cm (3in) pots when large enough. Plant in final growing positions when well established in summer. Alternatively, take semi-ripe cuttings in summer. Shelter the plants from cold, wet winds in winter.
FORAGE Unlikely to be found growing wild outside its native habitat. The fruits are edible and can be collected in summer, but are only suitable for jams or jellies.
HARVEST Collect aerial parts when flowering or in fruit.

CAUTION May cause drowsiness.

FLOWERS
The finely cut corona of each flower, which blossoms in summer, represents Jesus' crown of thorns, and the 10 sepals the Apostles present at the crucifixion

LEAVES
The lobed leaves were traditionally used by Mayan Indians as a poultice for swellings

9m (29ft)

GROWTH HABIT
Climbing perennial vine with ornate flowers and egg-shaped orange fruits.

Plantago lanceolata **Ribwort plantain**

Both ribwort plantain and its broad-leaved cousin common plantain (*Plantago major*) are among the most common European weeds likely to be found anywhere, from pavement cracks to hedgerows. The plants are also found in the temperate regions of Asia, and were introduced by settlers into North America and Australia. Both plantains are a first-aid standby in folk tradition.

LEAVES
The long, leathery leaves can be pulped for poultices or to extract a soothing juice useful for inflamed mucous membranes

FLOWERS
The tall flower stems and flowers make an interesting addition to a wild flower garden, and will attract small butterflies and moths

40cm (16in)

GROWTH HABIT
Perennial with long, ribbed leaves that form a rosette shape.

PARTS USED Leaves
MAIN CONSTITUENTS Flavonoids, iridoids, mucilage, tannins, minerals
ACTIONS Relaxing expectorant, tonifying to mucous membranes, anticatarrhal, antispasmodic, topically healing, haemostatic

HOW TO USE

TINCTURE Take 3–5ml (60 drops–1 tsp) 3 times daily for catarrhal conditions or digestive problems, including gastritis and irritable bowel syndrome.
JUICE Use fresh leaves to make a juice and take in 10ml (2 tsp) doses 3 times daily to soothe cystitis, diarrhoea, and lung infections. The juice can also be applied to wounds and sores.
INFUSION Take 1 cup of a standard infusion (p.342) 3 times daily for catarrhal conditions, or use as a gargle for sore throats.
SYRUP Add 225g (8oz) of honey to 300ml (10fl oz) of a standard infusion and take in 5ml (1 tsp) doses as required for sore throats or productive coughs.
POULTICE Use fresh leaves, mashed into a pulp, for slow-healing wounds and chronic ulcers, or apply the fresh leaves to insect bites and stings.

HOW TO SOURCE

GROW Prefers moist, poor to moderately fertile soil in sun, or partial shade. Usually found as a self-seeded garden weed, although seeds can be obtained from wild flower specialists. Sow seeds where you want them to grow in spring or in 7.5cm (3in) pots in a cold frame, and plant out when established. Flowers, usually produced in the second year, appear from early spring until first frosts. It is generally included in wild meadow plantings, but self-seeds enthusiastically and can easily become invasive.
FORAGE Easily found growing on wasteland, hedgerows, roadsides, and grassy areas. It is best to choose plants growing in uncultivated areas well away from traffic to reduce the risk of collecting contaminated specimens.
HARVEST Gather leaves in summer.

Plantago psyllium **Psyllium**

Both black psyllium seeds, and the pale beige ispaghula seeds from its near relative, *Plantago ovata*, are commonly used over-the-counter remedies for constipation. Psyllium originates in the Mediterranean region, while ispaghula is native to India and Pakistan. The seeds swell in water to produce a mucilaginous mass, which is used as a bulking laxative.

PARTS USED Seeds

MAIN CONSTITUENTS Mucilage, fixed oil (incl. linoleic, oleic, and palmitic acids), starch, vitamins, minerals

ACTIONS Demulcent, bulking laxative, antidiarrhoeal, anti-inflammatory

HOW TO USE

MACERATION Soak two rounded teaspoons of the seeds in a mug of warm water overnight. Take as a single dose in the morning for constipation. The mixture can be flavoured with fruit juice or mixed with porridge or yoghurt, which some people find more palatable. Drink a glass of water or fruit juice after taking the seeds.

POULTICE Mix 1 tsp of psyllium husks with ½ tsp of slippery elm powder, add a little water to make a paste, and apply to boils or abscesses.

POWDER The husks are generally sold in powdered form: stir ½ tsp into a cup of water and take 3 times daily for diarrhoea or to help reduce blood cholesterol levels.

HOW TO SOURCE

GROW Prefers well-drained soil in full sun. Sow seeds in spring in trays on the surface of compost; keep in a propagator at 15-21°C (59-70°F) and transplant to final growing positions in early summer when large enough to handle. The plant flowers about 60 days after planting and needs high temperatures to set seed.

FORAGE Likely to be found in southern Europe, North Africa, and western Asia in waste places and dry, scrubby ground. Both psyllium and ispaghula are widely cultivated commercially.

HARVEST Harvest the seeds when ripe in late summer or early autumn.

CAUTION Always take with plenty of water and do not exceed the stated dose. Although sometimes recommended for irritable bowel syndrome, psyllium can exacerbate symptoms in some cases, so use with caution. Take at least 1 hour before any other medication.

FLOWERHEADS
White flowers in summer give rise to capsules containing many black seeds. Both the seeds and their husks are made into various over-the-counter remedies for constipation

LEAVES
The narrow, linear leaves grow to 10cm (4in) long

40cm
(16in)

GROWTH HABIT
An annual with lance-shaped leaves, small white flowers, and a spread of 30cm (12in).

Platycodon grandiflorus **Chinese balloon flower**

Listed in the *Shen Nong Ben Cao Jing* – China's oldest herb book attributed to the legendary founder of herbal medicine, Shen Nong, who lived 5,000 years ago – the balloon flower, which is native to eastern Asia, is considered an important respiratory remedy in traditional Chinese medicine. In the West it is better known as a garden ornamental.

BUDS
Each large, inflated flower bud looks rather like a balloon and opens into a bell-shaped flower in summer

FLOWERS
In addition to the usual white or blue flowers, various double-flowered pink cultivars are grown as garden ornamentals

LEAVES
The ovate leaves are green and 5–10cm (2–4in) in length, with a downy underside

90cm (36in)

GROWTH HABIT
Erect, clump-forming perennial with a spread of 30cm (12in).

PARTS USED Root
MAIN CONSTITUENTS Saponins, stigmasterol, inulin, platycodin
ACTIONS Antifungal, antibacterial, expectorant, hypoglycaemic, reduces cholesterol levels

HOW TO USE

DECOCTION Take 1 cup of a standard decoction of the root 3 times daily for productive coughs and sore throats associated with common colds.
SYRUP Combine 450g (1lb) of sugar or honey with 600ml (1pint) of strained standard root decoction, bring to the boil, and simmer gently for 10 minutes; take in 5–10ml (1–2 tsp) doses as required for bronchitis and other coughs producing profuse phlegm. Seek medical help if a productive cough does not improve after 2–3 days.
PATENT REMEDY Included in a number of commercially available pills and powders used in traditional Chinese medicine, including *sang ju yin* (a decoction of mulberry leaf with chrysanthemum), which is used for coughs, bronchitis, and the early stages of some feverish diseases.
GARGLE Use 1 cup of a standard decoction 2–3 times daily as a gargle for laryngitis and sore throats.

HOW TO SOURCE

GROW Prefers a well-drained site in sun or partial shade and forms in broad clumps 45cm (18in) in diameter when well established. Sow seeds in a seed tray in spring or early summer and transplant to 7.5cm (3in) pots when large enough to handle. Transplant to a permanent position when large enough to handle.
FORAGE Unlikely to be found naturalized outside China and Japan, although cultivated plants that self-seed may occur.
HARVEST Dig the root of established plants in autumn.

CAUTION Avoid this herb if there is blood in the phlegm.

Prunella vulgaris **Self-heal**

As with so many plants, the common name of this herb – self-heal – gives a good indication as to its use; it was once highly regarded as a wound remedy and cure-all. Native to Europe and Asia, self-heal is used as a wound healer and general tonic, and the flowers are a significant remedy in traditional Chinese medicine for soothing liver problems.

PARTS USED Aerial parts, flowers
MAIN CONSTITUENTS Flavonoids (incl. rutin), vitamins A, B1, C, K, fatty acids, volatile oil, bitter principle
ACTIONS Aerial parts: antibacterial, hypotensive, diuretic, astringent, haemostatic, wound herb
Flower spikes: liver stimulant, hypotensive, antibacterial, febrifuge

HOW TO USE

TINCTURE Best made from the freshly gathered leaves and stems. Take 5ml (1 tsp) 3 times daily for all sorts of bleeding, including heavy periods or traumatic injuries.
MOUTHWASH/GARGLE Use ½ tsp of dried herb to 1 cup of boiling water and allow to cool; use for bleeding gums and mouth inflammations or as a gargle for sore throats.
INFUSION Use a standard infusion (p.342) of flower spikes for liver problems linked to irritability and anger, over-excitability, high blood pressure, eye problems, headaches, or hyperactivity in children. (Consult a herbalist to treat children.) Often combined with Chinese chrysanthemum flowers, another herb used in Chinese medicine for liver problems.
POULTICE Use the fresh leaves on clean wounds.
CREAM/OINTMENT Use for bleeding piles.

HOW TO SOURCE

GROW Prefers moist, well-drained soil in full sun or partial shade, but will tolerate a wide range of conditions. Propagate from seeds sown in a cold frame in spring and transplant when established or by root division in spring or autumn. A prolific self-seeder that can become invasive.
FORAGE A common weed throughout Europe and many parts of Asia, it is found in grassland, roadsides, and sunny meadows. Collect the leaves and stems in early summer or harvest the flowers while in full bloom in mid- to late summer.
HARVEST In the West the leaves and young shoots are traditionally gathered before flowering.

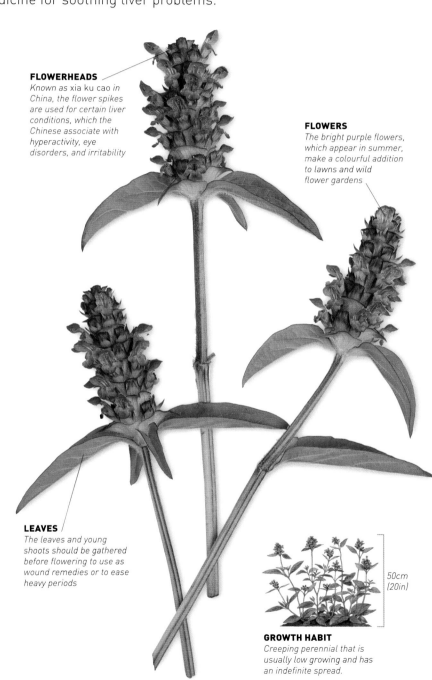

FLOWERHEADS
Known as xia ku cao in China, the flower spikes are used for certain liver conditions, which the Chinese associate with hyperactivity, eye disorders, and irritability

FLOWERS
The bright purple flowers, which appear in summer, make a colourful addition to lawns and wild flower gardens

LEAVES
The leaves and young shoots should be gathered before flowering to use as wound remedies or to ease heavy periods

50cm (20in)

GROWTH HABIT
Creeping perennial that is usually low growing and has an indefinite spread.

Ribes nigrum **Blackcurrant**

Native to temperate regions of Europe and Asia, blackcurrants are extensively cultivated for their juice and as a flavouring. Demand for the juice is so high that the fruits are rarely available in stores and should be grown in gardens for home use. While the fruits are rich in vitamin C, the leaves are largely used as a diuretic.

LEAVES
Blackcurrant leaves are believed to increase the production of cortisol by the adrenal glands, so they can help stimulate the sympathetic nervous system

FRUITS
The fruits were traditionally made into syrups taken as a prophylactic for colds and chills in winter due to their high vitamin C content

An established bush can produce around 5kg (11lb) of fruit in a summer

1.5m (5ft)

GROWTH HABIT
Small deciduous perennial shrub with a spread of around 1.5–2m (5–6ft).

PARTS USED Leaves, fruits, seed oil
MAIN CONSTITUENTS Leaves: volatile oil, tannins
Fruits: flavonoids, anthocyanosides, tannins, vitamin C, potassium
Seeds: Essential fatty acids incl. gamma-linolenic acid
ACTIONS Astringent, mild febrifuge, diuretic, antirheumatic; the fruits are a rich source of vitamin C

HOW TO USE

INFUSION Take ½–1 cup of a standard infusion (p.342) of the leaves as desired during the early stages of colds and feverish infections.
SEED OIL Rich in gamma-linolenic acid, blackcurrant seed oil capsules are available commercially as an alternative to evening primrose oil for treating eczema, menstrual irregularities, arthritis, etc. Follow dosage directions on the pack.
JUICE Take 10ml (2 tsp) 3 times daily (ideally as freshly made, unsweetened juice) for diarrhoea and digestive upsets; also provides additional vitamin C for infections such as flu or pneumonia.
GARGLE/MOUTHWASH Use 1 cup of a standard leaf infusion 2–3 times daily for sore throats and mouth ulcers.
TINCTURE Take 5ml (1tsp) of leaf tincture in a little water 3 times daily to increase elimination of fluids in high blood pressure.

HOW TO SOURCE

GROW Prefers full sun and rich, well-drained soil, but tolerates other conditions. Usually propagated by hardwood cuttings in autumn. Pot on until well established and plant in final positions in early winter or up to mid-March. Plant bushes 5cm (2in) deeper than the top of their pot; they produce stems from just below the surface: Water regularly and keep well weeded.
FORAGE Rarely found growing wild in Europe, although bushes may grow in hedgerows. Unlikely to be found growing wild in the US (it is host to a rust fungi and is therefore banned in some states).
HARVEST Pick fruits in midsummer when ripe and leaves through the growing season.

Rosa canina **Dog rose**

Native to Europe, western Asia, and north-west Africa, dog roses are now found throughout North America and New Zealand, where they are regarded as an invasive weed. The name reputedly derives from a Roman tradition that the root was, erroneously, a cure for rabies caused by dog bites. The hips are rich in vitamins, especially vitamin C, and can be made into syrups and jellies.

PARTS USED Fruits (hips), leaves
MAIN CONSTITUENTS Vitamins (A, B1, B2, B3, C, and K), flavonoids, tannins, polyphenols, carotenoids, volatile oil
ACTIONS Nutrient, astringent, diuretic, anti-inflammatory

HOW TO USE

SYRUP Popular form of nutritional supplement for young children. It is also used to flavour other medicines, and is added to cough mixtures. Add 225g (8oz) of honey to 300ml (10fl oz) of a strong decoction of hips (simmer a standard decoction gently until reduced in volume by half, then strain through a fine sieve or muslin cloth to remove the hairs from the seeds). Take 5ml (1 tsp) doses as required.
TINCTURE Take up to 5ml (1 tsp) of rose hip tincture 3 times daily for diarrhoea, gastritis, to relieve colicky pains, or as a mild diuretic.
FRESH HIPS The ripe hips can be eaten as a food supplement (remove the seeds before eating). They were traditionally baked in tarts or made into fruit jellies, often combined with apples.
INFUSION Once used as a substitute for tea, infused rose leaves can be made into a pleasant tisane for everyday drinking.

HOW TO SOURCE

GROW Usually grown from softwood cuttings in summer, it will self-seed freely once established. Often regarded as a weed by gardeners, dog rose is fast-growing and can be invasive. It will grow well in any well-drained moist soil in sun or partial shade, although it does not generally grow well in coastal areas. It is often grown as part of a mixed hedge.
FORAGE Found in hedgerows, roadside borders, and wasteland. The hips are best gathered in late autumn when they start to fall from the plant. If picked any earlier, they can be hard and will need to be cooked before use.
HARVEST Gather the bright red hips in autumn when ripe, and the leaves at any time for tea. Gather the rose petals in the summer to use in jam and jelly making.

FLOWERS
The white or pink petals are not used medicinally, but can be used to make jellies, crystallized sweets, or pot pourri.

LEAVES
Mid-green toothed leaflets can be used to make a delicious tisane

STEM
Vigorous arching or climbing stems with strong, downward-hooked prickles

GROWTH HABIT
Fast-growing, deciduous shrub with a spread of 3m (10ft).

5.5m (18ft)

Rosa x *damascena* **Damask rose**

Damask roses originated in the near East and were introduced into Europe in the 13th century. Today, they are regarded as a cross between *Rose gallica* and *Rosa moschata*. The flowers vary in colour from pink to light red. Rose oil – known as rose otto – is extracted by steam distillation, mainly in Bulgaria and Turkey, and is said to be good for "the skin and the soul".

FLOWERS
The petals were once used in tinctures as an astringent remedy for sore throats and to flavour other medicines

THORNS
The thorns can be particularly vicious

GROWTH HABIT
A deciduous shrub with sprawling growth; spread 1.5m (5ft).

2.2m (7ft)

PARTS USED Flowers, essential oil, hydrosol

MAIN CONSTITUENTS Geraniol, nerol, citronellol, geranic acid (rose oil contains around 300 chemicals, of which about 100 have been identified)

ACTIONS Sedative, antidepressant, anti-inflammatory, reduces cholesterol levels, astringent

HOW TO USE

MASSAGE OIL Use 1 drop of rose oil in 5ml (1 tsp) of almond oil to massage into the temples and neck for stress or exhaustion.

BATHS Add 2 drops of rose oil to bath water for depression, sorrows, or insomnia.

CREAM Made from the petals, or by adding a few drops of rose oil to a base cream. For dry or inflamed skin conditions.

LOTION Rosewater – the waste water from the steam distillation process (hydrosol) – can be used as the basis of various lotions: add 10% lady's mantle tincture for vaginal itching, or mix 50:50 with distilled witch hazel as a cooling lotion for skin prone to spots or acne.

TINCTURE Take 1–2 ml (20–40 drops) of a tincture made from the rose petals for nervous disorders, poor digestion, or to help reduce cholesterol levels.

HOW TO SOURCE

GROW Prefers fertile, moist but well-drained soil and needs at least 5 hours of sunlight a day during the growing season. Will tolerate temperate to sub-tropical temperatures. Usually propagated by hardwood cuttings in autumn.

FORAGE May be found growing wild, but more likely to be cultivated in hedges.

HARVEST Gather flowers in summer.

CAUTION Avoid during pregnancy. Do not take essential oils internally without professional advice. Rose oil is often adulterated or synthesized, so only buy from reputable sources.

Rosmarinus officinalis **Rosemary**

Originally found in dry coastal areas around the Mediterranean region, rosemary is now cultivated worldwide and is grown both as a culinary herb and for its essential oil. Medicinally, the herb is largely used as a stimulating tonic and digestive remedy, while the oil is used for arthritic pains. It is an important ingredient in the cosmetics and fragrance market.

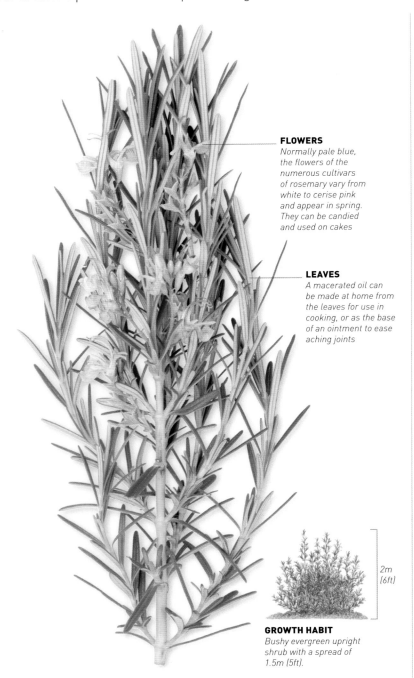

FLOWERS
Normally pale blue, the flowers of the numerous cultivars of rosemary vary from white to cerise pink and appear in spring. They can be candied and used on cakes

LEAVES
A macerated oil can be made at home from the leaves for use in cooking, or as the base of an ointment to ease aching joints

GROWTH HABIT
Bushy evergreen upright shrub with a spread of 1.5m (5ft).

2m (6ft)

PARTS USED Leaves, flowers, essential oil
MAIN CONSTITUENTS Volatile oil (incl. borneol, camphene, cineole), flavonoids, rosmarinic acid, tannins
ACTIONS Astringent, nervine, carminative, antiseptic, diaphoretic, antidepressive, circulatory stimulant, antispasmodic, cholagogue, diuretic
ESSENTIAL OIL Topically rubefacient, analgesic

HOW TO USE

INFUSION A standard infusion (p.342) can taste unpleasant, so use a weaker mix; take 1 cup for tiredness and headaches, or after meals to improve digestion.
HAIR RINSE Use a standard infusion, strained, as a final rinse for dandruff.
INHALATION Inhaling a drop of essential oil from a tissue is an energising brain stimulant and concentration aid.
TINCTURE Take up to 2.5ml (50 drops/ ½ tsp) 3 times daily for tiredness and nervous exhaustion; combine with an equal amount of wild oat or vervain tincture for depression.
MASSAGE RUB Add ¼ml (5 drops) of the essential oil to 15ml (1 tbsp) of almond oil and massage aching joints and muscles. Massage also into the temples to ease tension headaches.
COMPRESS Use 1 cup of hot standard infusion in a compress to ease sprains. Alternating a very hot infusion with an ice pack every 2–3 minutes works best.

HOW TO SOURCE

GROW Can be grown from seed, although cultivars do not come true and must be propagated from semi-ripe cuttings. Prefers neutral to alkaline soil.
FORAGE Found in native areas – scrub and open woodland around the Mediterranean.
HARVEST Gather in spring and summer.

CAUTION Avoid therapeutic doses of the herb during pregnancy.

Rubus idaeus **Raspberry**

Familiar as a summer fruit, raspberry is native to Europe, Asia, and North America, and has been cultivated in kitchen gardens since at least the 16th century. The leaves are commonly taken in tea to strengthen the womb for childbirth, while the fruits can be made into vinegar to use in salad dressings or to add to cough mixtures.

PARTS USED Leaves, fruit

MAIN CONSTITUENTS Leaves: fragarine (uterine tonic), tannins, polypeptides Fruit: vitamins A, B, C, and E, sugars, fruit acids, pectin

ACTIONS Astringent, prepares the womb for childbirth, stimulant, digestive remedy, increases urination, laxative

HOW TO USE

INFUSION 1 cup of a standard infusion (p.342) of the leaves can be taken daily in the last two months of pregnancy to help strengthen and prepare the womb for childbirth; drink the infusion as often as needed during labour. Take 1 cup 3 times daily to ease painful or heavy menstruation.

TINCTURE Take 3–5ml (60 drops–1 tsp) of the tincture 3 times daily for mild diarrhoea, or add to 100ml (3½fl oz) of warm water and use to bathe wounds, varicose veins, or skin inflammations. Put 2–5 drops into an eyebath of boiled, cooled water for conjunctivitis and eye inflammations.

MOUTHWASH/GARGLE Use 1 cup of an infusion for mouth ulcers or sore throats.

JUICE Take 10ml (2 tsp) 3–4 times daily of the juice (made from pulped berries) as a cooling remedy in mild fevers.

HOW TO SOURCE

GROW Prefers moist, slightly acidic soil. Propagate from rooted suckers, root division, or softwood cuttings, and plant out in winter/early spring; prune canes to 25cm (10in) above ground after planting. Cut fruited canes back to ground level after harvesting, and select and support young canes for the following year's crop.

FORAGE Found on scrubland and waste areas. Collect the leaves in early- to midsummer, and the berries when ripe.

HARVEST Gather the fruits in summer or autumn and the leaves in early summer.

CAUTION Therapeutic doses of raspberry leaf should only be taken in the last trimester of pregnancy, and avoided completely in the early stages.

FRUITS
Both summer and autumn varieties of raspberry are available, and the fruits, which can be red or yellow, are astringent and nutritious

LEAVES
The leaves can be used for both menstrual cramps and to strengthen the womb for childbirth. The leaves are gathered in early summer

GROWTH HABIT
Deciduous shrub with prickly, woody stems and a spread of 1–2m (3–6ft).

2m (6ft)

Rumex crispus **Yellow dock**

Native throughout Europe and Africa, yellow dock is a common wayside plant and garden weed that thrives on scrubby waste ground and grass verges. Its main use today is as a detoxifying herb and as a mild laxative. It is often combined with other herbs, such as burdock root, in the treatment of chronic skin conditions.

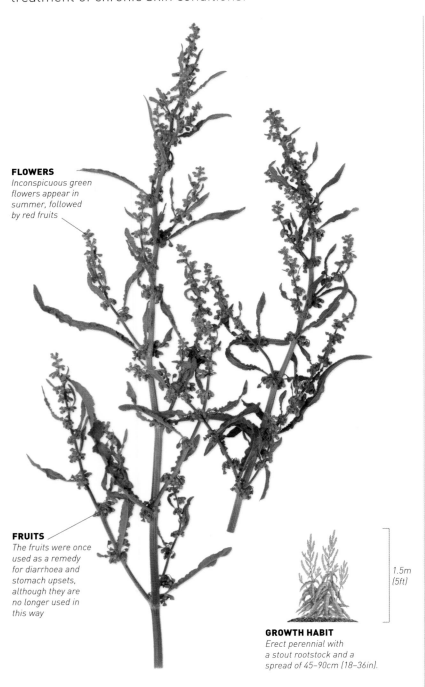

FLOWERS
Inconspicuous green flowers appear in summer, followed by red fruits

FRUITS
The fruits were once used as a remedy for diarrhoea and stomach upsets, although they are no longer used in this way

GROWTH HABIT
Erect perennial with a stout rootstock and a spread of 45–90cm (18–36in).

1.5m
(5ft)

PARTS USED Root
MAIN CONSTITUENTS Anthraquinones (incl. emodin and chrysophanol), tannins, oxalates, volatile oil
ACTIONS Blood and lymphatic cleanser, bitter tonic, stimulates bile flow, laxative

HOW TO USE

DECOCTION Take ½–1 cup 3 times daily of a decoction made from 15g (½oz) of root to 550ml (17fl oz) of water simmered gently for 20 minutes for mild constipation, or to stimulate bile flow to improve the digestion and help clear toxins from the system.
TINCTURE Take 1–2ml (20–40 drops) of tincture 3 times daily as part of a cleansing regime for conditions such as irritant skin rashes and eczema, boils, acne, shingles, rheumatism, and osteoarthritis.
MOUTHWASH Use ½ cup of the decoction (made as above) diluted with an equal amount of warm water 2–3 times daily for mouth ulcers.
HOMOEOPATHIC EXTRACTS In homoeopathy, yellow dock root is used for coughs, sore throats, and hoarseness made worse by cold air and damp weather. Take 1–2 tablets up to 3 times daily.

HOW TO SOURCE

GROW A perennial weed that self-seeds enthusiastically, and which few people would want to cultivate in their gardens. Seeds can be gathered from hedgerows in autumn if required and scattered where you want them to grow. Once established, the plant can be difficult to eradicate thanks to its tough root. It will tolerate any soil and grows in both sun and shade.
FORAGE The roots are long and can be difficult to dig up unless the ground has been well wetted first. Gather in autumn.
HARVEST Dig up the roots in autumn, wash thoroughly, chop, and dry.

CAUTION Do not take in pregnancy or when breast-feeding. Use for occasional constipation; for chronic constipation, consult a herbalist.

Salix alba **White willow**

Originally found in temperate or cold regions in the northern hemisphere, white willow was classified as a cool and moist remedy due to its preference for growing near water. In 1828 the Bavarian pharmacist, Johann Buchner (1783–1852), extracted bitter-tasting crystals – which he named salicin – from the bark; these were synthesized as aspirin by Bayer in 1899.

PARTS USED Bark, leaves
MAIN CONSTITUENTS Salicin, salicylic acid, tannins, flavonoids
ACTIONS Antirheumatic, anti-inflammatory, febrifuge, antihidrotic (reduces sweating), analgesic, antiseptic, astringent, bitter digestive tonic

HOW TO USE

FLUID EXTRACT Take 1–2ml (20–40 drops) of the bark extract in water 3 times daily for rheumatic conditions, lumbago, sciatica, and neuralgia. Combine with an equal amount of rosemary tincture for headaches.
TINCTURE Use 5–10ml (1–2 tsp) doses of the bark tincture (p.342) 3 times daily for fevers: generally combined with other herbs such as boneset (*Eupatorium perfoliatum*) or elderflower. Add 20–40 drops to menopausal remedies to help reduce night sweats and hot flushes.
DECOCTION Take 1 cup of a standard decoction of the bark 3 times daily for feverish chills, headaches, or as part of arthritic treatments with herbs such as St John's wort and crampbark.
INFUSION Take 1 cup of a standard infusion (p.342) of the leaves after meals for indigestion.

HOW TO SOURCE

GROW Prefers moist but well-drained soil. Propagate from semi-ripe cuttings in summer or hardwood cuttings in winter, although it can be grown from seed.
FORAGE Often found growing near water such as rivers or canals. The leaves were once collected in summer and used in infusions as a fever remedy, for colicky pains, or for digestive problems, although they are no longer commercially harvested. The bark should not be stripped from wild trees.
HARVEST The bark is stripped in spring from branches of two- to five-year-old trees that have been pollarded.

> **CAUTION** Avoid if allergic to aspirin or salicylates. Avoid during pregnancy.

LEAVES
The narrow, tapering silvery leaves were once associated with the moon, so the tree was regarded as cooling

25m (80ft)

GROWTH HABIT
A large tree with deeply fissured grey-brown bark and a spread of 10m (30ft).

Salvia officinalis **Sage**

Saliva officinalis originates in Mediterranean regions, and is well known as a culinary and medicinal herb. It is largely used for digestive and menopausal problems, particularly hot flushes, and is traditionally associated with longevity: modern research has shown that it can slow the progress of Alzheimer's disease.

LEAVES
Both green- and purple-leaved sage can be used in herbal medicine

The leaves were once used to wrap cheeses, and are used in dishes such as saltimbocca or to flavour stuffings

90cm (36in)

GROWTH HABIT
Shrubby evergreen perennial with usually blue flowers in early summer; spread 1m (3ft).

PARTS USED Leaves, essential oil
MAIN CONSTITUENTS Volatile oil (incl. thujone, linalool, and borneol), diterpene bitter, tannins, flavonoids, oestrogenic substances
ACTIONS Carminative, antispasmodic, astringent, antiseptic, reduces sweating, salivation, and lactation, uterine stimulant, stimulates bile flow

HOW TO USE

INFUSION Take 1 cup of a standard infusion (p.342) of the leaves 3 times daily for diarrhoea, to help improve digestive function in debility, or to ease menopausal symptoms, including night sweats. It can also help dry off milk at the weaning stage.
GARGLE/MOUTHWASH Use 1 cup of a standard infusion of the leaves as a gargle for sore throats, tonsillitis, quinsy, or as a mouthwash for mouth ulcers, gingivitis, etc.
TINCTURE Take 1–2ml (20–40 drops) of tincture 3 times daily for the menopause or as a tonic for digestive function.
HAIR RINSE Use 500ml (16fl oz) of a standard infusion as a final rinse to control dandruff or restore colour to greying hair.
CREAM/OINTMENT/LOTION Used as a household standby in many parts of Europe for treating minor cuts and grazes.

HOW TO SOURCE

GROW Prefers neutral to alkaline soil and full sun. Sow seeds in 7.5cm (3in) of compost in spring or summer and plant out the following year when sturdy, or propagate from softwood cuttings in summer. Prune after flowering and in early spring to stop the plant becoming too straggly.
FORAGE Found growing wild on dry, sunny hillsides in temperate regions.
HARVEST Cropped just before flowering in summer, or collect the leaves to use in cooking throughout the year.

CAUTION Due to its high thujone content, sage should not be taken in therapeutic doses by epileptics. Avoid therapeutic doses in pregnancy.

Sambucus nigra **Elder**

A common woodland tree throughout Europe, north Africa, and south-west Asia, elder was once regarded as a complete medicine chest: the root and bark made strong purgatives, while the leaves were made into a green ointment for use on bruises and sprains. Today, the flowers are most commonly used in refreshing elderflower cordials and medicinal brews.

FLOWERS
The creamy flowers appear in early summer, and can be made into an anti-inflammatory hand cream

LEAVES
The pinnate leaves were traditionally made into a green ointment, known as unguentum sambuci viride, to use on bruises and sprains

GROWTH HABIT
Vigorous, deciduous tree or bushy shrub; spread 6m (20ft).

6m (20ft)

PARTS USED Leaves, flowers, fruits
MAIN CONSTITUENTS Volatile oil, flavonoids, mucilage, tannins, cyanogenic glycosides, viburnic acid, phenolic acid, sterols. Berries contain vitamins A and C.
ACTIONS Flowers: expectorant, anticatarrhal, circulatory stimulant, diaphoretic, antiviral, topically anti-inflammatory
Berries: diaphoretic, diuretic, laxative
Leaves: topically wound-healing

HOW TO USE

INFUSION Take 1 cup of a standard infusion (p.342) of the flowers 3 times daily for feverish and catarrhal conditions and coughs; combine with yarrow, boneset, and peppermint in equal proportions for seasonal colds.
MOUTHWASH/GARGLE Use 1 cup of a standard infusion of the flowers as a mouthwash and gargle for mouth ulcers, sore throats, or tonsillitis.
CREAM/OINTMENT Made from the flowers to soothe inflamed or chapped hands, or from the leaves for bruises, sprains, chilblains, or piles.
SYRUP Add 600ml (1 pint) of a standard decoction of berries to 450g (1lb) honey and take in 10ml (2 tsp) doses for colds and flu.
TINCTURE Take 2–4ml (40–80 drops) elderberry tincture three times a day for coughs, colds, and flu symptoms. Combines well with echinacea.

HOW TO SOURCE

GROW Tolerates almost any soil, but prefers a moist, well-drained site. Propagate from hardwood cuttings in winter or ripe seeds sown in a cold frame; it will also self-seed easily. Can be invasive.
FORAGE Collect from hedgerows away from busy roads to avoid pollutants.
HARVEST Gather flowers in early summer and berries in early autumn, removing them from the stalk before use.

CAUTION Excessive consumption of fresh berries can have a laxative effect.

Saussurea costus **Costus**

Native to the eastern Himalayas, costus has been used in Ayurvedic tradition (in which it is known as *kuth*) for digestive and respiratory problems for at least 2,500 years. It was soon exported to China (where the root is called *mu xiang*) and also to the Middle East, where it is still used in Unani Tibb medicine.

FLOWERS
The small flowers appear in clusters of two or three in the summer and are variously described as purple or blue-black

STEM
The thick, yellowish stems can grow up to 3m (10ft) long in the plant's natural habitat, although cultivated specimens are more likely to be 2m (6ft) in height

GROWTH HABIT
Perennial, growing to 3m (10ft), with thick tapering root and irregular leaves; spread 1m (3ft).

3m (10ft)

PARTS USED Root, essential oil
MAIN CONSTITUENTS Alkaloid (sausserine), volatile oil (incl. linalool, terpenes and sesquiterpenes), stigmasterol, inulin, tannins
ACTIONS Antispasmodic, anodyne, aphrodisiac, astringent, bronchodilator, carminative, stimulant, stomachic, tonic

HOW TO USE

DECOCTION Generally used in Chinese medicine in combination with other herbs, such as cardamom (*Elettaria cardamomum*) or tangerine peel (*Citrus reticulata*), to relieve abdominal distention and pain, or for poor appetite, nausea, and vomiting. Typical dosage is 1–5g (½–1 tsp) of root, usually added in the last 5 minutes of heating.
PATENT REMEDIES Included in patent pills and powders marketed by Chinese pharmaceutical companies. These include *mu xiang shun qi wan* and *mu xiang bing lang wan* for digestive problems. Usual dosage is 8 tiny pills 3 times daily.
OINTMENT Kuth oil is traditionally used in ointments in Ayurvedic medicine for wounds, ulceration, and skin disease.
HAIR RINSE Use 1 cup of a decoction made from ½–1 tsp of dried root to 600ml (1pint) of water.

HOW TO SOURCE

GROW Prefers moist soil in sun or partial shade. Sow seeds in a cold frame when ripe and transplant when large enough to handle or by root division in spring.
FORAGE Unlikely to be found growing wild outside its native region. As it is listed as "most endangered" (Appendix I) by CITES, it should not be gathered in the wild.
HARVEST The roots of mature plants are gathered in spring or autumn.

CAUTION Avoid during pregnancy. Seek professional advice before taking patent Chinese remedies. As costus is so endangered, substitutes are often used. Only use costus plants from sustainable sources.

Schisandra chinensis **Schisandra**

Native to north-eastern China and Japan, schisandra is valued as an aphrodisiac, although it is also used for coughs, diarrhoea, insomnia, and skin rashes. The berries are called *wu wei zi* in Mandarin, which translates as "five taste seeds", as the pulp, skin, and seeds combine the five classic tastes identified in traditional Chinese medicine.

PARTS USED Fruit
MAIN CONSTITUENTS Phytosterols (incl. sigmasterol and beta-sitosterol), lignans, volatile oil, vitamins C and E
ACTIONS Antibacterial, astringent, tonic, aphrodisiac, circulatory stimulant, digestive stimulant, expectorant, hypotensive, sedative, uterine stimulant

HOW TO USE

LOTION Dilute 30ml (1fl oz) of tincture with 300ml (10fl oz) of water to make a lotion to bathe irritant skin rashes.
BERRIES Traditionally, a few berries are chewed as a tonic every day for 100 days.
DECOCTION Take 1 cup of a standard decoction (p.342), with a tiny pinch of powdered ginger added, 3 times daily for coughs and wheezing For insomnia, drink ¹/₂–1 cup, without the ginger, before bedtime.
TINCTURE Take 5ml (1 tsp) in water 3 times daily for poor liver function.
TONIC WINE Put 115g (4oz) of berries in a jar and cover with 600ml (1 pint) of rice wine. Seal and leave in a cool place for 1 month, shaking the bottle occasionally. Strain and take a sherry-glass dose daily as a tonic or to improve sexual energy.

HOW TO SOURCE

GROW Prefers rich, well-drained, moist soil against a sheltered, shady wall. Sow ripe seeds in autumn in a cold frame; soak seeds sown in spring overnight first. Grow on until well established before planting in final positions. Must be trained against a wall or fence; remove unwanted shoots in late winter. Both male and female plants are required to produce berries.
FORAGE Unlikely to be found growing wild outside its native habitat, although it is cultivated as a garden ornamental.
HARVEST Collect the fruits after the first frosts and sun-dry them.

CAUTION Avoid in pregnancy or in feverish chills and conditions involving heat. Large doses may cause heartburn.

LEAVES
The leaves are green, pointed, egg-shaped, and up to 15cm (6in) long

STEM
Scratching the stem produces a fragrant scent with a hint of lime

8m (25ft)

GROWTH HABIT
Deciduous, dioecious, climbing shrub with solitary flowers that appear in late spring.

Scutellaria lateriflora **Virginian skullcap**

Native to North America, Virginian skullcap was once known as "mad dog herb" due to an erroneous belief that it could cure rabies. Today it is mainly used as a sedative. Its European relative, marsh, or hooded, skullcap (*Scutellaria galericulata*) has similar properties, while the root of the Chinese species (*Scutellaria baicalensis*), known as *huang qin*, is used in hot, feverish conditions.

FLOWERS
The lobed flowers are generally blue, although pink or white varieties sometimes occur, and are produced in one-sided axillary racemes in summer

LEAVES
The toothed leaves are green and oval- to lance-shaped

STEM
Like other members of the mint family, the stems are square

GROWTH HABIT
Herbaceous perennial spreading to 45cm (8in), often with blue flowers.

60cm (2ft)

PARTS USED Aerial parts
MAIN CONSTITUENTS Flavonoids, tannins, bitter iridoids, volatile oil, minerals
ACTIONS Relaxing and restorative nervine, sedative, antispasmodic, mild bitter

HOW TO USE

INFUSION Take 1/2–1 cup of a standard infusion (p.342) 3 times daily for nervous exhaustion, excitability, anxiety, or stress.
TEA Use 1 tsp of dried herb per cup, or 3–4 whole sprigs in a small teapot, to make a soothing tea to ease tensions at the end of the working day or to ease emotional upsets associated with premenstrual syndrome. A cup before bedtime can also help with insomnia.
TINCTURE Take 1–2ml (20–40 drops) in a little water 3 times daily for nervous tension, stress, anxiety, or associated headaches.
TABLETS/CAPSULES Commercially available, and often combining skullcap with passionflower. Follow dosage directions on the pack and use for anxiety and stress.

HOW TO SOURCE

GROW Prefers moist but well-drained soil in sun or partial shade. Sow seeds in autumn or spring in seed trays and transplant to 7.5cm (3in) pots when large enough to handle. Grow on until well established before planting in their final positions. Alternatively, divide plants in spring. Self-seeds enthusiastically and can become invasive.
FORAGE Found in hedgerows or riverbanks in the USA and Canada; likely elsewhere only in isolated groups that may have self-seeded in grass verges or hedgerows from neighbouring herb gardens. Common skullcap (*Scutellaria galericulata*) can be used in similar ways and is likely to be found along riverbanks or in fens.
HARVEST Cut while flowering and dry immediately; the aerial parts will contain both flowers and seed pods.

Senna alexandrina **Senna**

Native to Egypt, Sudan, Somalia, and Arabia, senna was used in the 9th century by Arabian physicians as a cathartic, or strong laxative. Its use soon spread, and both pods and leaves are still used as laxatives. The leaves are known as *fan xie ye* in traditional Chinese medicine, while their Indian name, *rajavriksha*, translates as "king of trees".

PARTS USED Leaves, pods
MAIN CONSTITUENTS Anthraquinone glycosides (incl. sennosides, dianthrone diglycosides) polysaccharides, mucilage, flavonoids (incl. kaempferol), salicylic acid
ACTIONS Stimulating laxative, antibacterial, anthelmintic, cooling

HOW TO USE

INFUSION For constipation, soak 3–6 pods (15–30mg) in 1 cup of warm water and drink last thing at night. Add a slice of fresh ginger root or 1 tsp of fennel seeds to combat griping pains caused by an increase in bowel movement. Use half the adult dose for children over 10 years.
FLUID EXTRACT Take ¼–½ml (5–10 drops) of senna leaf extract in a little water at night for constipation.
TINCTURE Take ½ml–1½ml (10–30 drops) in a little water at night for constipation.
TABLETS/POWDERS Take 1–2 tsp of granules or 2–4 tablets at night for occasional constipation.

HOW TO SOURCE

GROW Prefers rich, moist, sandy soil in full sun. Requires a minimum of 5°C (41°F) to grow, but can be grown in containers in cooler regions. Sow seeds in spring and transplant to containers or final growing positions when well established, or take semi-ripe cuttings in spring.
FORAGE Unlikely to be found growing wild outside its native habitat.
HARVEST Pick leaves before and during flowering; gather pods in autumn when ripe.

CAUTION Can cause abdominal cramps. Do not take in cases of inflammatory bowel disease (such as Crohn's disease or ulcerative colitis), or if pregnant or breast-feeding. Avoid in intestinal obstruction. Excessive use can cause diarrhoea and can damage the colon. Do not take leaf extracts or infusions for more than seven days at a time and take a break of at least two weeks before repeating the treatment.

LEAVES
Hand-collected senna leaves are known as Tinnevally senna, while leaves that have been harvested and graded mechanically are called Alexandria senna

The hairy, divided leaves are used in Ayurveda for constipation following fevers. They have a stronger action than the pods, so are less commonly used

STEM
The stem is branched, erect, and pale green

90cm
(36in)

GROWTH HABIT
Low-branching, shrubby perennial with small yellow flowers in spring; spread 50–60cm (20–24in).

Silybum marianum **Milk thistle**

Native to stony areas in the Mediterranean region and south-west Asia, milk thistle is also known as Mary thistle, as the white veins on its leaves are reputedly due to splashes of the Virgin Mary's milk falling on them while she fed the Christ child. Although it encourages milk flow, it is probably now better known for its liver-protective qualities.

FLOWERHEADS
The flowerheads, which can be boiled and eaten as a vegetable, were once taken for "melancholia", a condition associated with a surfeit of "black bile" in traditional Western (Galenic) medicine

LEAVES
The white splashes on the leaves are said to resemble drops of milk, and give the plant its common name, milk thistle

GROWTH HABIT
Biennial with spiny green leaves marbled with white; spread 60–90cm (24–36in).

1.5m
(5ft)

PARTS USED Seeds, leaves, flowerheads
MAIN CONSTITUENTS Flavolignans (incl. silymarin), bitters, polyacetylenes
ACTIONS Bitter tonic, cholagogue, antiviral, choleretic, antidepressant, antioxidant, galactagogue, liver protector

HOW TO USE

TINCTURE Take 20–50 drops of the seed tincture with a little water 3 times daily for liver and gall bladder problems, or to stimulate the digestion. Take up to 5ml (1 tsp) daily in water as a preventative if you have a history of gallstones or liver disease. Treatment of gallstones requires professional advice.
CAPSULES Regular use of milk thistle capsules may help in the treatment of liver diseases.
INFUSION Drink 1–2 cups of a standard leaf infusion (p.342) daily to stimulate milk production when breast-feeding. The infusion can be used to stimulate a sluggish digestion.
DECOCTION Take ½ cup of a standard decoction (p.342) of the cracked seeds daily for liver disorders, including infections.

HOW TO SOURCE

GROW Prefers full sun in poor to moderately fertile soil that is well drained and neutral to alkaline. Sow seeds where you want to grow them in spring for annual growth or in late summer or early autumn for flowers the following year. Thin to at least 45cm (18in) between plants.
FORAGE May be found in hedgerows and waste areas in many parts of Europe, North and East Africa, and western Asia. The flowerheads can be cooked and eaten as a vegetable (rather like globe artichoke), the young leaves are used as a spinach substitute, and the root tastes rather like salsify.
HARVEST Collect the seeds in late summer; other parts of the plant can be gathered for culinary use during the summer.

Stellaria media **Chickweed**

Found throughout Europe and Asia, chickweed has long been used as a soothing and healing remedy for skin problems and wounds. Regarded by many as a weed, it is a favourite food for chickens – as the name implies – and other small birds: in the 16th century it was regularly fed to caged linnets.

PARTS USED Aerial parts
MAIN CONSTITUENTS Mucilage, saponins, coumarins, minerals, vitamins A, B, and C.
ACTIONS Astringent, antirheumatic, wound herb, demulcent, emollient, mild laxative

HOW TO USE

INFUSED OIL Fill a jar with fresh chickweed and cover completely with sunflower oil; steep for 2 weeks, then strain and use on eczema and irritant skin rashes – or add 25ml (5 tsp) to bath water for eczema sufferers.

CREAM/OINTMENT Use regularly on itching skin rashes and eczema. Can also soothe minor burns and be used to draw out thorns and splinters – put a little on the embedded splinter, cover with a sticking plaster, and leave overnight; the next morning the splinter can usually be found on the sticking plaster pad.

INFUSION Take 1 cup of a standard infusion (p.342) 3 times daily for muscular rheumatism, urinary tract inflammations, or whenever a cooling and cleansing remedy is required.

POULTICE Apply the crushed, fresh plant on gauze or in a muslin bag for boils, abscesses, skin sores, or gout.

HOW TO SOURCE

GROW Prefers moist soil and full sun, but will tolerate many conditions. Sow seeds directly at any time. Usually regarded as a weed, but worth growing as a useful source of food for domestic chickens.

FORAGE Generally found in hedgerows, ditches, waste areas, or grassy areas. Cut the aerial parts as required through the growing period. Chickweed can be sweated like spinach as a vegetable and served with butter.

HARVEST Can be cut throughout the growing period and used fresh or dried.

> **CAUTION** If taken in excess, it may cause nausea and vomiting.

FLOWER BUDS
The buds open into the star-shaped flowers that give the plant its botanical name, Stellaria, *from the Latin,* stella, *meaning "star"*

LEAVES
The plant and its leaves are a useful source of vitamin C, and can be eaten in salads or cooked as a vegetable

40cm
(16in)

GROWTH HABIT
Spreading annual weed with small, white, star-shaped flowers; spread 5–40cm (2–16in).

Symphytum officinale **Comfrey**

Growing throughout Europe, comfrey has been used to heal broken bones since ancient times. In the 1970s it became popular as a remedy for arthritis when taken internally, which led to extensive animal studies using the plant and a realization that the alkaloids it contains may cause liver cancer. Since then it has been banned in a number of countries.

FLOWERHEADS
The drooping flowerheads appear in summer and are rich in allantoin, which encourages cell division and repair

LEAVES
The large leaves have been used for centuries as a poultice for broken bones

1.3m
(4½ft)

GROWTH HABIT
Vigorous rhizomatous perennial spreading to 2m (6ft) or more.

PARTS USED Aerial parts, root
MAIN CONSTITUENTS Mucilage, steroidal saponins (root), allantoin, vitamin B12, tannin, pyrrolizidine alkaloids, rosmarinic acid
ACTIONS Cell proliferator, astringent, demulcent, anti-inflammatory, expectorant, wound herb

HOW TO USE

MACERATED OIL Use night and morning to massage arthritic joints, sprains, bruises, and other traumatic injuries.
OINTMENT: Use on clean cuts and grazes, or on skin sores such as nappy rash. Also useful for boils, acne, and psoriasis.
POULTICE Use puréed leaves as a poultice for minor breaks (broken toes, etc) not normally set in plaster. Make a paste with powdered root and a little water, and use on varicose ulcers, stubborn wounds, or bleeding piles.
COMPRESS Apply a pad soaked in a standard decoction of the root to bruises and sprains.

HOW TO SOURCE

GROW Prefers moist soil in a sunny or partially shaded site. Can be propagated from seed sown in autumn or spring, by root division in spring, or root cuttings in winter. Does not tolerate dry winters. Once established, it can be difficult to eradicate.
FORAGE Usually found in damp field borders or hedgerows. When not in flower, the plant can be confused with foxglove.
HARVEST Gather leaves and flowering tops in summer and roots in autumn.

CAUTION Avoid during pregnancy. Do not take comfrey internally; it contains compounds that may be carcinogenic when taken internally. Do not use on dirty wounds, as rapid healing may trap pus or dirt.

Tanacetum parthenium **Feverfew**

Found throughout northern temperate regions, feverfew is widely used today as a migraine remedy. Earlier herbalists thought of it as "a general strengthener of the womb" (Nicholas Culpeper, 1653). It has also traditionally been used to treat arthritis and rheumatism. Numerous cultivars have been developed as garden ornamentals.

PARTS USED Aerial parts
MAIN CONSTITUENTS Sesquiterpene lactones (parthenolide), volatile oil, pyrethrin, tannins, camphor
ACTIONS Anti-inflammatory, vasodilator, relaxant, digestive stimulant, emmenagogue, anthelmintic, bitter

HOW TO USE

TINCTURE Use 5–10 drops at 30-minute intervals at the onset of a migraine. It is most effective for preventing and treating "cold" type migraines involving vasoconstriction, which are eased by applying a hot towel to the head. For the acute stages of rheumatoid arthritis, add up to 2ml (40 drops) 3 times a day to herbal remedies such as celery seed, white willow, or devil's claw (*Harpagophytum procumbens*).
POULTICE Fry a handful of leaves in a little oil and apply to the abdomen as a poultice for colicky pains.
INFUSION Drink 1 or 2 cups of a weak infusion made from 15g (½oz) of the aerial parts to 600ml (1pint) of water after childbirth to encourage cleansing and tonifying of the womb; take 1 cup 3 times daily for period pain associated with sluggish flow and congestion.

HOW TO SOURCE

GROW Prefers full sun and well-drained soil, but tolerates a range of conditions. Sow seeds in a propagator at 10–18°C (50–64.4°F) in late winter or early spring, or take softwood cuttings in early summer. A prolific self-seeder that can be invasive.
FORAGE Often found in hedgerows and waste places. Easily confused with other daisy-like plants; look for its characteristic leaves, which have a very bitter taste.
HARVEST Collect the leaves as required throughout the growing period and the whole plant in summer while flowering.

CAUTION Mouth ulcers can occur after eating the fresh leaves. Avoid if taking anticoagulant drugs such as warfarin. Avoid during pregnancy.

FLOWERS
Its daisy-like flowers, which bloom in summer, mean that feverfew is easily confused with similar plants such as annual mayweeds

LEAVES
The bitter-tasting pale green leaves were traditionally fried and made into a poultice for headaches, rather than taken internally

60cm (24in)

GROWTH HABIT
Short-lived, bushy perennial with deeply scalloped leaves and a spread of 60cm (24in).

Taraxacum officinale **Dandelion**

Several species of dandelion are found throughout the temperate regions of Europe, Asia, and South America. The plant is a comparative newcomer to the medicinal repertoire, and was first mentioned in Arabic herbals in the 11th century, as a remedy to increase urination. The root, an effective liver tonic, was not used until much later.

LEAVES
The leaves are rich in potassium, which helps balance the increased urination they cause by maintaining the body's sodium/potassium balance

FLOWERS
The bright yellow flowers appear from spring to autumn. The English name is derived from dent de lion or dens leonis (lion's tooth) – a description of the leaves

GROWTH HABIT
Tap-rooted perennial; spread 45cm (18in).

30cm (12in)

PARTS USED Leaves, root
MAIN CONSTITUENTS Sesquiterpene lactones, vitamins A, B, C, D, choline, minerals (incl. potassium)
Leaf only: coumarins, carotenoids.
Root only: taraxacoside, phenolic acids.
ACTIONS Diuretic, liver and digestive tonic, cholagogue, stimulates pancreas and bile duct, mild laxative (root only)

HOW TO USE

DECOCTION Take 1 cup of a standard decoction of the root 3 times daily for any condition – such as osteoarthritis, gout, rheumatism, acne, psoriasis, and eczema – where liver stimulation and detoxification may help.
INFUSION Take 1 cup of a standard infusion (p.342) of the leaves 3 times daily to encourage urination in conditions such as cystitis, fluid retention, or high blood pressure.
JUICE Process the leaves in a juicer and take up to 20ml (4 tsp) 3 times daily as a stronger alternative to the infusion.
TINCTURE Take 2–5ml (40 drops–1 tsp) of combined root and leaf tincture 3 times daily to stimulate bile flow, act as a mild laxative, or help dissolve small gallstones.

HOW TO SOURCE

GROW Tolerates a wide range of soils and will grow in full sun or partial shade. Sow the seeds in spring. It self-seeds enthusiastically. The plant is also cultivated for salad leaves in parts of Europe.
FORAGE Found in many parts of the world growing in hedgerows, field borders, waste areas, and even in city pavement cracks. Avoid collecting plants where traffic pollution may be a problem.
HARVEST Gather young leaves for salads in the spring, and the larger leaves in summer for medicinal use. The two-year-old roots are collected in autumn.

CAUTION If suffering from gallstones, only use dandelion root under professional supervision.

Thymus vulgaris **Common thyme**

Originating from the dry, grassy areas of southern Europe, thyme is now widely grown worldwide as a culinary herb. It is mainly used as an expectorant and antiseptic for the lungs to clear productive coughs and infections, while the essential oil is used in aromatherapy. Research in the 1990s also suggested antioxidant and anti-ageing properties.

FLOWERS
The aerial parts are harvested in summer when the leaves and flowers can be collected and used together

LEAVES
The essential oil is made by steam-distilling the aerial parts. Thyme leaves and oil are strongly antiseptic and used to clear chest infections

GROWTH HABIT
Low-growing, evergreen, woody-based perennial; spread 40cm (16in).

25cm (10in)

PARTS USED Aerial parts, essential oil
MAIN CONSTITUENTS Volatile oil (incl. thymol, cineole and borneol), flavonoids, bitter, tannins, saponins
ACTIONS Antiseptic expectorant, antispasmodic, antiseptic, astringent, antimicrobial, diuretic, antitussive, antibiotic, wound herb, topically rubefacient

HOW TO USE

INFUSION Take 1 cup of a standard infusion (p.342) 3 times daily for seasonal colds, chest infections, mild asthma, hayfever, stomach chills, or irritable bowel syndrome.
SYRUP Add 450g (1lb) of honey to 600ml (1 pint) of strained infusion to make a syrup for coughs and chest infections and take in 5ml (1 tsp) doses as required.
MOUTHWASH/GARGLE Use 1 cup of standard infusion morning and night for gum disease and sore throats.
CHEST RUB/MASSAGE OIL Use 10 drops of thyme oil in 25ml (5 tsp) of almond oil as a chest rub for bronchitis and infections. Use with an equal amount of lavender oil for rheumatic pains and strained muscles.
LOTION Dilute 1ml (20 drops) of thyme oil in 60ml (2fl oz) of water and use for insect bites and infected wounds.

HOW TO SOURCE

GROWS Prefers dry alkaline soil in full sun. Sow seeds in trays in a greenhouse or cold frame in spring, potted into 7.5cm (3in) pots when large enough to handle, and planted out when well established. Alternatively, take softwood cuttings in summer as flowering starts.
FORAGE Found in scrubby, rocky wasteland or dry grassland throughout Europe and Asia.
HARVEST Gather aerial parts in mid- to late summer, and sprigs for cooking throughout the growing period.

CAUTION Avoid therapeutic doses in pregnancy. Do not take the essential oil internally, and always use well diluted.

Tilia cordata **Lime flowers**

Native to central and eastern Europe, the lime, or linden tree, is popular in urban street plantings in many countries – perhaps most notably in the iconic avenue, the *Unter den Linden*, leading to the Brandenburg Gate in Berlin. The flowers are mainly used in sedative mixtures, although they can also be used in soothing lotions.

FLOWERS
Whole flowers are harvested in summer and crushed for use in relaxing teas, which can also help reduce blood pressure

FRUITS
Distinctive pale green spherical fruits form in autumn

GROWTH HABIT
Medium-large columnar tree; spread 10–30m (30–100ft).

40m (130ft)

PARTS USED Flowers
MAIN CONSTITUENTS Flavonoids (incl. quercetin and kaempferol), caffeic acid, mucilage, tannins, volatile oil
ACTIONS Antispasmodic, diaphoretic, diuretic, sedative, hypotensive, anticoagulant

HOW TO USE

INFUSION Take 1 cup of a standard infusion (p.342) up to 3 times daily to soothe tension, stress or nervous headaches, or to relieve colds, flu, and nasal catarrh. Commercial teabags often combine lime with chamomile, or mix the dried flowers with equal amounts of lemon balm and chamomile and use 1–2 tsp of the dried mix in a cup of boiling water for a relaxing and calming tea.
TINCTURE Take 5ml (1 tsp) of the tincture in water 3 times daily, for high blood pressure associated with stress and anxiety or arteriosclerosis. Usually used in combination with other herbs such as valerian or hawthorn.
OINTMENT/LOTION Use as required for itching skin caused by rashes or insect bites.
CHILDREN'S TEA Can be used as a soothing remedy in the early stages of childhood infections such as flu, seasonal colds, or chicken pox. Consult a herbalist for advice on dosage.

HOW TO SOURCE

GROW Prefers fertile, moist but well-drained soil that is neutral to alkaline. The seeds need to be stratified over winter and planted in a seed bed outside in the spring, but it can be slow to germinate. It is a large tree, so is not suitable for small or congested gardens.
FORAGE Limes are found throughout Europe and in many other temperate zones, often as part of a street-planting scheme. The flowers can be collected in early to mid-summer, but it is best to avoid trees in high traffic areas to minimize pollution.
HARVEST Gather the flowers in midsummer. They can be collected with the sepals and crushed when dry.

Trifolium pratense **Red clover**

Native to temperate regions of Europe and Asia, red clover is now naturalized in many parts of North America and Australia. The plant was known as "honey stalk", as children sucked the sweet sap from its stems. In the 1930s it became popular for treating breast cancer. Today it is mainly used for coughs, skin problems and menopausal symptoms.

PARTS USED Flowerheads

MAIN CONSTITUENTS Flavonoids, salicylates, coumarins, phenolic glycosides, cyanogenic glycosides, volatile oil (incl. methyl salicylate and benzyl alcohol), sitosterol

ACTIONS Antispasmodic, diuretic, lymphatic cleanser, possible oestrogenic activity, expectorant

HOW TO USE

INFUSION Take 1 cup of a standard infusion (p.342) 3 times daily for coughs, menopausal problems, or as part of a cleansing regime for skin problems.

SYRUP Make a standard infusion and use 600ml (1 pint) to make a syrup with 450g (1lb) of honey. Take in 5ml (1 tsp) doses as required for stubborn coughs, especially whooping cough or bronchitis.

MOUTHWASH/GARGLE Use 1 cup of a standard infusion for mouth ulcers and sore throats.

TINCTURE Take 5–10ml (1–2 tsp) 3 times daily for eczema, psoriasis, and old sores that are slow to heal. Combines well with heartsease for childhood eczema.

CREAM/OINTMENT Use frequently for lymphatic swellings.

FRESH HERB Use the crushed flowers directly on insect bites and stings.

HOW TO SOURCE

GROW Prefers moderate summer temperatures and adequate moisture throughout the growing period. Scatter seeds where you want them to grow in late winter or early spring, and then cover with a light dusting of good compost.

FORAGE Widely cultivated as a fodder crop and as part of a crop-rotation programme, red clover can be found growing in many parts of the world. Look for it growing in hedgerows and meadows and collect the flowerheads when they are newly opened.

HARVEST Gather throughout the summer, choosing newly opened flowerheads.

CAUTION Avoid during pregnancy.

FLOWERHEADS
The distinctive purple-pink globe-shaped flowerheads appear in late spring and early summer

LEAVES
Red clover has leaves of three oval leaflets, often marked with a pale crescent

45cm (18in)

GROWTH HABIT
Biennial or perennial; spread 45cm (18in).

Tropaeolum majus **Nasturtium**

Originally found in the Andes from Bolivia to Colombia, nasturtiums have now spread worldwide as a popular and easy-to-grow garden ornamental. They naturalize readily and are classified as an invasive weed in New Zealand and other areas. Valued both as an antiseptic and respiratory remedy, the flowers and seeds also have many culinary uses.

LEAVES
The almost circular leaves reduce the amount of nasal catarrh produced in colds and flu and increase resistance to bacterial infections

FLOWERS
Yellow or red nasturtium flowers, which bloom from early summer, make a colourful and nutritious addition to salads

LEAVES
The leaves make a spicy addition to summer salads, and are rich in vitamin C

GROWTH HABIT
Fast-growing trailing annual with a spread of 1.5m–2m (5–6ft).

3m (10ft)

PARTS USED Flowers, leaves, seeds
MAIN CONSTITUENTS Glucocyanates, spilanthol, myrosin, mineral salts (incl. iodine, iron, and phosphates), oxalic acid, vitamin C
ACTIONS Antibiotic, antitussive, diuretic, expectorant

HOW TO USE

INFUSION Take 1 cup of a standard infusion (p.342) of the leaves 3 times daily to increase resistance to bacterial infection; also effective for clearing catarrh due to colds and flu.
TINCTURE Take 5–10ml (1–2 tsp) of a leaf tincture 3 times daily for colds, influenza, and dry coughs.
JUICE Pulp the whole plant in a food processor or juicer and take 20ml (4 tsp) 3 times daily in a little milk for chronic lung conditions such as emphysema; the juice rubbed into the scalp is said to stimulate hair growth in alopecia.
LOTION Use 1 cup of a standard infusion of the leaves as an antiseptic wash for cuts and grazes.
FRESH LEAVES AND FLOWERS Add both to salads – the leaves have a spicy flavour and are rich in vitamin C.

HOW TO SOURCE

GROW Nasturtiums will grow almost anywhere, but prefer well-drained soil and a sunny site. A rich soil encourages leaf growth rather than flowers. Sow the seeds where you want to grow them in early summer, or plant in trays in mid-spring at 13–16°C (55–61°F) and transplant when all danger of frost has passed.
FORAGE An invasive weed in some parts of the world, in temperate zones they may be found in urban areas outside gardens as self-seeded plants. Gather the flowers as required and the whole plant in late summer for use in tinctures.
HARVEST Gather leaves and flowers as required for salads, or the whole plant in summer for drying.

Tussilago farfara **Coltsfoot**

Once a remedy for coughs, as the botanical name suggests (from *tussis*, the Latin for "cough"), coltsfoot has fallen from favour in recent years since pyrrolizidine alkaloids, which are carcinogenic and have been linked to liver cancer, were identified in the plant. Found throughout Europe, western Asia, and North Africa, the plant is an invasive weed. It is restricted in some countries.

LEAVES
The leaves only appear once the flowers have completely died down

GROWTH HABIT
A creeping perennial with large, heart-shaped leaves; it has an indefinite spread.

30cm (12in)

PARTS USED Leaves, flowers
MAIN CONSTITUENTS Mucilage, tannins, pyrrolizidine alkaloids, inulin, zinc, bitter principle, sterols, flavonoids (incl. rutin), potassium, calcium
ACTIONS Relaxing expectorant, anticatarrhal, demulcent

HOW TO USE

NB: Do not take internally without professional guidance
POULTICE Chop fresh leaves in a blender or food processor, spread on gauze, and use as a poultice for ulcers, sores, and other slow-healing wounds.
SYRUP Add 450g (1lb) of honey or sugar to 600ml (1 pint) of a strained standard leaf infusion (p.342), bring to the boil, and simmer gently for 5–10 minutes to form a syrup. Use in 5ml (1 tsp) doses for dry, unproductive, irritating coughs or asthma.
TINCTURE Use 2–5 ml (40 drops–1 tsp) of leaf tincture 3 times daily for whooping cough or bronchitis.
DECOCTION Simmer 15g (½oz) of dried flowers in 600ml (1 pint) of water for 15 minutes and take ½–1 cup 3 times daily for asthma, bronchitis, or persistent coughs.

HOW TO SOURCE

GROW Prefers moist neutral to alkaline soil in sun or partial shade. Sow seeds in spring in a prepared seed bed, or divide clumps after the flowers, which appear before the leaves, fade, or in autumn as the leaves die down. Extremely invasive.
FORAGE Found in hedges and waste ground.
HARVEST Gather the flowers as soon as they open and use fresh or dried; collect the leaves when fully grown in summer.

CAUTION Contains pyrrolizidine alkaloids; do not take internally without professional guidance. Do not use if pregnant or if breast-feeding.

Ulmus rubra **Slippery elm**

One of the most widely used herbal remedies, slippery elm is native to eastern areas of North America from Quebec to Mexico. It is used to heal and soothe damaged tissues – both external wounds and internal mucous membranes – and is also extremely nutritive, so is used as a food in debility and convalescence.

PARTS USED Inner bark
MAIN CONSTITUENTS Mucilage, starch, tannins
ACTIONS Soothing demulcent, emollient, laxative, expectorant, antitussive, nutritive

HOW TO USE

FOOD SUPPLEMENT Use as a food in debility or for infants. Mix ¼–1 level tsp of the powder with a little water to make a paste and add boiling water or hot milk, stirring constantly, to make up to 1 cup of thin gruel. Alternatively, sprinkle the powder on porridge or muesli.
OINTMENT Use to "draw" pus, thorns, or splinters; often combined with marshmallow powder.
POULTICE Mix 1 tsp of powder with a little water or calendula infusion to form a paste, spread on gauze, and apply to boils, abscesses, varicose ulcers, or suppurating wounds.
CAPSULES/TABLETS Take 200mg 3 times daily for gastric or oesophageal inflammation or ulceration or chronic indigestion. Take 1 tablet or capsule before a journey to allay travel sickness.

HOW TO SOURCE

GROW Prefers moist, deep soil in full sun. Usually propagated by seed sown in autumn, from suckers, or from semi-ripe cuttings in summer. Not generally grown in gardens. Susceptible to pests, fungal infections, and Dutch elm disease.
FORAGE Planted as a street tree in parts of the USA, but rarely cultivated elsewhere, and unlikely to be found in the wild outside its native habitat. Stocks have been depleted by elm leaf beetle and Dutch elm disease, so great care needs to be taken when gathering the bark to avoid damaging trees further.
HARVEST Strip the inner bark from the trunks and branches of mature trees in spring.

CAUTION Availability of the whole bark is restricted in some countries.

LEAVES
The leaves are hairy and deeply veined, and grow up to 20cm (8in) in length

LEAVES
The leaves were once used in poultices or decoctions to bathe wounds and encourage healing.

20m (65ft)

GROWTH HABIT
Tree with a broad crown, teardrop-shaped leaves, and a spread of 18m (60ft).

Urtica dioica **Nettle**

Found throughout the temperate regions of Europe and Asia, the stinging nettle is an all-too-familiar weed that thrives in the rich soil of cultivated land. The "sting" is caused by hairs on the plant that contain histamine and formic acid. Nettles are said to rob the soil of its minerals and vitamins by absorbing them and concentrating them in its leaves, so becoming highly nutritious.

LEAVES
Collect the young leaves in spring to use in seasonal tonic soups, or cook and eat them like spinach

The lance-shaped leaves are a rich source of minerals, making the plant an ideal tonic remedy for conditions such as iron-deficient anaemia

GROWTH HABIT
Creeping perennial; spread indefinite.

1.5m
(5ft)

PARTS USED Aerial parts, root
MAIN CONSTITUENTS Amines (histamine, acetylcholine, choline, serotonin), flavonoids, formic acid, glucoquinones, minerals (incl. silica and iron), vitamins A, B, and C, tannins
ACTIONS Astringent, diuretic, tonic, nutritive, haemostatic, circulatory stimulant, galactogogue, hypotensive, antiscorbutic, anti-allergenic

HOW TO USE

JUICE Pulverize or process the whole fresh plant to obtain juice. Take in 10ml (2 tsp) doses 3 times daily as a tonic for debilitated conditions and anaemia.
INFUSION Take 1 cup of standard infusion (p.342) of leaves 3 times daily as part of a cleansing regime in arthritis, rheumatism, gout, and eczema, or use as a final hair rinse for dandruff.
CREAM/OINTMENT Use for minor cuts and grazes, skin rashes including eczema, or piles.
FRESH LEAVES AND STEMS Lashing arthritic joints (urtication) is an uncomfortable but traditional remedy with some recent studies showing its efficacy.
COMPRESS Use a pad soaked in a strong infusion or diluted tincture of leaves to relieve pain in arthritis, gout, neuralgia, sprains, tendonitis, and sciatica.
TINCTURE Take 2–4ml (40–80 drops) of the leaf tincture 3 times daily for allergic skin conditions and hay fever. Take 2–4ml (40–80 drops) of the root tincture 3 times daily for benign prostatic hypertrophy.

HOW TO SOURCE

GROW It is not usually necessary to cultivate nettles, as they grow freely in the wild.
FORAGE Found growing in hedgerows, waste areas, and scrub.
HARVEST Gather aerial parts when in flower. Dig up roots in autumn, and young leaves in spring.

CAUTION Wear rubber gloves when harvesting the plant.

Vaccinium myrtillus **Bilberry**

Native to temperate regions of Europe and Asia, bilberry is closely related to the North American blueberry. It has become renowned as a "superfood" thanks to the potent antioxidant proanthocyanidins contained in the fruit. Bilberry jam was eaten by fighter pilots during World War II as it was believed to improve night vision.

PARTS USED Fruit, leaves
MAIN CONSTITUENTS Tannins, sugars, fruit acids, anthocyanosides, glucoquinone, glycosides, vitamin A
ACTIONS Astringent, hypoglycaemic, tonic, antiseptic, anti-emetic, anti-inflammatory, diuretic, venous tonic

HOW TO USE

MOUTHWASH Use 1 cup of a standard infusion (p.342) of the leaves as a gargle or mouthwash for mouth ulcers and throat inflammations; 10ml (2 tsp) of the fresh berry juice diluted in 120ml (4fl oz) of water can be used in the same way.
LOTION Mix 30ml (1fl oz) of unsweetened berry juice with 30ml (1fl oz) of distilled witch hazel and use as a cooling lotion for sunburn and other skin inflammations.
DECOCTION Use 1 cup of a standard dried berry decoction daily for chronic diarrhoea.
FRESH RAW BERRIES Eat a large bowl of fresh berries with sugar and milk or cream for constipation.
INFUSION Take 1 cup of a standard infusion (p.342) of the leaves 3 times daily to support dietary control in late-onset, non-insulin dependent diabetes mellitus.

HOW TO SOURCE

GROW Prefers moist, very acid soil (pH5.5 or less) in sun or partial shade and water, as it is shallow-rooted. Sow seeds in a cold frame in autumn and transplant to final growing positions when large enough. Or propagate by semi-ripe cuttings in summer. Prune in spring to encourage bushy growth. Grow in a sheltered position. Best grown in large containers in alkaline soil areas.
FORAGE Grows wild in acidic, poor soil such as peat bogs, moors, and similar areas in temperate and sub-arctic regions.
HARVEST Gather the leaves in spring and the fruits when ripe in late summer.

CAUTION Insulin-dependent diabetics should not use bilberry leaf teas without professional guidance. Do not use the leaves for more than four weeks.

The oval leaves grow on erect stems

LEAVES
The leaves can be helpful in the early stages of late-onset diabetes while under dietary control and without medication

FRUIT
The berries are softer than blueberries and can be difficult to transport without being crushed

60cm (24in)

GROWTH HABIT
A deciduous shrub with creeping rhizomes and a spread of 60cm (24in) or more.

Valeriana officinalis **Valerian**

Sometimes described as "nature's tranquillizer", valerian originates in temperate areas from Europe to Japan. It has been extensively researched in recent years. Chemicals called valepotriates, which seem to have a depressant effect on the nervous system, are now known to develop in extracts and the dried plant. The fresh plant is more sedating.

FLOWERS
The cream or pale pink flowers, which should not be confused with red valerian, appear in summer

GROWTH HABIT
Clump-forming rhizomatous perennial.

2m (6ft)

PARTS USED Root and rhizome
MAIN CONSTITUENTS Volatile oil (incl. isovalerianic acid, borneol), valepotriates, alkaloids
ACTIONS Tranquillizer, antispasmodic, expectorant, diuretic, hypotensive, carminative, mildly analgesic

HOW TO USE

MACERATION Valerian root is best made into a maceration rather than a decoction. Soak 25g (scant 1oz) of the chopped, preferably fresh, root for 8–10 hours in 600ml (1 pint) of cold water. Take 1 cup up to 3 times daily for anxiety, nervous tension, or high blood pressure linked to stress. Take a cup before bed for insomnia.
CAPSULES The ground root may be added to capsules (also commercially available).
TINCTURE Take 1–5ml (20 drops–1 tsp) up to 3 times daily for nervous problems. Dosage can vary considerably between individuals, with higher doses causing headaches in some, so start with low doses.
COMPRESS Soak a pad in a cup of maceration or the diluted tincture and apply to muscle cramps or the abdomen for period pain and colic.

HOW TO SOURCE

GROW Prefers moist soil in a sunny or partially shaded area; suitable for a woodland garden. Sow seeds in a cold frame in spring, transplant to pots, and plant out when established, or propagate by root division in spring or autumn.
FORAGE Usually found in woodland edges or damp grass. Easily confused with the popular garden plant red, or American, valerian (*Centranthus ruber*).
HARVEST Dig roots and rhizomes of plants that are at least 2 years old in autumn.

CAUTION Enhances the action of sleep-inducing drugs, so avoid if taking such medication.

Verbascum thapsus **Mullein**

Found from Europe to western China, mullein was traditionally used to ward off evil spirits and cure wasting diseases, such as tuberculosis, which it was once believed such spirits caused. Simply carrying the plant or using it in an amulet was thought to be sufficient. Today it is mainly used in cough remedies and for respiratory disorders.

PARTS USED Flowers, leaves, aerial parts
MAIN CONSTITUENTS Mucilage, saponins, volatile oil, bitter, flavonoids (incl. rutin), glycosides (incl. aucubin)
ACTIONS Expectorant, demulcent, mild diuretic, sedative, wound herb, astringent, anti-inflammatory

HOW TO USE

SYRUP Make a syrup by combining 600ml (1 pint) of a standard infusion of fresh flowers with 450g (1lb) of honey or golden syrup: combine the ingredients, bring to the boil, and simmer gently for 10–15 minutes. Take 5ml (1tsp) doses as required.
INFUSED OIL Macerate the fresh flowers in sunflower oil for 2 weeks, strain, and use to relieve the pain of ear infections (add 2 drops to a piece of cotton wool and place in the outer ear) or as a salve on wounds, skin ulcers, piles (haemorrhoids), eczema, frostbite, blepharitis, or as a chest rub for respiratory complaints.
INFUSION Use an infusion of dried leaves or aerial parts made from 30g (1oz) of the herb to 600ml (1 pint) of boiling water for chronic coughs and throat inflammations or feverish chills with hard coughs.
TINCTURE Take 5–10ml (1–2 tsp) 3 times daily of a tincture of the leaf or aerial parts for chronic respiratory disorders.

HOW TO SOURCE

GROW Prefers well-drained to dry soil in full sun, and will spread to 90cm (3ft). Sow seeds in a cold frame in autumn or spring and transplant to 7.5cm (3in) pots when the seedlings are large enough to handle. Plant out in their final positions when well-established. Self-seeds enthusiastically if growing conditions are ideal.
FORAGE Found in hedgerows, roadsides and open, uncultivated land and can be easily spotted in summer by its statuesque flower spikes. Collect and dry the different parts separately for maximum use.
HARVEST Collect individual yellow blossoms when in full bloom. Cut the aerial parts while flowering and gather the leaves separately.

FLOWERS
The yellow flowers can be macerated in sunflower or almond oil and used for wounds, piles, eczema, blepharitis, frostbite, or painful ear infections

LEAVES
The egg-shaped woolly leaves can be up to 45cm (18in) long and were once used as a preservative wrapped around fresh fruits

The flowers, which appear in summer, are rarely separated from the leaves in commercial production, so are best foraged for

STEM
The tall stems of mullein were once burned as torches for funeral processions and were believed to ward off evil spirits

GROWTH HABIT
A tall biennial with soft, grey-green downy leaves; spread 1m (3ft).

1.8m (6ft)

Verbena officinalis **Vervain**

Once regarded as a cure-all, and sacred to the ancient Greeks, Romans, and Druids, vervain – which grows throughout much of Europe, Asia, and North Africa – is associated with a wealth of folklore and was once used in fortune-telling. Today it is a favourite after-dinner "tisane" to stimulate the digestion, and is also used to ease headaches, nervous tension, and depression.

FLOWERS
The tiny pale lilac flowers are carried on tall flower spikes in the summer, when the plant is harvested

LEAVES
The dried leaves and stems are used in after-dinner tisanes, and are especially popular in France

60cm (24in)

GROWTH HABIT
Straggly perennial with oval leaves and long flower stems; spread 60cm (24in).

PARTS USED Aerial parts
MAIN CONSTITUENTS Volatile oil (incl. citral), bitter iridoids (incl. verbenin and verbenalin), alkaloids, tannins
ACTIONS Relaxant tonic, galactagogue, diaphoretic, nervine, sedative, antispasmodic, hepatic restorative, laxative, uterine stimulant, cholagogue

HOW TO USE

TINCTURE Take 2–4ml (40–80 drops) 3 times daily for nervous exhaustion, stress, anxiety, or depression; as a liver stimulant for sluggish digestion, toxic conditions, or jaundice; and with other urinary herbs for stones and excess uric acid.
INFUSION Take 1 cup of a standard infusion (p.342) of the aerial parts 3 times daily as a digestive stimulant, or in feverish conditions; take 1 cup at night for insomnia.
CREAM/OINTMENT Use on eczema, wounds, and running sores or for painful neuralgia.
FLOWER REMEDY Dilute 2 drops in 10ml (2 tsp) of water in a dropper bottle and take in drop doses as required for mental stress and over exertion with related insomnia and an inability to relax.

HOW TO SOURCE

GROW Prefers a sunny site in well-drained soil, but tolerates other conditions. Sow the seeds in a seed bed in spring or autumn and transplant (60cm/24in apart) when established, or propagate by division in late spring. Self-seeds in the right conditions.
FORAGE An inconspicuous plant that is easily missed, it can be found growing wild, mainly in hedgerows and dry grassy areas, throughout its native region and elsewhere. Collect the aerial parts while flowering in summer.
HARVEST Traditionally collected when the plant is in flower.

CAUTION Avoid in pregnancy. May cause vomiting if taken in excess.

Viburnum opulus **Crampbark**

As with many plants, the common name of this herb aptly describes its properties. It is effective at treating cramping and spasmodic pains affecting both smooth and skeletal muscles – so, for example, it is a useful treatment for colic as well as for leg cramps. Native to Europe, northern Asia, and North America, the shrub is an attractive and popular garden plant.

PARTS USED Bark
MAIN CONSTITUENTS Bitter (viburnin), valerianic acid, tannins, coumarins, saponins
ACTIONS Antispasmodic, sedative, astringent, muscle relaxant, cardiac tonic, sedative, anti-inflammatory

HOW TO USE

TINCTURE Take 5ml (1 tsp) 3 times daily as a relaxant for nervous or muscular tension, or for colicky pains affecting the digestive tract or urinary system. Add 1ml (20 drops) to remedies for IBS or combine with rhubarb root for constipation.
DECOCTION Take ½–1 cup of a standard decoction (p.342) every 3–4 hours for period pain or colic. Can also be used with other remedies for excessive menstrual bleeding associated with the menopause.
CREAM/LOTION Use regularly for muscle cramps, including night cramps in the legs, or for shoulder tension.
MASSAGE RUB Use the macerated oil as a basis for massage rubs for muscular aches and pains associated with cramps and spasm. Add 10 drops of lavender, thyme, or rosemary essential oil to 5ml (1 tsp) of the macerated oil.

HOW TO SOURCE

GROW Prefers moist yet well-drained soil in sun or dappled shade, and can be a useful addition to a hedge or woodland garden. Propagate by softwood cuttings in summer, or plant seed as soon as it is ripe and over-winter in a cold frame or unheated greenhouse.
FORAGE May be found growing in woodlands in Europe or North America. As always when collecting bark, it is important not to damage the bush. Only harvest a small amount from each shrub.
HARVEST Bark from the branches is collected in spring and summer when the plant is flowering.

> **CAUTION** Avoid during pregnancy except under professional supervision.

BERRIES
Bright red berries, which form in autumn, are popular with some bird species

BARK
Harvested from branches in spring and summer, the bark can be used in both internal and external preparations, to ease muscle cramps

5m
(15ft)

GROWTH HABIT
Vigorous, bushy shrub with lace-capped white flowers in spring; spread 4m (12ft).

Viola tricolor **Heartsease**

The name "heartsease" is reputedly derived from its use in medieval love potions, although it was also once used for heart problems. Also known as wild pansy, the herb is native to Europe, North Africa, and temperate regions of Asia. Today it is mainly used for skin disorders and coughs, as well as making an attractive garnish in cooking.

AERIAL PARTS
Heartsease acts on blood vessels, tonifying and strengthening them thanks to the flavonoids it contains

FLOWERS
Its distinctive cream, white, and violet flowers, which bloom in summer, make wild pansy one of Europe's favourite wild flowers

LEAVES
The leaves are variable, with the lower leaves oval and the upper ones lance-shaped and lobed

12cm (5in)

GROWTH HABIT
Tufted annual, biennial, or short-lived perennial, with a spread of 38cm (15in).

PARTS USED Aerial parts
MAIN CONSTITUENTS Saponin, salicylates, flavonoids (incl. rutin), volatile oil, mucilage
ACTIONS Expectorant, anti-inflammatory, diuretic, antirheumatic, laxative, stabilizes capillary membranes

HOW TO USE

CREAM/OINTMENT Use regularly for skin rashes, eczema, nappy rash, or cradle cap.
INFUSION Take 1 cup of a standard infusion (p.342) 3 times daily as a cleansing remedy for toxic conditions, or as a gentle stimulant for the circulation and immune system in rheumatic disorders, chronic skin conditions, urinary infections, and chronic infections.
WASH Use 1 cup of a standard, well-strained infusion (p.342) to bathe nappy rash, cradle cap, weeping sores, varicose ulcers, or oozing insect bites.
SYRUP Add 450g (1lb) of honey or sugar to 600ml (1 pint) of strained infusion, bring to the boil, and simmer gently for 5–10 minutes to form a syrup. Use in 5ml (1 tsp) doses to soothe bronchitis and asthma.
TINCTURE Take 5ml (1 tsp) in a little water 3 times daily for capillary fragility, urinary disorders, or skin disorders

HOW TO SOURCE

GROW Prefers moist but well-drained soil in full sun or dappled shade. Sow seeds in seed trays in a cold frame in summer or in spring when ripe; transplant to final positions when large enough to handle. Alternatively, take basal cuttings in spring or divide established clumps in autumn.
FORAGE Found in grassy places, such as meadows and waste ground. Gather in summer while flowering. The flowers are edible and can be added to salads or used to garnish pasta dishes.
HARVEST Collect all the aerial parts in summer.

CAUTION Very high doses may cause nausea due to the saponin content.

Viscum album **Mistletoe**

Traditionally associated with fertility rites, and significant in Norse legend as the only plant capable of killing the Norse god Baldur, mistletoe has been used as a cancer treatment since the days of the Druids. Some modern research has confirmed this action, although its most common use is to lower high blood pressure. It is native to Europe and northern Asia.

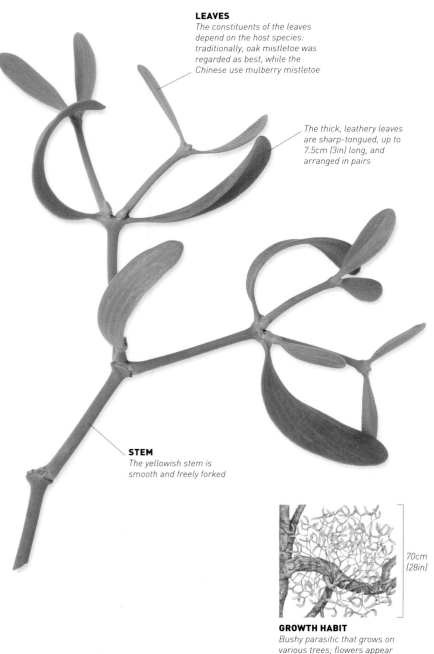

LEAVES
The constituents of the leaves depend on the host species: traditionally, oak mistletoe was regarded as best, while the Chinese use mulberry mistletoe

The thick, leathery leaves are sharp-tongued, up to 7.5cm (3in) long, and arranged in pairs

STEM
The yellowish stem is smooth and freely forked

70cm (28in)

GROWTH HABIT
Bushy parasitic that grows on various trees; flowers appear in autumn and fruits in winter.

PARTS USED Leaves, branches, berries
MAIN CONSTITUENTS Alkaloids, glycoproteins, viscotoxin, flavonoids, acetylcholine, polysaccharides (berries)
ACTIONS Hypotensive, sedative, anti-inflammatory, diuretic, immune tonic

HOW TO USE

NB Use only under medical supervision
INFUSION Take ½–1 cup of a standard leaf infusion (p.342) 3 times daily for high blood pressure, petit mal, or to assist with withdrawal in benzodiazepine addiction. Combine with skullcap, valerian, or betony (*Stachys officinalis*) for nervous disorders. Take ½ cup of a half-strength infusion 3 times daily for panic attacks or headaches.
TINCTURE Best made from the fresh plant; take 10 drops 3 times a day to lower blood pressure.
FLUID EXTRACT Consult a herbalist for usage to strengthen the immune system during treatments for cancer, including after surgery and during radiotherapy.
BERRY EXTRACTS Used in anthroposophical medicine to treat cancer.

HOW TO SOURCE

GROW Encourage mistletoe to grow on garden trees by making a small incision in the bark and crushing freshly gathered ripe berries into the cut. The berries are ripe in late winter/early spring. Collect berries only from the same type of tree (i.e. mistletoe berries from an oak tree will usually only grow on another oak). Once established, the plant is spread to other parts of the tree by birds.
FORAGE Often found growing high up on deciduous trees, it can easily be seen in winter; use secateurs on an extendable pole to cut the stems in autumn.
HARVEST Gather leaves and branches in late autumn and ripe berries in late winter.

CAUTION Avoid during pregnancy. Can be toxic (especially the berries); take only under professional supervision.

Vitex agnus-castus **Agnus castus**

Native to the Mediterranean region, agnus castus was known as the "chaste tree", while its berries were called "monk's pepper" – a reference to their medieval use as an anaphrodisiac to reduce the libido of celibate monks. The herb has the opposite effect on women, stimulating the production of female hormones, and is used for a wide range of gynaecological problems.

FLOWER BUD
When in full bloom in early autumn, the lilac to dark-blue flowers grow in long spikes

LEAVES
The leaves are darker than those of Vitex negundo, *the Chinese chaste tree*

GROWTH HABIT
Spreading shrub or small tree with pale lilac flowers in early autumn; spread 2–8m (6–25ft).

5m (16ft)

PARTS USED Fruit
MAIN CONSTITUENTS Iridoid glycosides (incl. aucubin and agnuside), volatile oil (incl. cineol), flavonoids, alkaloids (incl. viticine), bitter, fatty acids
ACTIONS Hormone regulator, progesterogenic, galactagogue

HOW TO USE

TINCTURE Take up to 2ml (40 drops) first thing in the morning during the second half of a menstrual cycle to stimulate hormone production in irregular menstrual cycles or PMS. It is easy to overdose, so start with a low dose and gradually increase the amount if there are no side effects (see Caution). It will also ease migraine or acne related to the menstrual cycle.
TABLETS/ CAPSULES Readily available commercially; follow the dosage directions on the pack and take to ease PMS.

HOW TO SOURCE

GROW Prefers well-drained soil in full sun and a warm site. Sow seeds in a cold frame in autumn or spring; transplant to 10cm (4in) pots when large enough to handle. Alternatively, take semi-ripe cuttings in summer. Grow on until well established before planting in permanent positions. Protect from cold, dry winds and severe winters. Prune in spring while still dormant.
FORAGE Generally cultivated, but can be found growing wild in southern Europe and naturalized in other sub-tropical regions. Can be confused with *Vitex negundo* (Chinese chaste tree), which has paler leaves and flowers and is native to India, Taiwan, and China. Does not always set seed to form berries in cooler climates.
HARVEST Gather ripe berries in autumn.

CAUTION Excess can cause formication – a sensation like ants crawling over the skin. Do not use if taking progesterone drugs. Avoid during pregnancy except under professional supervision.

Withania somnifera **Ashwagandha**

Also known as Indian ginseng, ashwagandha is found in the drier regions of India and the Middle East. The name translates as "that which has the smell of a horse" and the plant is traditionally associated with the strength and sexual energy of a stallion. Traditionally used as a tonic, modern research has shown it to have significant antitumour activity.

PARTS USED Root, leaves
MAIN CONSTITUENTS Alkaloids (incl. anaferine and isopelietierine), steroidal lactones (incl. withanolides and withaferins), saponins, iron
ACTIONS Tonic, nervine, sedative, adaptogen, anti-inflammatory, antitumour

HOW TO USE

POWDER/CAPSULES Take 250mg–1g of powdered root or capsule equivalent 3 times daily as a restorative tonic for over-work, exhaustion, sleep problems, and debility caused by chronic disease. Regular use can also help in degenerative disorders such as arthritis.
FLUID EXTRACT Take 2–4ml (40–80 drops) in water 3 times daily as an energy tonic, a calming remedy for insomnia, to nourish the blood in anaemia, or for stress or debility.
DECOCTION Take 1/2–1 cup of a decoction made from 1 tsp of dried root and 120ml (4fl oz) of milk or water simmered for 15 minutes for stress or exhaustion.

HOW TO SOURCE

GROW Prefers dry, stony soil in full sun. Sow seeds in spring in seed trays and transplant to 7.5cm (3in) pots when the seedlings are large enough to handle. Alternatively, propagate by heeled greenwood cuttings in late spring. Rarely seen cultivated in the West.
FORAGE Unlikely to be found growing wild outside its native region.
HARVEST The leaves are collected in spring and the root is dug in autumn.

CAUTION Avoid during pregnancy.

LEAVES
An infusion of the leaves is a traditional folk remedy for exhaustion, fevers, and insomnia

Studies suggest that the oval leaves have anticancer activity

BERRIES
Both the berries and leaves have been used in poultices for boils, carbuncles, and ulcers

1.5m (5ft)

GROWTH HABIT
Upright evergreen shrub with inconspicuous yellow flowers; spread 1m (3ft).

Zea mays **Cornsilk**

Cultivated for 4,000 years both as a cereal crop and for fodder, maize was originally grown by the Aztecs and Mayans in South America and is now the continent's most widely grown crop. Cornsilk, used medicinally, consists of the brown whiskery parts of the styles and stigmas that can be seen at the top of the cobs, and is mainly used for urinary disorders.

FLOWER
The male inflorescence is called a tassel and is made up of many small flowers, while the female forms the cob and only the silky stigma can be seen

LEAVES
The leaves form at nodes on the stem, and can grow up to 1m (3ft) in length and up to 10cm (4in) wide. The ears of corn are produced under the leaf and close to the stem

GROWTH HABIT
Annual cereal crop. Each plant has a spread of 45–60cm (18–24in).

70cm (28in)

PARTS USED Styles and stigmas (cornsilk), maize meal
MAIN CONSTITUENTS Allantoin, saponins, flavonoids, mucilage, volatile oil, vitamins C and K, potassium
ACTIONS Diuretic, urinary demulcent, mild stimulant

HOW TO USE

INFUSION Generally regarded as more effective than the tincture. Take 1 cup of a standard infusion (p.342) up to 6 times daily for cystitis, urethritis, benign prostate gland enlargement, urinary retention, or urinary gravel.
TEA Combine 1 tsp each of dried cornsilk and agrimony with 1 cup of boiling water, infuse for 15 minutes, and strain. Give to children with bed-wetting problems; consult a herbalist for advice on dosage.
TINCTURE Take 5–10ml (1–2 tsp) 3 times daily for acute or chronic inflammation of the urinary system.
POULTICE Mix 2 tsp of powdered maize meal with a little water into a paste, spread on gauze, and use as a poultice for ulcers and boils.

HOW TO SOURCE

GROW Prefers moist but well-drained soil in full sun. Sow seeds directly in spring when the ground is not too wet. Can be grown in kitchen gardens and allotments with the ripe cobs used as a food.
FORAGE Maize is widely cultivated worldwide and cornsilk can be gleaned from standing crops just before harvest, as long as landowners do not object. Snip the brown whiskery parts of the styles and stigmas from the cob with scissors.
HARVEST The cornsilk is harvested with the ripe cobs in summer, then separated and dried.

Use Herbs

Learn how to use herbs to help treat ten common health concerns, and discover over 150 inspiring recipes for effective home-made herbal remedies to help you heal from the inside and outside.

✋ Healthy skin and hair

Our skin may form a wonderfully protective barrier against the outside world, but it is also a mirror of our inner health. Effective cleansing and care can maintain skin and hair health from the outside, but most skin problems require both internal and external remedies to effectively relieve and treat symptoms such as rashes, spots, and itching. This chart is not comprehensive, but it does contain the key herbs for skin health.

Herb	Action
Calendula *Calendula officinalis* (p.36)	A soothing herb that also stimulates healing of the skin. Take an infusion of the herb or dilute the tincture for abrasions, wounds, ulcers, or as a mouthwash. Use as a cream or macerated oil to relieve eczema, rashes, or sore skin.
Oats *Avena sativa* (p.33)	Cleansing and soothing, oats make a good alternative to soap or detergents for very sensitive skin. Grind oats to a powder and add to the bath water, or mix with a little water or oil to make a soothing mask or cleanser.
Chamomile *Matricaria recutita* (p.80)	Soothing and anti-inflammatory. Use cooled chamomile tea as a lotion to relieve any hot, inflamed skin condition (e.g. sunburn, hives, or rashes). Drink the tea, with its calming and anti-allergenic properties, to alleviate eczema, rashes, and so on.
Chickweed *Stellaria media* (p.111)	A wonderfully cooling and soothing herb for the skin, chickweed will relieve any irritation such as eczema, psoriasis, hives, or ulcers. Mash the fresh plant, adding a little boiling water, wrap in a muslin cloth, and apply once cold as a poultice to the skin.
Burdock root *Arctium lappa* (p.28)	One of the most effective cleansing herbs, which is used internally to treat chronic skin problems such as psoriasis, eczema, acne, persistent boils, ulcers, and so on. Combine with dandelion and make a decoction of the root, or take the tincture.
Lavender *Lavandula angustifolia* (p.74)	The soothing, anti-inflammatory, and antiseptic properties of lavender make it a very versatile herb. Use the essential oil or a cooled infusion to calm rashes, redness, eczema, sunburn, thrush, and so on.
Dandelion leaf *Taraxacum officinale* (p.114)	One of the best-known cleansing herbs, dandelion leaf can be combined with burdock and red clover and taken as an infusion three times a day for several weeks to help clear acne, eczema, psoriasis or problem skin.
Nettle *Urtica dioica* (p.124)	Taken internally as an infusion, nettles help to reduce inflammation and have an anti-allergenic action. Combine with chamomile for urticaria (hives) or any itchy rash. Allow the infusion to cool and use as an excellent final rinse for dandruff or psoriasis of the scalp.
Thyme *Thymus vulgaris* (p.116)	An effective antiseptic and antifungal herb. Dilute the essential oil in a base oil to treat fungal infections such as ringworm, thrush, and athlete's foot. Make a strong infusion to use as a lotion to prevent infection, for example in wounds, ulcers, or gum disease.
Red clover *Trifolium pratense* (p.119)	A cleansing herb that promotes healing of the skin. Combine with dandelion and burdock and drink as an infusion or as tinctures to help clear eczema, psoriasis, recurrent boils, or any chronic skin disease.

Recipes

Red clover *Trifolium pratense*

HEAL FROM THE INSIDE

- Goji berry and
pine nut smoothie
(see page 164)

- Almond and rose smoothie
(see page 165)

- Ginger and fennel juice
(see page 171)

- Dandelion and burdock tea
(see page 180)

- Red clover and cleavers tincture
(see page 205)

- Goji berry and mint soup
(see page 216)

- Nettle and sweet potato soup
(see page 218)

- Courgette spaghetti with
coriander and pine nut pesto
(see page 228)

HEAL FROM THE OUTSIDE

- Minty fresh foot cream
(see page 254)

- Stimulating body oil
(see page 266)

- Lavender and bergamot soothing
skin oil
(see page 265)

- Detox body oil
(see page 267)

- Geranium and orange body oil
(see page 266)

- Rosemary gardener's soap
(see page 282)

- Calendula and chamomile soap
(see page 284)

- Neem cleansing soap
(see page 285)

- Relaxation soap
(see page 286)

- Exotic soap
(see page 287)

- Soothing lavender cleanser
(see page 289)

- Spicy witch hazel deodorant
(see page 271)

- Bergamot and mint deodorant
(see page 272)

- Blackcurrant and sage
foot powder
(see page 280)

- Aloe and elderflower
body scrub
(see page 259)

- Honey and avocado body scrub
(see page 260)

- Lavender salt scrub
(see page 260)

- Calendula and oat body scrub
(see page 261)

- Honey and orange body scrub
(see page 261)

Lavender and rosemary conditioner
Restores vitality to dull hair
(see page 324).

Thyme *Thymus vulgaris*

- Cleansing chamomile
hand scrub
(see page 262)

- Mandarin and myrrh foot scrub
(see page 263)

- Rose and honey face scrub
(see page 290)

- Elderflower and aloe vera
face polish
(see page 291)

- Rosemary conditioner
(see page 321)

- Enriching coconut conditioner
(see page 323)

- Lavender and
rosemary conditioner
(see page 324)

- Stimulating hair oil
(see page 326)

- Calendula and banana
hair treatment
(see page 327)

- Nettle shampoo
(see page 320)

- Thyme and cider rinse
(see page 322)

- Nourishing conditioner
(see page 321)

- Horsetail shampoo
(see page 320)

Digestion

Careless eating habits, drugs, emotional upsets, and stress can all trigger a variety of symptoms, so keeping the digestive system in good working order is essential to our well-being and is the foundation of good health. If any symptoms worsen or are persistent, seek professional advice, as they may mask a more serious underlying complaint. This chart is not comprehensive, but it does contain the key herbs for digestive health.

Herb	Action
Fennel *Foeniculum vulgare* (p.57)	A gentle digestive stimulant suitable for delicate stomachs. Chew a few seeds or make an infusion to dispel wind, griping pains, and colic.
Peppermint *Mentha x piperita* (p.84)	A versatile herb for the effective relief of a range of digestive complaints. Drink as an infusion for symptoms of indigestion, flatulence, travel sickness, colic, nausea, and vomiting. Essential oil capsules are used to treat IBS.
Chamomile *Matricaria recutita* (p.80)	A gentle herb that calms digestive problems. Drink an infusion or use the tincture to relieve indigestion, gastrointestinal spasm, and "nervous" tummy. This herb is a favourite remedy for babies and children.
Meadowsweet *Filipendula ulmaria* (p.56)	A natural antacid that will relieve the symptoms of a range of gastrointestinal problems associated with flatulence or hyperacidity. Drink an infusion to treat wind, peptic ulcers, reflux, mild diarrhoea, and gastritis.
Lemon balm *Melissa officinalis* (p.83)	A wonderfully soothing and gentle herb for an overwrought digestive system in both adults and children. Drink an infusion to relieve colic, flatulence, stomach cramps, and any stress-related digestive symptoms.
Liquorice *Glycyrrhiza glabra* (p.62)	Soothing to the digestive tract and mildly laxative. Combine with chamomile and meadowsweet and take as an infusion for symptoms of indigestion, acidity, and gastritis, or combine with senna to relieve constipation.
Marshmallow *Althaea officinalis* (p.23)	Soothes inflammation of the entire digestive tract. Combine with chamomile and drink as an infusion to relieve symptoms of acidity or discomfort or irritation of the mouth, stomach, or duodenum.
Slippery elm *Ulmus rubra* (p.123)	Adds a protective and healing coating to the digestive tract. Mix the herb with a little water and drink the resulting paste to relieve symptoms of acidity, reflux, gastritis, gastroenteritis, and diarrhoea.
Ginger *Zingiber officinale*	Acts as an antispasmodic and anti-emetic: use to relieve symptoms of flatulence, colic, nausea, irritable bowel, hiccups, and vomiting. It is also anti-inflammatory and antiseptic, so is beneficial for gastrointestinal infections.
Senna *Senna alexandrina* (p.109)	A stimulant laxative that will relieve occasional constipation. Make an infusion to drink at bedtime that will stimulate a bowel motion the following morning. Adding a little liquorice or ginger powder will help prevent any griping pain.

Recipes

Chamomile *Matricaria recutita*

HEAL FROM THE INSIDE

- Plum and fennel smoothie
  (see page 167)

- Garden greens juice
  (see page 170)

- Red pepper and sprouted
  seeds juice
  see page 170)

- Ginger and fennel juice
  (see page 171)

- Fennel and broccoli sprouts juice
  (see page 171)

- Tomato salsa juice
  (see page 172)

- Artichoke leaf and fennel juice
  (see page 173)

- Sunflower greens and
  wheatgrass juice
  (see page 173)

- Chamomile and fennel tea
  (see page 178)

- Dandelion and burdock tea
  (see page 180)

- Blackberry and wild strawberry
  leaf tea
  (see page 181)

- Nettle and cleavers tea
  (see page 184)

- Peppermint and thyme tincture
  (see page 198)

- Dandelion and burdock tincture
  (see page 208)

- Onion squash and ginger soup
  (see page 213)

- French bean and coriander soup
  (see page 214)

- Burdock root and carrot soup
  (see page 215)

- Nettle and sweet potato soup
  (see page 218)

- Ginseng and astragalus soup
  (see page 219)

- Sprouted puy lentil and
  turmeric soup
  (see page 223)

- Nasturtium and sprouted
  seed salad
  (see page 226)

- Courgette spaghetti with
  coriander and pine nut pesto
  (see page 228)

- Dandelion and primrose
  leaf salad
  (see page 230)

- Broccoli and rosemary salad
  (see page 232)

Fennel *Foeniculum vulgare*

- Sauerkraut and avocado salad
  (see page 234)

- Nori rolls
  (see page 235)

- Mint and cucumber salad
  with cashew nut cream
  (see page 236)

- Cayenne-toasted almond
  and kale salad
  (see page 237)

- Linseed and chilli bars
  (see page 241)

Broccoli and rosemary salad A salad full of nutrients that improves digestion
(see page 232).

⦾ Circulation

Cardiovascular disease is caused by lack of exercise, obesity, diets that are rich in saturated fats, smoking, and excessive stress. Improving your diet and regular exercise helps, as can simple herbal remedies to reduce cholesterol levels and alleviate stress. If you take medication, seek medical advice first. This chart is not comprehensive, but it does contain the key herbs for improving circulation.

Herb	Action
Nettle *Urtica dioica (p.124)*	Nettle tea is an excellent iron tonic in the treatment of anaemia. It helps to lower blood pressure when combined with hawthorn and lime flowers, and is a traditional remedy for varicose veins when combined with motherwort and melilot.
Ginger *Zingiber officinale*	An effective circulatory stimulant and vasodilator that has an anti-cholesterol action. Add powdered ginger to hot water, or take the tincture or capsules, to relieve cold hands and feet and to support the treatment of atherosclerosis.
Hawthorn *Crataegus laevigata (p.44)*	Traditionally used as a restorative for the heart and circulation, hawthorn helps to regulate heartbeat and high blood pressure. Take it as an infusion, tincture, or as capsules.
Yarrow *Achillea millefolium (p.12)*	Combined with lime flowers and hawthorn as a tea or tincture, yarrow will reduce high blood pressure and treat arteriosclerosis. Soak a cotton wool pad in the diluted tincture or cooled tea to stop a nosebleed.
Lime flowers *Tilia cordata (p.118)*	Helps to relieve the stress and tension associated with high blood pressure, and also used to treat hardening of the arteries and relieve headaches associated with high blood pressure. Often combined with hawthorn and taken as an infusion or tincture.
Garlic *Allium sativum (p.19)*	Helps prevent the build-up of cholesterol and has an anticoagulant action that is beneficial in thrombosis and arteriosclerosis. Eat garlic raw or take the juice or capsules.
Rosemary *Rosmarinus officinalis (p.98)*	A circulatory tonic traditionally used to strengthen the heart, improve varicose veins, and help prevent arteriosclerosis. Combine with lime flowers as an infusion to relieve headaches associated with high blood pressure.
Ginkgo *Ginkgo biloba (p.61)*	A circulatory stimulant and peripheral vasodilator. Combine with hawthorn to treat coronary artery disease. Combine with yarrow to treat varicose veins. Combine with ginger to treat cold extremities, intermittent claudication, and chilblains.
Goji *Lycium barbarum (p.79)*	A traditional Chinese tonic, believed to promote long life. The berries, now thought of as a "superfood" in the West, are a tonic for the circulatory system and blood, and can relieve dizziness and tinnitus. The root relaxes the artery muscles and lowers blood pressure.
Witch hazel *Hamamelis virginiana (p.63)*	Soak a cotton wool pad in distilled witch hazel and apply locally to relieve the heat, inflammation, and itching of varicose veins, piles (haemorrhoids), phlebitis, and chilblains.

Recipes

HEAL FROM THE INSIDE

- **Blackcurrant booster smoothie**
  (see page 164)

- **Pistachio and avocado smoothie**
  (see page 166)

- **Power berry smoothie**
  (see page 167)

- **Red pepper and sprouted seeds juice**
  (see page 170)

- **Buckwheat greens and pea shoots juice**
  (see page 172)

- **Hawthorn flower and lavender tea**
  (see page 184)

- **Four fruits bars**
  (see page 239)

- **Lime flower and hawthorn berry tincture**
  (see page 201)

- **Yarrow and calendula tea**
  (see page 180)

Four fruits bars High in nutrients and low in saturated fats *(see page 239)*.

Yarrow *Achillea millefolium*

Ginger and juniper warming foot soak *(see page 314)*.

HEAL FROM THE OUTSIDE

- **Detox body oil**
  (see page 267)

- **Detox bath infusion**
  (see page 313)

- **Ginger and juniper warming foot soak**
  (see page 314)

♀ Women's health

Herbs can help treat a range of problems associated with menstruation (such as painful or heavy periods), premenstrual syndrome, boosting fertility, vaginal infections, and menopausal symptoms. For persistent problems, consult an experienced herbalist. This chart is not comprehensive, but it does contain the key herbs for women's health. Do not use the herbs listed during pregnancy without checking their appropriateness.

Herb	Action
Lady's mantle *Alchemilla xanthochlora (p.18)*	An astringent herb that is a menstrual regulator. Use to relieve heavy and painful periods: combine with shepherd's purse and raspberry leaf and drink as an infusion three times a day. Or use a cooled infusion as a douche for vaginal inflammation, thrush, or pruritis.
Chamomile *Matricaria recutita (p.80)*	A soothing and antispasmodic herb with a multitude of uses. As an infusion or tincture, it can help to relieve painful periods and alleviate stress. A cooled infusion or diluted essential oil can be used externally to relieve vaginal itching or irritation.
Raspberry leaf *Rubus idaeus (p.99)*	An astringent and toning herb with a special affinity for the uterus. Drink as an infusion to relieve heavy or painful periods.
Chaste berry *Vitex agnus-castus (p.134)*	A hormonal regulator used in the treatment of an irregular menstrual cycle, symptoms of premenstrual syndrome, and to relieve symptoms of the menopause. It is often used in the treatment of polycystic ovary syndrome (PCOS). Most often used as a tincture.
St John's wort *Hypericum perforatum (p.68)*	An effective antidepressant herb, proven to relieve symptoms of mild or moderate depression. Also important for anxiety and stress, it can be helpful for premenstrual syndrome and emotional problems arising during the menopause.
Rose *Rosa x damascena (p.96)*	A soothing, uplifting, and balancing herb and essential oil. Take as an infusion combined with motherwort for stress or headaches associated with premenstrual syndrome or the menopause. Use a cooled infusion or essential oil to soothe vaginal dryness and irritation.
Chinese angelica *Angelica sinensis*	An essential women's tonic herb of traditional Chinese medicine, Chinese angelica is taken to increase vitality and libido, treat infertility, regulate periods, and for anaemia due to blood loss. Take as a tincture or add to soups.
Schisandra *Schisandra chinensis (p.107)*	An excellent Chinese tonic herb and restorative. It is helpful for night sweats and as a tonic to support the body through menopause. It also helps to improve stamina, fatigue, and physical stress. Best taken as a tincture.
Black cohosh *Actaea racemosa (p.14)*	A North American herb traditionally used for gynaecological complaints. It helps to relieve pain and is used for painful periods and the bloating and discomfort associated with premenstrual syndrome. Combine with sage to relieve menopausal symptoms.
Vervain *Verbena officinalis (p.128)*	An antispasmodic herb that helps to relieve pain, stress, and tension. Use for headaches associated with periods or during the menopause, premenstrual syndrome, scanty periods, and nervous exhaustion. Best taken as an infusion or tincture.

Recipes

Damask rose *Rosa* x *damascena*

St John's wort *Hypericum perforatum*

Raspberry *Rubus idaeus*

HEAL FROM THE INSIDE

- Goji berry and cranberry smoothie
  (see page 164)

- Jasmine and lemon grass tea
  (see page 176)

- Goji berry and damiana tea
  (see page 176)

- Yarrow and calendula tea
  (see page 180)

- Peppermint and calendula infusion
  (see page 183)

- Horsetail and cornsilk tea
  (see page 185)

- Rose petal syrup
  (see page 194)

- Chaste berry and dang gui tincture
  (see page 203)

- Black cohosh and sage tincture
  (see page 210)

- Birch leaf and nettle root tincture
  (see page 211)

- Courgette and sea greens soup
  (see page 222)

- Red clover sprouts and lemon balm salad
  (see page 229)

Peppermint and calendula infusion This infusion relieves PMS and period pains *(see page 183)*.

⚲ Men's health

In the West we tend to look to herbs to treat specific problems (unlike traditional Chinese medicine, where herbs are recognized for their virtues as energy tonics), and modern research is backing up the benefits of certain herbs to deal with prostate health, infertility, erectile dysfunction, and stress. If any symptoms worsen or are persistent, seek medical advice. This chart is not comprehensive, but it does contain the key herbs for men's health.

Herb	Action
Saw palmetto *Serenoa repens*	Proven to relieve the symptoms of an enlarged prostate by reducing elevated testosterone levels. It acts as an antiseptic diuretic in the treatment of cystitis or urethritis. Traditionally used as a male aphrodisiac, and to treat infertility. Best taken as a tincture or capsules.
Ginkgo *Ginkgo biloba (p.61)*	Proven to stimulate peripheral circulation. It has a direct effect on the blood flow to the penile arteries and veins, and is used in the treatment of erectile dysfunction and impotence. Combine with cinnamon in an infusion, or drink the tincture regularly for a few months.
Damiana *Turnera diffusa*	Acts as an antidepressant and energy tonic and helps to combat chronic exhaustion and anxiety. It is also used to treat premature ejaculation, impotence, and a loss of interest in sex. Take in combination with other appropriate herbs as an infusion or tinctures.
Ashwagandha *Withania somnifera (p.135)*	A traditional energy tonic from the Ayurvedic tradition, this herb is used to combat stress and as an aphrodisiac. Used in the treatment of chronic stress, anaemia, impotence, and infertility. Best taken as a tincture or capsules.
Ginseng *Panax ginseng (p.88)*	The most famous of all energy or "chi" tonics from the Chinese tradition, ginseng has a long tradition as an aphrodisiac and to generally improve stamina and boost natural immunity and resistance to stress. Best taken as capsules, a tincture, or in soups.
Goji berries *Lycium barbarum (p.79)*	Goji berries have established a reputation in the West as a "superfood", and are used in traditional Chinese medicine as a blood tonic and to promote longevity. Eat the berries or combine the tincture with damiana as an energy tonic and as an aphrodisiac.
Schisandra *Schisandra chinensis (p.107)*	A major tonic herb that acts to protect the liver, it is also frequently used as a sexual tonic and aphrodisiac. Combine with ginkgo to improve concentration, or with damiana to treat stress, erectile dysfunction, or loss of interest in sex. Best taken as a tincture.
Gotu kola *Centella asiatica (p.40)*	A herb from the Ayurvedic tradition that is used as a tonic and to revitalize. Combine with ginkgo to improve memory and concentration and help erectile dysfunction, or with other aphrodisiac herbs to improve libido and general energy levels. Take as an infusion or tincture.
Nettle root *Urtica dioica (p.124)*	Several studies have shown the root of this versatile herb to be of value in the relief of benign prostate hypertrophy (enlargement). Combine with saw palmetto and take as a decoction or tinctures.
Pumpkin seeds *Cucurbita* spp.	Pumpkin seeds are a rich source of zinc, which is essential for reproductive health and for a healthy prostate and bladder in particular. Eat a few of the seeds every day, or take the cold-pressed oil, which is also an excellent source of omega fatty acids.

Recipes

HEAL FROM THE INSIDE

- Strawberry and
  macadamia smoothie
  (see page 163)

- Goji berry and
  pine nut smoothie
  (see page 164)

- Jasmine and lemon grass tea
  (see page 176)

- Goji berry and damiana tea
  (see page 176)

- Horsetail and cornsilk tea
  (see page 185)

- Birch leaf and nettle
  root tincture
  (see page 211)

- Courgette and sea greens soup
  (see page 222)

Gotu kola *Centella asiatica*

Strawberry and macadamia smoothie The ingredients in this smoothie are both cooling for the body and act as a male reproductive tonic *(see page 163)*.

Goji *Lycium barbarum*

🗝 Coughs and colds

Early treatment is the key to preventing coughs, colds, and flu from becoming too serious or developing complications. This chart is not comprehensive, but it does contain key herbs that help to combat a fever, reduce catarrh or inflammation, and boost natural immunity. They work best if you take the opportunity to rest and reduce excess stress in your life. If symptoms become serious or do not clear up in a couple of days, seek medical advice.

Herb	Action
Garlic *Allium sativum (p.19)*	An excellent respiratory antiseptic and anticatarrhal. Take for all types of chest infections, bronchitis, colds, flu, ear infections, and for excess catarrh. Add to food or take capsules or make a cough syrup.
Mullein *Verbascum thapsus (p.127)*	A soothing expectorant for irritating coughs, tracheitis, and bronchitis. Helps to dispel excess catarrh. Combine with coltsfoot and take as an infusion. The macerated oil is a traditional remedy for earache: place on cotton wool and position in the outer ear.
Yarrow *Achillea millefolium (p.12)*	Reduces the fever of colds and flu by promoting sweating, and also boosts natural immunity. It can be made into a traditional cold and flu tea when combined with elderflower and peppermint; drink three times a day. Avoid during pregnancy.
Echinacea *Echinacea purpurea (p.50)*	A natural antibiotic and immune booster, echinacea has been proven to shorten the duration of colds and flu. Best taken as a tincture, and combines well with elderberry. Use for coughs, colds, flu, earache, sore throats, and any infection or viruses.
Eucalyptus *Eucalyptus globulus (p.53)*	A native Australian tree renowned for its antibacterial, decongestant, and immune-boosting properties. Add the leaves to hot water or use the essential oil and use as a steam inhalation or chest salve for colds, flu, catarrh, sinusitis, coughs, bronchitis, asthma, and throat infections.
Elecampane *Inula helenium (p.71)*	An important herb for chest complaints, as it clears mucus off the chest and has a warming and tonic effect on the lungs. It is also antibacterial, so is great for lung infections. Use to treat any chest infection, bronchitis, asthma, or chronic cough. Take as a decoction or tincture.
Liquorice *Glycyrrhiza glabra (p.62)*	An anti-inflammatory and expectorant herb, liquorice is well loved in Chinese and European medicine. Add liquorice powder or tincture to combinations of other appropriate herbs for coughs, catarrh, respiratory infections, and bronchitis.
Thyme *Thymus vulgaris (p.116)*	A highly effective respiratory antiseptic and expectorant herb useful for infections that involve coughing. Used to treat throat and chest infections, bronchitis, pleurisy, and whooping cough. Take as an infusion or combine the tincture with other appropriate herbs.
Sage *Salvia officinalis (p.102)*	An astringent and tonic herb that is excellent for the relief of sore throats. Use as an infusion or tincture to drink or gargle for sore throats, tonsillitis, laryngitis, and mouth or gum problems. Avoid during pregnancy.
Elderberry *Sambucus nigra (p.104)*	A traditional remedy for both adults and children in the prevention and treatment of colds, coughs, and sore throats. Has an antiviral and immune-boosting action and is proven to shorten the duration of colds and flu. Take as a decoction, syrup, or tincture.

Recipes

HEAL FROM THE INSIDE

- **Early autumn rambler's delight** *(see page 168)*
- **Chrysanthemum and elderflower tea** *(see page 177)*
- **Mullein and marshmallow tea** *(see page 185)*
- **Blackberry and lime cordial** *(see page 186)*
- **Elderberry and elderflower cordial** *(see page 188)*
- **Sweet violet and ginger syrup** *(see page 189)*
- **Mullein and aniseed syrup** *(see page 193)*
- **Echinacea and thyme syrup** *(see page 197)*
- **Elderberry and liquorice tincture** *(see page 200)*
- **Echinacea and elderberry winter guard tincture** *(see page 206)*
- **Raw carrot and almond soup** *(see page 221)*

Raw carrot and almond soup This restorative remedy strengthens the lungs against winter ailments such as colds and flu *(see page 221)*.

Elder *Sambucus nigra*

Mullein *Verbascum thapus*

Elecampane *Inula helenium*

✚ First Aid

Every home should have a few simple herbal remedies to hand in addition to a first-aid kit. Many situations that need a first-aid solution – such as minor accidents and injuries, insect bites and stings, abrasions, and minor burns and scalds – will also benefit from the healing properties of a herbal remedy. If you are in any doubt, seek urgent medical advice first. This chart is not comprehensive, but it does contain the key herbs for emergency aid.

Herb	Action
Aloe vera *Aloe vera (p.20)*	Highly effective soothing and cooling properties. Break off a leaf from a fresh plant, split it open, and use the fresh gel to soothe rashes, minor burns, scalds, or sunburn. Alternatively, buy aloe vera juice.
Calendula *Calendula officinalis (p.36)*	An antiseptic and healing herb. Combine the tincture with St John's wort and dab neat onto spots, or dilute 1 teaspoon in half a cup of boiled water to use as an antiseptic and cleansing lotion for abrasions, or use as a healing cream.
Chamomile *Matricaria recutita (p.80)*	Soothing and calming. Sip the tea to ease fevers, insomnia, and nausea, or sweeten with honey to relieve shock. The cooled tea can be used as a cooling and soothing lotion for inflamed skin and rashes.
Comfrey *Symphytum officinale (p.112)*	Traditionally known as "knitbone" because of its healing properties. Pound the fresh leaves into a pulp and apply as a poultice for sprains, bruises, and ulcers. Alternatively, apply as a macerated oil or cream.
Echinacea *Echinacea purpurea (p.50)*	Known as "nature's antibiotic'", echinacea should be used whenever necessary to prevent an infection. Dilute the tincture and use as a lotion for wounds, insect or animal bites, and stings. Also take internally to boost immunity.
Garlic *Allium sativum (p.19)*	A pungent but effective kitchen herb with antiseptic and anticatarrhal properties. Eat a raw clove twice daily to alleviate congestion and help prevent infections. A fresh clove rubbed onto an infected spot or boil is also effective.
Lavender *Lavandula angustifolia (p.74)*	Healing, calming and anti-inflammatory, this versatile essential oil can be dabbed onto the skin to relieve insect bites, sunburn or minor burns, and scalds. Inhaling the oil can relieve shock, or dab a little on the temples to alleviate tension headaches or insomnia.
Plantain *Plantago lanceolata (p.90)*	A naturally soothing herb with an antihistamine action. Bruise the fresh leaves and apply to rashes, insect bites, and stings to calm the irritation. Combine the tincture with calendula as a healing mouthwash or for cuts and abrasions.
Slippery elm *Ulmus rubra (p.123)*	Lines the stomach and reduces inflammation: mix with water and drink to relieve indigestion, gastritis and stomach upsets. Mix a little water into a paste to make a poultice to draw out splinters, boils, and abscesses.
Witch hazel *Hamamelis virginiana (p.63)*	This plant is well known as an instantly cooling and soothing herb. Soak some cotton wool in distilled witch hazel and apply liberally to relieve discomfort from insect bites, bruising, minor burns, sunburn, and piles (haemorrhoids).

Recipes for first aid

Calendula *Calendula officinalis*

HEAL FROM THE INSIDE

- Crampbark and valerian tincture
  (see page 209)

HEAL FROM THE OUTSIDE

- Soothing herbal balm
  (see page 251)

- Citronella spray
  (see page 274)

- After-bite soother
  (see page 274)

- Calendula and St John's wort soothing oil
  (see page 267)

- Tea tree and thyme foot balm
  (see page 305)

- Ginger and juniper warming foot soak
  (see page 314)

Aloe vera *Aloe vera*

Echinacea *Echinacea purpurea*

⚡ Muscles and joints

The key to healthy muscles and joints is to balance a strong structure with flexibility; this can become a challenge as we grow older. If you do have long-standing problems with muscles or joints, a combination of manipulation, diet, lifestyle changes, and herbal remedies to detoxify and reduce inflammation will all help. This chart is not comprehensive, but it does contain key herbs that help to prevent pain and inflammation.

Herb	Action
Arnica *Arnica montana*	The first remedy to think of following any injury to muscles or joints such as bruising, sprains, or strains. Can also be used to relieve backache and the pain of arthritis and rheumatism. Apply locally as a cream, macerated oil, or salve.
Comfrey *Symphytum officinale* (p.112)	Traditionally known as "knitbone" because of its remarkable healing properties. The fresh leaves can be pulverised to make a poultice for sprains, strains, aches and pains, and arthritis. Alternatively, use the cream or macerated oil.
Celery *Apium graveolens* (p.26)	Detoxifying and anti-inflammatory, celery seeds are an important remedy in the treatment of gout, rheumatism, and arthritis. Combine with white willow and drink three times a day for several weeks as a decoction, or use the tinctures.
Meadowsweet *Filipendula ulmaria* (p.56)	With its anti-inflammatory and antirheumatic properties, meadowsweet is helpful in relieving the pain and inflammation of rheumatism and arthritis. Take as an infusion or tincture three times daily.
Rosemary *Rosmarinus officinalis* (p.98)	Stimulates the circulation and brings a feeling of warmth and comfort to aching muscles and joints. Dilute the essential oil in a massage base and rub into painful areas. Excellent for sports injuries such as pulled muscles; rub into the muscle before and after any exertion.
St John's wort *Hypericum perforatum* (p.68)	With its analgesic and anti-inflammatory properties, St John's wort is particularly appropriate for treating areas rich in nerves. Massage the macerated oil into the skin to treat backache, sciatica, and neuralgia.
Juniper *Juniperus communis* (p.73)	A diuretic, detoxifying, and antirheumatic essential oil. Make a compress using the essential oil to relieve gout. Combine with ginger essential oil in a vegetable base oil to relieve muscular aches and pains.
Crampbark *Viburnum opulus* (p.129)	An effective antispasmodic and sedative herb. Use to relieve the pain of backache (combine with white willow) and muscular cramp. Best used as a tincture. Combine with devil's claw (*Harpagophytum procumbens*) for swollen joints and arthritis.
Devil's claw *Harpagophytum procumbens*	An effective anti-inflammatory herb useful in the treatment of swollen joints and arthritis. Take as a tincture or capsules. Works well combined with crampbark or white willow.
White willow *Salix alba* (p.101)	Analgesic and anti-inflammatory, white willow relieves pain in a similar way to aspirin. Helpful in the treatment of painful joints and muscles, arthritis, neuralgia, and sciatica. Take as a decoction or tincture in combination with other appropriate herbs.

Recipes

Roasted barley and chestnut soup This beneficial tonic soup is worth having weekly if you suffer from lower back pain (see page 224

HEAL FROM THE INSIDE

- Fennel and broccoli sprouts juice
  (see page 171)
- Rosehip syrup
  (see page 192)
- Sour cherry syrup
  (see page 196)
- Sprouted puy lentils and
  turmeric soup
  (see page 223)
- Roasted barley and
  chestnut soup
  (see page 224)

HEAL FROM THE OUTSIDE

- Citrus bath bombs
  (see page 307)
- Exotic bath bombs
  (see page 308)
- Sunshine bath bombs
  (see page 309)
- Rose and calendula bath infusion
  (see page 310)
- Lavender and aloe vera
   bath infusion
  (see page 312)
- Lemon grass and rosemary
  bath infusion
  (see page 312)
- Seaweed and arnica
  bath infusion
  (see page 313)
- Detox bath infusion
  (see page 313)
- Relax and restore bath herbs
  (see page 316)

Meadowsweet *Filipendula ulmaria*

Citrus bath bombs These fizzing balls contain grapefruit, lemon, and lime oils and fresh rosemary to uplift.

◉ Mind and emotions

Modern life can be stressful. Herbs can help us to cope better with stress and relieve symptoms of depression, exhaustion, and tension, but to bring about lasting benefits, we must change our lifestyles and use remedies to support us during that change. Refer any severe or long-standing complaints to a medical practitioner for professional help. This chart is not comprehensive, but it does contain the key herbs for emotional and mental well-being.

Herb	Action
Oats *Avena sativa (p.33)*	An excellent tonic for the nervous system, oats help to improve nervousness, exhaustion, anxiety, and decrease stress. Eat as porridge every morning or use the tincture in combination with other appropriate herbs.
St John's wort *Hypericum perforatum (p.68)*	Proven to relieve the symptoms of mild to moderate depression, and also helpful in cases of SAD, anxiety, and exhaustion. Take as an infusion, tincture, or capsules. Not to be used in conjunction with any other medication without medical advice.
Lemon balm *Melissa officinalis (p.83)*	An uplifting antidepressant and calming remedy. It lifts the spirits and calms anxiety, nervousness, and panic attacks. Also good for treating insomnia and headaches. This very safe, pleasant-tasting herb is suitable for everyone. Best taken as an infusion or tincture.
Vervain *Verbena officinalis (p128)*	A tonic herb that is strengthening for the nervous system and useful for the relief of tension, headaches, depression, exhaustion, and stress. Combines well with lemon balm and skullcap. Take as an infusion or as tincture.
Skullcap *Scutellaria lateriflora (p.108)*	An important nervine tonic with antispasmodic action that has mild sedative qualities. Useful in the treatment of stress, anxiety, overwork, migraine, and following an emotional shock. Combines well with lemon balm and chamomile. Use as an infusion or tincture.
Lavender *Lavandula angustifolia (p.74)*	With its calming and sedative properties, lavender is useful in the treatment of restlessness, shock, and stress. Drink as an infusion combined with lemon balm to relieve tension headaches. Use the essential oil to relieve insomnia.
Passionflower *Passiflora incarnata (p.89)*	A mild sedative herb that is excellent in the treatment of sleeplessness and anxiety. Combines well with chamomile to make an infusion for the relief of insomnia.
Ashwagandha *Withania somnifera (p.135)*	A herb from the Ayurvedic tradition that is known as an adaptogen – helping the body to cope with the effects of long-term stress. Helps to restore energy and vitality to those suffering from exhaustion. Best taken as a tincture or powder.
Damiana *Turnera diffusa*	An effective antidepressant herb that helps to restore an enthusiasm and vitality for life. Use to relieve symptoms of anxiety and depression. Take as an infusion or tinctures combined with other appropriate herbs such as lemon balm.
Borage *Borago officinalis (p.34)*	The phrase "borage for courage" indicates its use in strengthening the adrenal glands of those fatigued by long-term stress. Used for stress, depression, and exhaustion, but only for short periods of time and only under the advice of a qualified herbalist.

Recipes

Borage *Borago officinalis*

HEAL FROM THE INSIDE

- Almond and rose smoothie
  (see page 165)
- Maca and mango smoothie
  (see page 166)
- Pistachio and avocado smoothie
  (see page 166)
- Power berry smoothie
  (see page 167)
- Tomato salsa juice
  (see page 172)
- Artichoke leaf and fennel juice
  (see page 173)
- Sunflower greens and wheatgrass juice
  (see page 173)
- Lemon balm and rose tea
  (see page 175)
- Jasmine and lemon grass tea
  (see page 176)
- Yarrow and calendula tea
  (see page 180)
- Skullcap and orange flower tea
  (see page 181)
- Peppermint and calendula infusion
  (see page 182)
- Hawthorn flower and lavender tea
  (see page 184)
- Blackberry and lime cordial
  (see page 186)

- Lemon balm and honey cordial
  (see page 190)
- Rose petal syrup
  (see page 194)
- Sour cherry syrup
  (see page 196)
- Lime flower and hawthorn berry tincture
  (see page 201)
- Passionflower and chamomile tincture
  (see page 202)
- Goji berry and Siberian ginseng tincture
  (see page 204)
- Ginseng and astragalus soup
  (see page 219)
- Roasted barley and chestnut soup
  (see page 224)
- Edible flower salad
  (see page 231)
- Cranberry and apricot bars
  (see page 240)
- Blackcurrant and walnut bars
  (see page 242)

HEAL FROM THE OUTSIDE

- Minty fresh foot cream
  (see page 254)
- Lavender and bergamot soothing skin oil
  (see page 265)

Blackcurrant and walnut bars Eat as an energizing snack *(see page 242).*

- Stimulating body oil
  (see page 266)
- Geranium and orange body oil
  (see page 266)
- Baby massage oil
  (see page 269)
- Baby bath oil
  (see page 269)
- Geranium and orange body splash
  (see page 273)
- Rose body splash
  (see page 275)
- Frankincense body splash
  (see page 275)
- Rosemary gardener's soap
  (see page 283)
- Relaxation soap
  (see page 286)
- Exotic soap
  (see page 287)
- Refreshing facial spritz
  (see page 295)
- Citrus bath bomb
  (see page 307)
- Exotic bath bomb
  (see page 308)
- Sunshine bath bomb
  (see page 309)
- Rose and calendula bath infusion
  (see page 311)
- Lavender and aloe vera bath infusion
  (see page 312)
- Lemon grass and rosemary bath infusion
  (see page 312)
- Seaweed and arnica bath infusion
  (see page 313)
- Relax and restore bath herbs
  (see page 316)

( ) Pregnancy and childbirth

No medicinal herb other than those known to be safe as everyday foods should be taken during early pregnancy or while breast-feeding without the advice of a qualified herbalist. However, some dietary plants and external lotions can relieve common ailments such as morning sickness or varicose veins, and heal the body after childbirth. This chart contains the key herbs that are beneficial for pre- and postnatal mothers.

Herb	Action
Ginger *Zingiber officinale*	A highly effective anti-emetic that helps to relieve the symptoms of nausea and morning sickness. Add a couple of slices of fresh ginger root to a cupful of hot water and sip as required.
Chamomile *Matricaria recutita* (p.80)	A versatile and gentle everyday herb that is calming and soothing to the nerves and digestion. Drink a cupful of infusion to relieve morning sickness, stress and tension, to aid relaxation before going to sleep, and as an aid to the digestion.
Witch hazel *Hamamelis virginiana* (p.63)	A cooling and astringent herb that benefits veins. Soak a pad of cotton wool in distilled witch hazel and apply to aching legs, varicose veins, or haemorrhoids.
Lavender *Lavandula angustifolia* (p.74)	A calming and anti-inflammatory essential oil that promotes healing after childbirth. Add 4–5 drops of lavender oil to the bath water. To relieve mastitis, add 3–4 drops of essential oil to warm water and apply using a clean facecloth as a compress.
Linseed *Linum usitassimum*	Acts as a gentle laxative and bowel lubricant, and is also very rich in omega fatty acids – particularly essential during pregnancy. Add a tablespoon to breakfast cereal or muesli and increase your fluids to help prevent constipation.
Calendula *Calendula officinalis* (p.36)	Highly nourishing and healing to the skin. Combine the tincture with St John's wort and dilute to use as a lotion to bathe any tearing or stitches after childbirth. Massage the macerated oil into the skin during pregnancy to help prevent stretch marks.
St John's wort *Hypericum perforatum* (p.68)	Has effective antiseptic and pain-relieving properties. Combine the tincture with calendula and dilute to use as a lotion to heal tearing or stitches after childbirth; also use to bathe cracked nipples, although rinse with clear water before breast-feeding.
Raspberry leaf *Rubus idaeus* (p.99)	A uterine tonic that helps to prepare the body for childbirth. Drink the infusion daily during the last trimester of pregnancy (not suitable during early pregnancy). Continue drinking it for two to three weeks after the birth to help contract the muscles and promote breast milk.
Dill *Anethum graveolens*	The seeds make an excellent infusion to drink during breast-feeding, as dill helps to promote the breast milk and also relieves any colic or wind in the baby. May be combined with fennel seeds.
Jasmine *Jasminum officinale* (p.72)	A delightfully fragrant essential oil that is traditionally used during labour for its relaxing properties and to help instil feelings of calmness and confidence. Dilute in a base oil and ask your partner to massage it into your lower back.

Herbs to avoid in pregnancy

This list of herbs should not be used internally in pregnancy unless prescribed by a qualified medical herbalist trained in the appropriate use of these substances. Please note that this list is not exhaustive. Culinary herbs marked with an asterisk are acceptable, but avoid them in large therapeutic doses.

- *Achillea millefolium* **Yarrow**
- *Actaea racemosa* **Black cohosh**
- *Agastache rugosa* **Purple giant hyssop***
- *Aloe vera* **Aloe vera**
- *Angelica archangelica* **Angelica root**
- *Apium graveolens* **Celery seed**
- *Aralia racemosa* **American spikenard**
- *Arctostaphylos uva-ursi* **Bearberry**
- *Artemisia absinthium* **Wormwood**
- *Borago officinalis* **Borage**
- *Calendula officinalis* **Calendula**
- *Curcuma longa* **Turmeric***
- *Cymbopogon citratus* **Lemon grass***
- *Eupatorium cannabinum* **Hemp agrimony**
- *Eupatorium purpureum* **Gravel root**
- *Filipendula ulmaria* **Meadowsweet**
- *Glycyrrhiza glabra* **Liquorice root***
- *Hydrastis canadensis* **Golden seal**

- *Hypericum perforatum* **St. John's wort**
- *Hyssopus officinalis* **Hyssop**
- *Inula helenium* **Elecampane**
- *Juniperus communis* **Juniper**
- *Leonurus cardiaca* **Motherwort**
- *Levisticum officinale* **Lovage**
- *Lycium barbarum* **Goji***
- *Nepeta cataria* **Catnip**
- *Panax japonicus* **Japanese ginseng**
- *Rosa x damascena* **Damask rose**
- *Rosmarinus officinalis* **Rosemary***
- *Rumex crispus* **Yellow dock**
- *Salix alba* **White willow**
- *Salvia officinalis* **Common sage**
- *Saussurea costus* **Costus**
- *Schisandra chinensis* **Schisandra**
- *Senna alexandrina* **Senna**
- *Symphytum officinale* **Comfrey**
- *Tanacetum parthenium* **Feverfew**
- *Thymus vulgaris* **Thyme***

- *Trifolium pratense* **Red clover**
- *Tussilago farfara* **Coltsfoot**
- *Verbena officinalis* **Vervain**
- *Viburnum opulus* **Crampbark**
- *Viscum album* **Mistletoe**
- *Vitex agnus castus* **Agnus castus/ Chaste berry**
- *Withania somnifera* **Ashwaghanda**

Jasmine *Jasminum officinale*
In labour, a few drops of jasmine essential oil added to a massage oil can help.

Recipes

HEAL FROM THE OUTSIDE
- **Baby massage oil**
  (see page 269)
- **Baby bath oil**
  (see page 269)
- **Baby powder**
  (see page 281)
- **Mother-to-be-balm**
  (see page 304)
- **Post-natal sitz bath**
  (see page 317)

Lavender *Lavandula angustifolia*

Raspberry *Rubus idaeus*

Heal from the inside

Drinks, tinctures, soups, and salads

MAKING JUICES AND SMOOTHIES

These juice recipes provide an instant means of detoxing and revitalizing your body, while the smoothies are a healthy yet tasty way to combine fruits, seeds, grains, and nuts to provide vitamins, minerals, phytonutrients (from fruit), essential fatty acids, and protein (from seeds).

Strawberry and macadamia smoothie

 ACTS AS A
MALE TONIC

INGREDIENTS
½ vanilla pod
50g (1¾oz) raw macadamia nuts
pulp of 1 young medium-sized
   coconut
250g (9oz) fresh strawberries
a little of the coconut juice (optional)

Makes 4 servings

This healthy twist on strawberries and cream uses an exotic version of cream made from coconut pulp and macadamia nuts. Macadamia nut oil is a rich source of monounsaturated fatty acids, which are reputed to lower cholesterol, while coconut pulp helps to clear the effects of summer heat in the body, quenches the thirst, and is a male reproductive tonic.

1 *Slit the vanilla pod* open with a sharp knife, then scrape out the seeds.

2 *Place the nuts* and the coconut pulp in a blender or food processor.

3 *Add the strawberries* and vanilla seeds. Pulse all the ingredients to give a smooth, silky texture. If the smoothie seems very thick, add enough coconut juice to give it a better texture. Pour into 4 glasses and serve.

Goji berry and pine nut smoothie

 **PURIFIES SKIN**  **SUPPORTS URINARY SYSTEM**  **SUPPORTS URINARY SYSTEM**

Makes 2 servings

Goji berries provide many amino acids and trace minerals – in particular germanium, a trace mineral thought to have anti-cancer properties. Not surprisingly, they have become known as a "superfruit". The berries are also a rich source of carotenoids, including zeaxanthin (which strengthens eyesight) and vitamins C, B complex, and vitamin E.

INGREDIENTS

50g (1¾oz) almonds
50g (1¾oz) goji berries
  (fresh or dried)
20g (¾oz) pine nuts
1 tsp linseed oil
2–3 leaves of fresh peppermint
350–400ml (12–14fl oz) mineral water
  (start with less water and adjust
  to a consistency and thickness
  you like)

METHOD

1 To sprout the almonds, soak them in cold water for half an hour, then rinse in a colander under running water. Place in a large bowl, cover with water, and leave overnight to soak. The next day, pop the skins off, place the almonds in a clean bowl, pour over mineral water, and refrigerate for up to 24 hours before draining.
2 Wash the goji berries and, if dried, soak them for few hours in a bowl of mineral water (allow enough space for the berries to expand and sufficient water – 150ml/5fl oz of water should be enough – for the fruit to remain submerged). Drain the berries.
3 Place all ingredients in a blender or food processor and blend with the mineral water to give a smooth silky texture. If the consistency is a bit too thick, add a little more water and blend.

Blackcurrant booster smoothie

 **RELIEVES INFLAMMATION**   **PROTECTS BRAIN**

Makes 2 servings

Blackcurrants are rich in vitamin C, rutin, and other flavonoids. Their high essential fatty acid levels may help to treat inflammatory conditions and manage pain, as well as regulate the circulatory system and enhance the immune system. Use warm rice milk and add a little more roasted barley and some nuts to turn this smoothie into a nourishing breakfast in winter.

INGREDIENTS

50g (1¾oz) fresh blackcurrants
  (or used dried and soak first)
50g (1¾oz) roasted barley (p.224)
4 tsp agave syrup
4 tsp coconut oil
250ml (9fl oz) rice milk (unsweetened)
A little mineral water

METHOD

Put all the ingredients except the mineral water in a blender or food processor and blend until smooth. Add enough mineral water to ensure the smoothie is of a pourable consistency.

Sour cherry and raw cocoa smoothie

 REGULATES SLEEP

Makes 2 servings

This smoothie is ideal before or after exercising and for long-distance runners, as the anti-inflammatory properties of cherries aid quicker muscle recovery and pain relief. Sour cherries are also a source of natural melatonin, a potent antioxidant with immune system-modulating properties. If eaten regularly, they may even help to regulate the body's natural sleep patterns.

INGREDIENTS

50g (1¾oz) sour cherries, stoned
  if fresh, or dried
300ml (10fl oz) rice or almond milk
4 tsp raw or regular cocoa powder
4 tsp hemp seeds, shelled
4 tsp flaxseed oil

METHOD

1 If using dried sour cherries, soak them for few hours in 150ml (5fl oz) of mineral water.
2 Combine half the rice or almond milk with the rest of the ingredients in a blender or food processor and blend to a smooth, silky, pourable consistency. Add the rest of the milk in stages until the texture of the smoothie is to your liking.

Almond and rose smoothie

 HARMONIZES EMOTIONS **MOISTURIZES SKIN**

Makes 2 servings

Almonds are a great food for strengthening the heart and blood vessels. They contain nutrients such as magnesium, potassium, copper, selenium, manganese, and vitamin E, which is known for its antioxidant activity. Almonds are also reported to lower cholesterol levels, while rose creates a sense of relaxed well-being.

INGREDIENTS

50g (1¾oz) almonds
300–400ml (10–14fl oz) mineral water
2½ tbsp rose syrup
4 tsp almond oil
1 drop rose attar essential oil
  (optional)
8 damask rose petals (optional)

METHOD

1 To sprout the almonds, soak them in cold water for half an hour, then rinse in a colander under running water. Place in a large bowl, cover with water, and leave overnight to soak. The next day, pop the skins off, place the almonds in a clean bowl, pour over filtered or bottled mineral water, and refrigerate for up to 24 hours before draining. Discard the soaking water.
2 Combine half the mineral water with the rest of the ingredients in a blender or food processor and blend to a smooth, silky, pourable consistency. Add the rest of the water in stages until the texture of the smoothie is to your liking.

Pistachio and avocado smoothie

 PROVIDES OMEGA-RICH OILS   **ENERGIZES**

Makes 2 servings

Pistachios are revered in Ayurvedic and Middle Eastern traditions as a tonic for the whole body. In traditional Chinese medicine they are believed to positively influence the liver, and especially the kidneys. The addition of avocado, hemp seed oil, and linseed oil add body and a rich blend of omega oils to this smoothie.

INGREDIENTS

50g (1¾oz) pistachios (plus a few for decoration)
1 small avocado, stoned, peeled, and quartered
1 tsp hemp seed oil
2 tsp linseed oil
juice of ½ lemon
fresh juice of 6 celery stems
freshly ground black pepper to taste
pinch of salt
3–4 fresh basil leaves
a little mineral water

METHOD

1 Put all the ingredients except the mineral water into a blender or food processor and blend until smooth. Add enough mineral water to ensure the smoothie is of a pourable consistency.
2 Serve in glasses, with a sprinkle of finely chopped pistachios on top of each.

Maca and mango smoothie

 ENERGIZES

Makes 2 servings

Maca root *(Lepidium meyenii)* does not taste tremendously interesting, but it has a reputation for invigorating the body and enhancing sexual stamina. Peruvians consider it to be a superfood. Coconut oil, linseeds, and hemp seeds all provide essential fatty acids, while fresh ripe mango provides body and flavour.

INGREDIENTS

2 large ripe mangoes
2 tsp maca root powder
2 tsp hemp seeds, shelled
2 tsp coconut oil
juice of 1 lemon
4 fresh peppermint leaves
a little mineral water (optional)

METHOD

Place all the ingredients in a blender or food processor and blend to a smooth, silky texture. Dilute with mineral water as desired, if necessary.

Plum and fennel smoothie

 DETOXES

Makes 2 servings

All the ingredients in this smoothie have a natural laxative quality. This is a good drink to take not only for occasional constipation, but also as a part of a more extensive detox regime. If you prefer a very smooth texture without bits, use a teaspoon each of linseed and hemp seed oils instead of the soaked seeds.

INGREDIENTS

9–10 large dark blue-skinned plums
½ tsp fennel seeds
2 tbsp linseeds, soaked
2 tbsp shelled hemp seeds, soaked

METHOD

1 Stew the plums first: put them in a saucepan with 250ml (9fl oz) of mineral water, add the fennel seeds, and bring to the boil. Put the lid on and simmer on a low heat for 10–12 minutes. Allow to cool.
2 Transfer to a blender or food processor, add the remaining seeds (or oils, if using) and blend to a smooth consistency.

Power berry smoothie

 NOURISHES BLOOD   REJUVENATES, REVITALIZES

Makes 2 servings

These fragrantly sweet but subtly tart fresh berries are a powerhouse of phytonutrients with antioxidant, antimicrobial, and anticarcinogenic properties. Their seed oil contains exceptionally high levels of vitamins E and A and omega-3 and omega-6 fatty acids, and they also protect the heart and nourish the liver.

INGREDIENTS

2 tbsp fresh raspberries
2 tbsp fresh blackberries
2 tbsp fresh blueberries
2 tbsp fresh blackcurrants
2 tsp acai berry powder
800ml (1¼ pints) lemongrass infusion, cold (p.342)
a little mineral water (optional)
a dash of maple syrup or a pinch of stevia powder (optional)

METHOD

1 Place the fresh berries and acai berry powder in a blender or food processor, add the lemongrass infusion, and blend to a smooth, silky texture.
2 If necessary, add a little mineral water to achieve a consistency you like. Ensure that most of the seeds from the fruit have been ground down so that they release their oils. Add the maple syrup or stevia powder to sweeten only if needed.

Early autumn rambler's delight

 **ENHANCES RESISTANCE
TO COLDS AND FLU**

Makes 2 servings

This is a great way to use freshly picked elderberries and blackberries, which contain high levels of antioxidants that help to fight free-radical damage and enhance the immune system. Blackberries are extremely high in phenolic compounds, which are known to be health-promoting, antiviral, and antibacterial, while elderberries contain potassium and vitamins C and E.

INGREDIENTS

3½ apples, peeled, cored, and chopped
⅓ pear peeled, cored, and chopped
12 ripe elderberries, rinsed, with all stalks removed
20 ripe blackberries, rinsed

METHOD

1 Put all the ingredients into a blender or a food processor and blend until smooth.
2 Divide between two glasses and top with elderberry and elderflower syrup (p.188) to enhance the antiviral content of the smoothie.

NOTE: Unripe raw elderberries and elder bark should be avoided, so make sure you use completely ripe elderberries with no stalk attached to make this smoothie.

Blackberry (Rubus fruticosus)
is an astringent, tonic, mildly diuretic herb, often to be found growing wild in hedgerows.

Garden greens juice

 DETOXES

Makes 2 servings

If you have a vegetable garden, a great way to use up any excess produce is to serve it as refreshing, detoxifying drinks. Courgettes, cucumber, and celery stems all provide a mild base to which you can add fragrant cabbage leaves, sour chard, and spinach. The marjoram added to this juice aids digestion and alleviates abdominal distension and wind.

INGREDIENTS
2 handfuls of kale leaves
2 Swiss chard leaves
1 large handful of spinach leaves
½ cucumber
1 small green courgette
3 stems celery
2 dandelion leaves (large)
2 stems fresh marjoram
a dash of lemon juice (optional)

METHOD
Wash and juice all the vegetables and herbs, and mix thoroughly. Add the lemon juice to taste if you wish or, if you prefer a more powerful lemon flavour, add an eighth of a lemon (organic is preferable) and mix well until blended.

Red pepper and sprouted seeds juice

 STIMULATES DIGESTION   **STIMULATES CIRCULATION**

Makes 2 servings

This fragrant, spicy juice is a great way to start the day. Chilli stimulates the body, particularly the circulation, strengthens the digestive system, and provides a sense of vigour and warmth, which is beneficial in winter. It also causes the body to perspire, and therefore cool down, which can help during periods of hot weather.

INGREDIENTS
1 red pepper, deseeded and
  cut into quarters
20g (¾oz) sprouted alfalfa seeds
20g (¾oz) sprouted red clover seeds
10g (¼oz) sprouted broccoli seeds
½ cucumber
2–3 fresh mint leaves
½ small fresh red chilli, deseeded

METHOD
Juice all the ingredients and mix thoroughly.

Ginger and fennel juice

 SOOTHES INFLAMED SKIN　　 **IMPROVES DIGESTION**

Makes 2 servings

Fennel bulb, celery, cucumber, and courgette have a cooling, anti-inflammatory effect on the body, and are beneficial for inflammatory conditions in the stomach, lungs, throat, skin, and vagina. They are also diuretic, as well as purifying the skin and moistening the lungs. Ginger and basil are included to add fragrance, remove any bloated feelings, and improve digestion.

INGREDIENTS

1 large fennel bulb
1cm (½in) cube fresh ginger
　root, peeled
2 celery stems
½ small cucumber
½ small green courgette
1 stem fresh basil

METHOD

Juice all the ingredients, mix well, and drink immediately.

Fennel and broccoli sprouts juice

 RESTORES PH BALANCE　　 **IMPROVES DIGESTION**

Makes 2 servings

This juice aims to expel body waste by increasing urination and clearing the bowels to eliminate putrefactive bacteria. Broccoli sprouts are also beneficial for inflammatory eye conditions, while carrots, fennel, and alfalfa seeds are alkaline-forming and help to clear acidic conditions, thus helping rheumatism.

INGREDIENTS

1 large fennel bulb
45g (1½oz) sprouted broccoli seeds
45g (1½oz) sprouted alfalfa seeds
1 large carrot
2 stems celery
2–3 fresh mint leaves
dash of lemon juice

METHOD

Juice all the ingredients, add the lemon juice to taste, and mix well.

Buckwheat greens and pea shoot juice

 STRENGTHENS BLOOD VESSELS

Makes 2 servings

Pea shoots and buckwheat greens are excellent sources of enzymes, vitamins, and chlorophyll. Buckwheat also contains rutin (4–6 per cent), which strengthens the capillaries (rutin belongs to a group of plant compounds called bioflavonoids – powerful antioxidants that fight free radicals) and is useful for reducing varicose veins and haemorrhoids.

INGREDIENTS
2 tbsp young buckwheat greens, finely chopped
4 tbsp fresh pea shoots
2 courgettes
1 cucumber
2 tbsp fresh marjoram leaves
a dash of lemon juice
200ml (7fl oz) mineral water

METHOD
Juice all ingredients, add the mineral water and lemon juice to taste, and mix well.

Tomato salsa juice

 IMPROVES DIGESTION   **ENHANCES WELL-BEING AND CONFIDENCE**

Makes 2 servings

This is a great juice to make when you feel like something substantial and savoury, but have no time to make a cooked meal. Basil has a reputation for restoring the vital spirits, quickening the brain, and awakening joy and courage. It also enhances digestion, clears respiratory congestion and phlegm, and lifts depression.

INGREDIENTS
5 ripe tomatoes
½ cucumber
1 small clove of garlic
½ fresh red chilli, deseeded
1 stem fresh basil leaves
2 stems celery
1 tsp virgin olive oil
salt to taste
1 red pepper, deseeded

METHOD
Juice all the vegetables and herbs, add the olive oil, season to taste with a little salt if you wish, and mix well. If you prefer your juice red, add 1 deseeded red pepper to the vegetables and herbs when you juice them.

Artichoke leaf and fennel juice

 DETOXES    **COMBATS NEGATIVE EMOTIONS**

Makes 2 servings

The liver needs help every now and then to eliminate wastes from the body. Artichoke leaves, which have a strong, bitter taste, contain cynarin, a compound that stimulates the liver to release these toxic substances and which also improves liver function. Fennel, dandelion leaves, celery stems, and courgette also enhance the elimination of waste through the kidneys.

INGREDIENTS
1 tsp artichoke leaves (from a globe artichoke plant), finely chopped
1 medium fennel bulb
4 fresh dandelion leaves
4 celery stems
½ courgette

METHOD
Juice all the ingredients, mix thoroughly, and drink. If you find the juice overly bitter, dilute it with some mineral water until it tastes palatable.

Sunflower greens and wheatgrass juice

 DETOXES   **REJUVENATES, REVITALIZES**

Makes 2 servings

The juice from wheatgrass and sunflower greens (young plants) is a natural aid that can be used in the treatment of degenerative diseases and to help slow cellular deterioration and relieve inflammation. Its high chlorophyll content also helps to detoxify the liver, so cleansing and energizing the body.

INGREDIENTS
100g (3½oz) sunflower greens
100g (3½oz) wheatgrass blades
300ml (10fl oz) or more mineral water to dilute to taste

METHOD
Juice the sunflower greens and wheatgrass, blend well, and add enough mineral water to dilute the flavour of the juice and give it a palatable taste.

MAKING TEAS

The recipes for the tea blends provided here allow you to explore the wonderful flavours of plants, with subtle nurturing and healing qualities in a single cup. All the plants mentioned here can be used either fresh or dry – and may inspire you to grow your own healing teas in your garden.

Lemon balm and rose tea

 ENHANCES MOOD

Makes 2–3 servings

This herbal tea contains a fusion of empowering yet relaxing lemon balm and mood-enhancing, sensual rose petals to make the ultimate summer refreshment. It can be enjoyed hot or cold, and is best drunk slightly bitter. For the best results, pick fresh lemon balm leaves and fresh perfumed rose petals from the damask rose (*Rosa* x *damascena*) or French rose (*Rosa gallica*).

INGREDIENTS

16 leaves of fresh lemon balm (the soft flowering tops can also be used), or 1 tbsp dried lemon balm

2 rose heads with petals removed, or 2 tbsp dried rose petals

METHOD

1 Put the fresh lemon balm leaves and rose petals in a large teapot. If using dried lemon balm and rose petals, spoon them into the teapot instead.

2 Boil 500ml (16fl oz) of water, allow to cool for 5 minutes, then pour it into the teapot. Allow to infuse for 5 minutes and then serve. More water can be added later if needed to re-infuse the leaves and rose petals.

Jasmine and lemongrass tea

 ALLEVIATES ANXIETY   **REVIVES PASSION**   **REVIVES PASSION**

Makes 2 servings

This tea, known for being an oriental love potion, is great to serve with oriental foods. Both jasmine flowers and lemongrass help to relax the mind, alleviate anxiety, improve communication, and revive passion. For the best flavour, buy fresh lemongrass from your local oriental greengrocer or a supermarket.

INGREDIENTS

1 stem lemongrass, chopped
1 tbsp jasmine flowers
a dash of lime juice

METHOD

1 Place the chopped lemongrass in a teapot and add the jasmine flowers.
2 Dilute 200ml (7fl oz) of boiled water with 100ml (3½fl oz) of cold water so that the temperature of the hot water is approximately 70°C (158°F).
3 Pour the water into the teapot, allow the aroma to develop, and serve. In hot weather this tea can be served chilled.

Goji berry and damiana tea

 ENHANCES SEXUAL EXPRESSION   **ENHANCES SEXUAL EXPRESSION**

Makes 2 servings

Damiana has a distinctive fragrance and flavour. It lifts depression, relieves anxiety, alleviates fatigue, and enhances reproductive energy. Goji berries also improve fertility, strengthen the heart, improve disease resistance, and alleviate menopausal symptoms. Liquorice is a tonic that is restorative to the adrenal glands and alleviates fatigue.

INGREDIENTS

1 tbsp goji berries, fresh or dried
1 tsp damiana (*Turnera diffusa*)
½ tsp liquorice root powder

METHOD

Place all the ingredients in a teapot, cover with 300ml (10fl oz) of boiling water, allow to stand for 10–15 minutes, then serve. The infusion can also be left to cool and served as a cold drink.

NOTE: This tea is not suitable for use during pregnancy.

Rosehip and bilberry tea

 REJUVENATES

Makes 2 servings

Rosehip helps to maintain healthy collagen in the skin, bilberries enhance blood perfusion to give skin a rosy, plumped complexion, and bilberries and goji berries are anti-inflammatory. These fruits are also known to be powerful antioxidants, while orange rind harmonizes the digestive system and helps to improve the absorption of nutrients. This tea is also delicious served cold.

INGREDIENTS
1 tbsp rosehip shells, fresh or dried
1 tbsp bilberries, fresh or dried
1 tsp orange rind
1 tsp goji berries, fresh or dried

METHOD
Place all ingredients in a teapot and cover with 300ml (10fl oz) of boiling water. Allow to infuse for 10–15 minutes, strain, and serve. (After straining, all the ingredients can be added to breakfast porridge and eaten.)

Chrysanthemum and elderflower tea

PROTECTS AGAINST HAY FEVER, COLDS, AND FLU

Makes 2 servings

This is a good tea to drink to alleviate symptoms of hay fever or to ward off colds or flu. All the ingredients reduce sweating, defend the body from pathogenic influences, have anti-allergic activity, and calm allergic reactions – especially to pollen and dust. Chrysanthemum also cools the body, neutralizes toxins, improves and brightens the eyes, and protects against liver damage.

INGREDIENTS
½ tbsp chrysanthemum flowers
  (*Chrysanthemum morifolium*)
½ tbsp elderflowers
½ tbsp peppermint
½ tbsp nettle leaves

METHOD
Place all the ingredients in a teapot, cover with 300ml (10fl oz) of boiling water, allow to infuse, and serve. Drink 3–4 cups a day during the hay fever season.

Chrysanthemum (*Chrysanthemum coronarium*) *The flowers are considered a valuable remedy against infection in the body, and have antibiotic properties.*

Chamomile and fennel tea

 IMPROVES DIGESTION

Makes 3 servings

This is a soothing, anti-inflammatory infusion of herbs that are well known for their beneficial effect on an unsettled, bloated or acidic digestive system. It will encourage better food assimilation, help to regulate the bowels and improve an over-acidic system.

INGREDIENTS

1 tsp chamomile flowers
1 tsp fennel seeds
1 tsp meadowsweet
1 tsp marshmallow root, finely chopped
1 tsp yarrow

METHOD

1 Put the herbs in a large teapot.
2 Boil 500ml (16fl oz) of boiling water, and add to the teapot. Allow to infuse for 5 minutes and serve. Drink 1 mug of the infusion 2–3 times a day.

NOTE: This tea is not suitable for use during pregnancy.

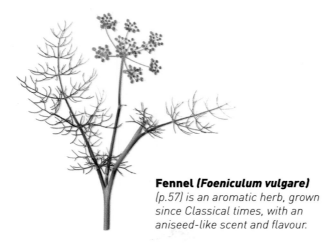

Fennel (Foeniculum vulgare)
(p.57) is an aromatic herb, grown since Classical times, with an aniseed-like scent and flavour.

Dandelion and burdock tea

 SOOTHES INFLAMED SKIN

 STIMULATES LIVER AND KIDNEY

Makes 3–4 servings

This classic blend of herbs helps to clear up blemished skin. It treats eczema and acne by gently invigorating the liver and kidneys to remove accumulated waste, while its anti-inflammatory activity helps to improve skin eruptions on the head, neck, and upper body. It is also appropriate for anyone who wishes to detox.

INGREDIENTS
1 tsp dandelion leaves
1 tsp burdock leaves
1 tsp cleavers herb
1 tsp red clover flowers

METHOD
Place all the ingredients in a teapot, pour in 500ml (16fl oz) of boiling water, allow to infuse for 10–15 minutes, and serve. Drink hot or cold through the day.

NOTE: This tea is not suitable for use during pregnancy.

Yarrow and calendula tea

 RELIEVES PMS

 HARMONIZES EMOTIONS

 IMPROVES CIRCULATION

Makes 3–4 servings

These herbs all benefit the female body. Yarrow and calendula relieve blood and energy stagnation in the abdomen and improve blood circulation to the womb. Vervain invigorates the liver, releases tension, and relaxes the mind. Lady's mantle, an astringent, relieves congestion through urination. Raspberry leaf will help to relieve period pains.

INGREDIENTS
1 tsp yarrow
1 tsp marigold flowers
1 tsp lady's mantle
1 tsp vervain
1 tsp raspberry leaf

METHOD
Place all the ingredients in a teapot, pour in 500ml (16fl oz) of boiling water, allow to infuse for 10–15 minutes, and serve. Drink hot or cold through the day. Take 2–4 cups with the onset of pain, and reassess with your health professional if the pain persists.

NOTE: This tea is not suitable for use during pregnancy.

Calendula (Calendula officinalis)
(p.36) has astringent and anti-inflammatory properties, and the flowers are rich in antioxidants.

Skullcap and orange flower tea

 RELIEVES DEPRESSION

Makes 3–4 servings

Herbal teas such as this can help you to relax and begin to put things into perspective – especially if you are suffering from feelings of depression. Skullcap, St John's wort, wood betony, lemon balm, and orange flower are all known to help to ease tensions, relax the body and mind, and lift the spirits.

INGREDIENTS
1 tsp skullcap
1 tsp orange flowers
1 tsp St. John's wort
1 tsp wood betony
1 tsp lemon balm

METHOD
Place all the ingredients in a teapot, pour in 500ml (16fl oz) of boiling water, allow to infuse for 10–15 minutes, and serve. Drink hot or cold through the day.

NOTE: This tea is not suitable for use during pregnancy.

Blackberry and wild strawberry tea

 DETOXES

Makes 3–4 servings

The leaves of these fruits are well known for their ability to heal, as well as for their revitalizing and rejuvenating qualities. Their ability to cleanse the body of the excesses of winter is remarkable. Use fresh leaves to make this tea in the spring, and harvest and dry some for use during the winter months.

INGREDIENTS
2 tsp blackberry leaves
1 tsp wild strawberry leaves
1 tsp raspberry leaves
1 tsp blackcurrant leaves

METHOD
Place all the ingredients in a teapot, pour in 500ml (16fl oz) of boiling water, allow to infuse for 10–15 minutes, and serve. Drink hot or cold through the day.

NOTE: This tea is not suitable for use during pregnancy.

Orange (Citrus aurantium) *The leaves, stems, flowers, and ripe fruits of the Seville orange tree can all be used for herbal remedies.*

Peppermint and calendula infusion

 IMPROVES MENSTRUAL IRREGULARITY   **RELAXES**

Makes 4 servings

This infusion works for premenstrual tension and period pains. Peppermint releases tension and calms the mind. Motherwort and vervain are used to treat menstrual irregularities, have a relaxing effect on the nervous system, and to relieve tension and pain. Calendula aids the other herbs in nurturing the womb, and roses have a healing influence.

INGREDIENTS

1 tsp peppermint leaves
1 tsp calendula flowers
1 tsp motherwort
1 tsp vervain
rose petal syrup (p.194)
  to sweeten

METHOD

1 Put all the herbs into a large teapot.
2 Boil 600ml (1 pint) of boiling water, and pour over the herbs. Allow to infuse for 20 minutes, then strain the liquid through a tea strainer into a clean jug. Drink 1 mug of the infusion 2–3 times a day, either hot or at room temperature.

NOTE: This tea is not suitable for use during pregnancy.

"This blend of herbs works well whether it is made from fresh plant material or from dry, and is best drunk slightly bitter"

Hawthorn flower and lavender tea

 STRENGTHENS HEART, RELAXES VESSELS   **MENDS A BROKEN HEART**

Makes 3–4 servings

There are some heartaches, such as overwhelming emotions, sense of loss, and lack of self-worth, that only the soft and enlightened fragrance of flowers can soothe. Hawthorn "lightens the heart", lavender relaxes the mind, rose eases a broken heart, and orange flower and jasmine encourage a desire to make things better and start anew.

INGREDIENTS
1 tsp hawthorn flowers
1 tsp lavender
1 tsp rosebuds
1 tsp orange flowers
1 tsp jasmine

METHOD
Place all the ingredients in a teapot, pour in 500ml (16fl oz) of boiling water, allow to infuse for 10–15 minutes, and serve. Drink hot or cold throughout the day.

Nettle and cleavers tea

 DETOXES

Makes 2 servings

This is a great tea for gentle cleansing at any time of the year. In spring, fresh nettles and cleavers can be juiced and drunk to cleanse and nourish the body. Cleavers helps to reduce fluid retention in the skin, reduce puffiness under the eyes, and improve the complexion. Nettles also nourish the blood and cleanse the body through increased urination.

INGREDIENTS
2 tsp nettle leaves
2 tsp cleavers

METHOD
Place the ingredients in a teapot, pour in 300ml (10fl oz) of boiling water, allow to infuse for 10–15 minutes, and serve. Drink hot or cold throughout the day.

Mullein and marshmallow tea

 RELIEVES A DRY COUGH

Makes 2 servings

Mullein leaves and flowers and marshmallow leaves, flowers, and roots all provide mucilaginous, anti-inflammatory protection for the respiratory and urinary system. This tea can also be used to treat dry coughs, nervous coughs, dry lungs, and inflamed bronchial tubes. Marshmallow leaf and plantain leaf also soothe an inflamed urinary tract.

INGREDIENTS
1 tsp mullein leaves
1 tsp marshmallow leaves
1 tsp ribwort plantain

METHOD
Place all the ingredients in a teapot, pour in 300ml (10fl oz) of boiling water, allow to infuse for 10–15 minutes, and serve. Drink hot or cold throughout the day.

Horsetail and cornsilk tea

 ACTS AS A DIURETIC　　 **ACTS AS A DIURETIC**

Makes 5–6 servings

This refreshing and cleansing tea is especially good for reducing occasional inflammatory conditions in the urinary system caused by non-specific micro-organisms, such as cystitis. These herbs not only increase urination, they also cool irritation and soothe inflammation of the urinary system, and contain potassium.

INGREDIENTS
2 tsp horsetail
2 tsp corn silk
2 tsp dandelion leaves
2 tsp cleavers
2 tsp ribwort plantain leaves

METHOD
Place all the ingredients in a teapot, pour in 600ml (1 pint) of boiling water, allow to infuse for 10–15 minutes, and serve. Drink hot or cold throughout the day.

Dandelion (Taraxacum officinale)
(p.114) The leaves are extremely rich in vitamins and minerals, and are a good source of calcium.

MAKING CORDIALS AND SYRUPS

Fruit cordials and syrups help to increase energy levels and nourish the body. The natural benefits of the plants in these cordial and syrup recipes are aided by sugar and honey, which help to alleviate dry coughs, sore throats, and general irritations of the respiratory system.

Blackberry and lime cordial

 **SOOTHES A SORE THROAT**    **REJUVENATES**

INGREDIENTS

1kg (2¼lb) fresh blackberries
juice of 4 limes
350g (12oz) caster sugar

Makes 500ml (16fl oz)

Blackberries are packed with antioxidants and are used in many recipes as a traditional remedy for colds and sore throats. This cordial also benefits from the antiseptic and refreshing taste of limes, which help to detoxify and cool the body.

1 *Over a low heat*, simmer the blackberries and lime juice in 600ml (1 pint) of water in a saucepan for approximately 15 minutes.

2 *Leave to cool* for 10 minutes or so, then push the mixture through a sieve and discard the pulp and pips. Pour the strained juice into a clean saucepan, and add the sugar. Stir over a low heat until the sugar has dissolved, and then simmer for about 5 minutes until the mixture is syrupy.

3 *Pour into sterilized bottles*, (p.194) seal, refrigerate, and use within a few days. Dilute to taste with fizzy or still mineral water and fresh mint or lime slices to make a refreshing drink.

Elderberry and elderflower cordial

 **ACTS AS A
WINTERTIME TONIC**

Makes 500ml (16fl oz)

This is a useful winter tonic: elderflowers, elderberries, and fresh ginger enhance the body's defence mechanisms that ward off seasonal colds and flu conditions, aniseed gently clears the lungs, and ginger and cinnamon bring warmth to the body. Sugar moistens the respiratory passages and alleviates the dry cough often caused by central heating.

INGREDIENTS

50g (1¾oz) fresh or dried elderflowers
100g (3½oz) elderberries (if using dried, rehydrate in water first)
1 small cinnamon stick
1 tsp aniseed
1 tbsp fresh ginger root, grated
400g (14oz) sugar
juice of ½ lemon

METHOD

1 Place all the ingredients except the sugar and lemon juice in a saucepan, add 1 litre (1¾ pints) of water, cover, and simmer over a low heat for 25–30 minutes.
2 Strain the liquid into a measuring jar. Decant 600ml (1 pint) into a saucepan and add the sugar. (Any extra liquid can be drunk as tea.)
3 Stir gently over a low heat to dissolve the sugar. When all the sugar has dissolved, add the lemon juice and simmer gently for another 10–15 minutes with the lid off. Then bring it to the boil for 2–3 minutes and remove from the heat.
4 Pour into a sterilized (p.194) 600ml (1 pint) glass bottle while still hot, seal, label with a list of the ingredients, and date. Keep refrigerated and use within 3–4 weeks.
5 Add a tablespoon of the cordial to a cup of cold or hot water, or drizzle on pancakes or breakfast cereals.

Elder (Sambucus nigra) (p.104)
*The black elder is a deciduous tree
of the honeysuckle family, and has
a long history of therapeutic use.*

Sweet violet and ginger honey

 **RELIEVES
INFLAMMATION**

Makes 400–500g (14oz–1lb 2oz)

This syrupy extract of fresh violets, ginger, plantain, and houttuynia should be made in spring when all these ingredients are growing fresh in the garden. Violets, plantain, and houttuynia are all good expectorants with strong anti-inflammatory actions. Fresh ginger is diaphoretic. Houttuynia, with its orange-like flavour, adds to the gingery taste.

INGREDIENTS

20g (¾oz) fresh violet leaves and
   flowers (or use viola, or heartsease,
   if not available)
30g (1oz) fresh ginger root
20g (¾oz) fresh plantain leaves
30g (1oz) fresh houttuynia leaves
500g (1lb 2oz) runny honey

METHOD

1 Carefully harvest the fresh leaves and flowers and wash and air-dry them.
2 Finely chop them, place in a clean jar, and cover completely with runny honey. Mix thoroughly to ensure all the herbs are well covered. Add extra honey if necessary.
3 Leave in a warm place, such as an airing cabinet, for 5 days. Then strain the honey through a clean muslin cloth and decant it into a smaller sterilized jar (p.194). Discard the strained herbs.
4 Seal the jar, label with a list of all the ingredients, and date.
5 The honey makes a great drink mixed either with cold or hot water. It will keep for a few weeks only.

Ginger (*Zingiber officinale*)
Warming ginger is known for its anti-inflammatory properties, helping to ease muscle aches and joint pain.

Lemon balm and honey purée

 RELAXES

Makes 125g (4½oz)

This purée, which uses fresh, young, juicy lemon balm leaves, is best prepared in late spring before the plant becomes somewhat woody and the leaves less juicy. It works well as a sweetener for other herbal infusions or summer cocktails, and can be served as a hot or cold drink by adding one or two teaspoons of the purée to boiling or chilled water.

INGREDIENTS

20g (¾oz) fresh lemon balm leaves
100g (3½oz) runny honey
Juice of ½ lemon

METHOD

1 Place the leaves in a blender or food processor, add the honey and lemon juice, and blend until you get a smooth green purée.
2 Dilute with water and drink. The purée will last for a week or two, if kept refrigerated.

Lemon balm (Melissa officinalis) (p.83) has cooling, sedative, and uplifting properties; it lowers fever and improves digestion.

Rosehip syrup

 IMPROVES JOINT HEALTH

 **NOURISHES SKIN**

Makes 700ml (1¼ pints)

This syrup is for beautiful skin and healthy joints. Rosehips contain vitamins A, B1, B2, and a high concentration of vitamin C, and are known for their anti-inflammatory activity in helping to reduce muscle and joint stiffness and arthritic pain. They also have antiscorbutic, antihaemorrhagic, and diuretic properties, skin-regenerating properties, and help to maintain healthy collagen.

INGREDIENTS

500g (1lb 2oz) fresh rosehips
400g (14oz) sugar

METHOD

1 Pick the rosehips when they are at their best; traditionally they are picked after the first few autumn frosts.

2 Slice the fruit in half and scoop out the seeds and hairs with a small spoon (rosehip fruit is full of these small hairs, which can irritate sensitive skin, so it is advisable to wear gloves to do this job). Wash the cleaned halves under running water to further remove the little hairs from the fruit.

3 Place the fruit in a saucepan, add 600ml (1 pint) of water, and simmer, uncovered, over a low heat for 20–30 minutes until the fruit is soft and the water has reduced slightly.

4 Strain the mixture and decant the liquid into a clean saucepan. Discard the fruit. Add the sugar to the strained liquid and allow it to dissolve over a low heat, stirring constantly.

5 Once all the sugar has dissolved, increase the heat and boil for 2–3 minutes. Decant the syrup into a sterilized bottle (p.194). Seal and label with the name and date. Keep refrigerated and use within 6 weeks.

Rose (Rosa canina) *(p.95) Rosehips are rich in antioxidant flavonoids, as well as being an excellent source of vitamin C.*

Mullein and aniseed syrup

 ACTS AN EXPECTORANT

Makes 200ml (7fl oz)

A mild expectorant to soothe winter coughs, this syrup uses tinctures of mullein, marshmallow root, thyme, and aniseed, combined with the anti-inflammatory action of plantain and liquorice, to soothe inflammation and relieve coughs. Manuka honey helps to moisten and soothe inflamed air passageways, and makes the tinctures more palatable. This is also a quick way to make a syrup.

INGREDIENTS

4 tsp mullein leaf tincture
4 tsp marshmallow
  root tincture
1 tbsp aniseed tincture
1 tbsp thyme tincture
4 tsp plantain tincture
2 tsp liquorice root tincture
100ml (3½fl oz) manuka honey

METHOD

Blend the tinctures and honey, mix thoroughly, and pour into a sterilized (p.194) 250ml (9fl oz) brown glass bottle. Seal, label with all the ingredients, and date. It will keep for 3–4 months.

NOTE: This syrup is not suitable for use during pregnancy. Persistent coughs must always be investigated in consultation with your medical professional.

Rose petal syrup

 RELAXES   **RELIEVES PERIOD PAIN**

Makes approximately 500ml (16fl oz)

This fragrant syrup can be served as a sweetener for herbal infusions, poured over pancakes and ice cream, or as a cordial diluted with water. The dark-coloured, perfumed rose petals of the damask rose (*Rosa x damascena*) or French rose (*Rosa gallica*) are best for this recipe. Keeping the temperature low is the key to making a successful syrup.

INGREDIENTS

225g (8oz) granulated sugar
juice of 1 lemon, strained
juice of 1 orange, strained
100g (3½oz) dried rose petals or
   10 fresh rose heads

METHOD

1 Dissolve the sugar in 300ml (10fl oz) of water in a small saucepan over a low heat, and do not allow it to boil, as this will make the mixture cloudy. Add the strained lemon and orange juices, turn the heat down and simmer over a low heat for 5 minutes.

2 Over the next 15 minutes, add the rose petals, a tablespoon at a time, and stir thoroughly before adding more. Remove from the heat, allow to cool, and strain. Pour into a sterilized glass bottle, seal, and label. Keep refrigerated and use within 6 weeks.

NOTE: To sterilize a glass jar or bottle, wash it and its lid in hot water, drain upside down, and put into a cool oven (140°C/275°F) for 15 minutes.

Sour cherry syrup

 QUICKENS MUSCLE RECOVERY

 REGULATES SLEEP

Makes approx 600ml (1 pint)

Long-distance runners take cherry juice concentrates before and after exercising, as the anti-inflammatory properties of cherries aid quicker muscle recovery and pain release. Sour cherries also help to preserve a youthful appearance, benefit liver function, and regulate sleep patterns. Approximately 200 cherries (660g/1lb 5oz) produce 400ml (14fl oz) of cherry juice.

INGREDIENTS

400ml (14fl oz) sour cherry juice, freshly pressed
250g (9oz) sugar

METHOD

1 Pour the juice into a saucepan, add the sugar, and heat gently. Dissolve the sugar in the juice, stirring constantly, then simmer for 20 minutes on a low heat.
2 Strain the syrup and bottle in a sterilized glass bottle (p.194) with a tight-fitting lid. Keep refrigerated and use within a few weeks.
3 Drink diluted with cold or hot mineral water.

Sour cherry (*Prunus cerasus*) *These cherries are rich in antioxidant anthocyanins, betacarotene, vitamins, and potassium, which all have health-boosting properties.*

Echinacea and thyme syrup

 **ENHANCES NATURAL IMMUNITY**

Makes 500ml (16fl oz)

When used regularly, this great all-year-round tonic helps the body to develop a natural resistance to viruses and other pathogens. Take it also at the onset of a cold, as it keeps the body warm and protected. Prepare the syrup in late spring, when ribwort and thyme are growing vigorously, and when fresh echinacea and elecampane can also be harvested.

INGREDIENTS

20g (¾oz) fresh thyme
20g (¾oz) fresh ribwort
  plantain leaves
20g (¾oz) fresh echinacea root,
  stem, and young green leaves
10g (¼oz) fresh ginger root, grated
10g (¼oz) fresh garlic, skinned
  and crushed
10g (¼oz) fresh elecampane root
1 whole fresh red chilli,
  finely chopped
400ml (14fl oz) good-quality vodka
100g (3½oz) manuka honey

METHOD

1 Wash all the herb ingredients once they have been harvested and allow to dry. Then chop them finely.
2 Place all the ingredients except the honey and vodka in a large glass jar with a lid. Pour in the vodka, close the lid tightly, and shake a few times. Label the jar with the ingredients and the date. Place the jar in a dark cupboard and shake it at least once a day for 3 weeks.
3 Strain the contents of the jar through the muslin bag into a measuring jug. Decant the manuka honey into a bowl and gently pour in the tincture, stirring continuously with a whisk until the honey and tincture are well blended. Pour the syrup into a 500ml (16fl oz) amber glass bottle with a lid, and label with the ingredients and the original starting date. Take 1 teaaspoon 2–3 times a day, or up to 6 teaspoons a day at the onset of a cold. This syrup should keep for up to 9 months.

NOTE: This syrup is not suitable for use during pregnancy.

HOW TO MAKE TINCTURES

Tinctures are concentrated, alcohol-based extracts of plant materials, and are much more portable and long-lasting than herbal teas. These recipes enable you to produce simple extracts and further explore the benefits of medicinal herbs.

Peppermint and thyme tincture

 CALMS A NERVOUS GUT

INGREDIENTS
25g (scant 1oz) peppermint
15g (½oz) thyme
25g (scant 1oz) chamomile
20g (¾oz) yarrow
15g (½oz) liquorice root
500ml (16fl oz) good-quality vodka

Makes approx 500ml (16fl oz)

This tincture tastes good enough to serve as an aperitif. It aids digestion and benefits the activity of the large intestine, and helps to expel wind and soothe a nervous stomach. Use within 6 months.

NOTE: This tincture is not suitable for use during pregnancy.

1 *Place all the ingredients* except the vodka in a large jar.

2 *Cover with the vodka,* stir, and make sure all the ingredients are well immersed. Seal the jar tightly and place it in a dark cupboard. Give the jar a few good shakes every day for 3 weeks.

3 *Open the jar* and strain the ingredients through a muslin-lined sieve into a shallow bowl. Discard the ingredients in the muslin and pour the liquid into an amber glass bottle. Label the tincture bottle with the names of all the ingredients and the date. Take 1 teaspoon in a glass of warm or cold water and sip before or after meals.

Elderberry and liquorice tincture

**ACTS AS A
WINTERTIME TONIC**

Makes 300–350ml (10–12fl oz)

In autumn, winter, and early spring, most of us require something to nurture our immunity, defend us from external pathogenic influences (rampant cold and flu viruses), stimulate our blood, warm our body, and keep our strength up. These plants are known to do just that. This blend may also be taken to shorten the duration of a cold or flu.

INGREDIENTS
25g (scant 1oz) elderberries
25g (scant 1oz) echinacea root
10g (¼oz) liquorice root
10g (¼oz) fresh ginger root, grated
10g (¼oz) cinnamon stick, broken into small pieces
20g (¾oz) peppermint
400ml (14fl oz) good-quality vodka

METHOD

1 Ensure that all the dried ingredients are finely chopped, but not powdered.
2 Place all the ingredients except the vodka into a large glass jar with a secure-fitting lid. Pour in the vodka, close the lid tightly, and shake a few times.
3 Label the jar with all the ingredients and the date. Place the jar in a dark cupboard and shake it at least once every day for 3 weeks.
4 Strain the contents of the jar through a muslin bag into a measuring jug and pour the tincture into an appropriately sized (350–400ml/12–14fl oz) sterilized amber glass bottle (p.194) Seal the bottle.
5 Label with all the ingredients and the original starting date. Start by taking a few drops each day and build up to 1 teaspoon 2–3 times a day. Use within 6 months.

NOTE: This tincture is not suitable for use during pregnancy.

Peppermint (Mentha x piperita) (p.84)
As well as having a refreshing taste, the menthol content of peppermint is cooling and helps to clear the lungs.

Lime flower and hawthorn berry tincture

 RELIEVES SYMPTOMS OF STRESS   **ACTS AS A HEART TONIC**

Makes 300–350ml (10–12fl oz)

This heart tonic is good for relieving nervous palpitations and discomfort due to stress and anxiety. Hawthorn berries and lemon balm have heart-strengthening and nourishing qualities, while lime flowers and lemon balm relax the mind and improve sleep patterns. Yarrow and cramp bark relax the blood vessels, enabling a better supply of blood to the heart, and also lower blood pressure.

INGREDIENTS

20g (¾oz) lime flowers
20g (¾oz) hawthorn berries
20g (¾oz) yarrow
20g (¾oz) lemon balm
20g (¾oz) crampbark
400ml (14fl oz) good-quality vodka

METHOD

1 Ensure that all the dried ingredients are finely chopped, but not powdered.
2 Place all the ingredients except the vodka into a large glass jar with a secure-fitting lid. Pour in the vodka, close the lid tightly, and shake a few times.
3 Label the jar with all the ingredients and the date. Place the jar in a dark cupboard and shake it at least once every day for 3 weeks.
4 Strain the contents of the jar through a muslin bag into a measuring jug and pour the tincture into an appropriately sized (350–400ml/12–14fl oz) sterilized amber glass bottle (p.194). Seal the bottle.
5 Label with all the ingredients and the original starting date. Start by taking a few drops each day and build up to 1 teaspoon 2–3 times a day. Use within 6 months.

NOTE: This tincture is not suitable for use during pregnancy or if taking prescribed medication.

Lime (Tilia cordata) (p.118) The Tilia tree is commonly known as lime or linden, and the flowers can be used as a gentle sedative.

Passionflower and chamomile tincture

 RELIEVES INSOMNIA

Makes 300–350ml (10–12fl oz)

All of these ingredients are known to regulate sleep patterns in their own way; when mixed together, they complement each other and work in synergy. Valerian is a sedative, while sour cherries are said to regulate the body's natural sleep pattern, improve sleep efficiency, and decrease the time it takes to fall asleep.

INGREDIENTS

20g (¾oz) passionflower
20g (¾oz) chamomile
20g (¾oz) valerian root
30g (1oz) sour cherries, fresh or dried
400ml (14fl oz) good-quality vodka

METHOD

1 Ensure that all the dried ingredients are finely chopped, but not powdered.
2 Place all the ingredients except the vodka into a large glass jar with a secure-fitting lid. Pour in the vodka, close the lid tightly, and shake a few times.
3 Label the jar with all the ingredients and the date. Place the jar in a dark cupboard and shake it at least once every day for 3 weeks.
4 Strain the contents of the jar through a muslin bag into a measuring jug and pour the tincture into an appropriately sized (350–400ml/12–14fl oz) sterilized amber glass bottle (p.194). Seal the bottle.
5 Label with all the ingredients and the original starting date. Start by taking a few drops each day and build up to 1 teaspoon in the late afternoon and another before going to bed. Use within 6 months.

NOTE: The best approach with this tincture is to ascertain the lowest beneficial dose and stick with it. More is not necessarily better; it is all about building an affinity with the ingredients.

German chamomile (*Matricaria recutita*) *(p.80) A gentle sleep remedy, chamomile is well known for its relaxing and soothing properties.*

Chaste berry and dang gui tincture

 **RELIEVES
PERIOD PAINS**

 **HARMONIZES EMOTIONS**

Makes 300–350ml (10–12fl oz)

This blend of herbs eases premenstrual tension and menstrual pain. Dang gui enhances the flow of blood and, with chaste berry, balances the hormones. These herbs alleviate blood and fluid congestion in the pelvic region to relieve pain, and harmonize the heart, mind, and emotions. They also alleviate anxiety, irritability, and mild forms of depression associated with hormonal changes.

INGREDIENTS

20g (¾oz) chaste berry (also called agnus castus)
20g (¾oz) Chinese angelica (dang gui) (*Angelica sinensis*)
20g (¾oz) motherwort
20g (¾oz) black haw root bark (*Viburnum prunifolium*)
20g (¾oz) chamomile
400ml (14fl oz) good-quality vodka

METHOD

1 Ensure that all the dried ingredients are finely chopped, but not powdered.
2 Place all the ingredients except the vodka into a large glass jar with a secure-fitting lid. Pour in the vodka, close the lid tightly, and shake a few times.
3 Label the jar with all the ingredients and the date. Place the jar in a dark cupboard and shake it at least once every day for 3 weeks.
4 Strain the contents of the jar through a muslin bag into a measuring jug and pour the tincture into an appropriately sized (350–400ml/12–14fl oz) sterilized amber glass bottle (p.194). Seal the bottle.
5 Label with all the ingredients and the original starting date. Start by taking a few drops each day and build up to 1 teaspoon 2–3 times a day. Use within 6 months.

NOTE: This tincture is not suitable for use during pregnancy.

Goji berry and Siberian ginseng tincture

 ENERGIZES

Makes 300–350ml (10–12fl oz)

This tincture enhances the body's natural defences and improves mental concentration, physical endurance, and a sense of well-being. It does this by energizing the body, especially the liver and the nervous, hormonal, and immune systems. If you can't find fresh oat tops (the top 20cm (8in) of the plant), use the dried oats available from grocers and supermarkets.

INGREDIENTS

25g (scant 1oz) goji berries
25g (scant 1oz) Siberian ginseng
  (*Eleutherococcus senticosus*)
25g (scant 1oz) oat tops or dried oats
20g (¾oz) schisandra berries
5g (⅛oz) liquorice root
400ml (14fl oz) good-quality vodka

METHOD

1 Ensure that all the dried ingredients are finely chopped, but not powdered.

2 Place all the ingredients except the vodka into a large glass jar with a secure-fitting lid. Pour in the vodka, close the lid tightly, and shake a few times.

3 Label the jar with all the ingredients and the date. Place the jar in a dark cupboard and shake it at least once every day for 3 weeks.

4 Strain the contents of the jar through a muslin bag into a measuring jug and pour the tincture into an appropriately sized (350–400ml/12–14fl oz) sterilized amber glass bottle (p.194). Seal the bottle.

5 Label with all the ingredients and the original starting date. Start by taking a few drops each day and build up to 1 teaspoon 2–3 times a day. Use within 6 months.

NOTE: This tincture is not suitable for use during pregnancy.

Red clover and cleavers tincture

 **SOOTHES INFLAMED SKIN**

Makes 300–350ml (10–12fl oz)

These herbs are all used for acute and chronic skin inflammation, including acne, eczema, psoriasis, and other skin conditions. They help to detoxify the body and eliminate waste via the urine, and have a laxative effect. They also stimulate the gall bladder and liver. It is worth noting that serious skin conditions always require professional advice.

INGREDIENTS

15g (½oz) red clover
15g (½oz) cleavers
20g (¾oz) viola (heartsease)
20g (¾oz) violet leaves (*Viola odorata*)
20g (¾oz) mahonia root (*Mahonia aquifolium*), finely chopped
20g (¾oz) gotu kola
400ml (14fl oz) good-quality vodka

METHOD

1 Ensure that all the dried ingredients are finely chopped, but not powdered.

2 Place all the ingredients except the vodka into a large glass jar with a secure-fitting lid. Pour in the vodka, close the lid tightly, and shake a few times.

3 Label the jar with all the ingredients and the date. Place the jar in a dark cupboard and shake it at least once every day for 3 weeks.

4 Strain the contents of the jar through a muslin bag into a measuring jug and pour the tincture into an appropriately sized (350–400ml/12–14fl oz) sterilized amber glass bottle (p.194). Seal the bottle.

5 Label with all the ingredients and the original starting date. Start by taking a few drops each day and build up to 1 teaspoon 2–3 times a day. Use within 6 months.

NOTE: This tincture is not suitable for use during pregnancy.

Echinacea and elderberry winter guard tincture

 ENHANCES RESISTANCE TO COLDS AND FLU

Makes 1 month's supply

This tincture is a delicious way of strengthening your immune system against winter ailments. It warms the body, expelling the cold, and strengthens non-specific immunity. Fresh ginger warms the body and is antimicrobial, while thyme, garlic, and chilli fortify antimicrobial and diaphoretic action. Echinacea root is well known for reducing the risk of catching colds and flu.

INGREDIENTS

20g (¾oz) fresh ginger root
80g (2¾oz) echinacea root, fresh
  or dried
20g (¾oz) thyme leaves, fresh or dried
2 garlic cloves (optional)
1 fresh chilli with seeds (optional)
80g (2¾oz) elderberries, fresh
  or dried
500ml (16fl oz) good-quality vodka

METHOD

1 Slice the fresh ginger and echinacea root thinly, pull the fresh thyme leaves from their stems, and mince the garlic and chilli (if using them).

2 Gently squeeze the elderberries. Place all the ingredients in a large jar with a securely fitting lid. Cover with the vodka, mix thoroughly, and make sure all the ingredients are completely immersed.

3 Close the top tightly and place the jar in a dark cupboard. Check it every day, shaking the jar a few times. After 3 weeks, open the jar, strain the ingredients through a muslin bag, collect the liquid in a sterilized amber glass bottle (p.194), label with the names of all the ingredients, and date. Take 5ml (1 tsp) 2–3 times a day in a cup of hot or cold water (the tincture can be used throughout the autumn, winter, and early spring).

Dandelion and burdock tincture

 DETOXES

Makes 300–350ml (10–12fl oz)

The toxic environment many of us now live in puts enormous strain on the liver, so good liver health is more important than ever before. This tincture of bitter herbs stimulates the liver to metabolize toxic residues, and influences the rest of the digestive system. It also improves the blood circulation and helps to make you feel calmer and less irritable.

INGREDIENTS

20g (¾oz) dandelion root
20g (¾oz) burdock root
20g (¾oz) schisandra berries
10g (¼oz) artichoke leaves
20g (¾oz) milk thistle
10g (¼oz) gentian root
   (*Gentiana lutea*)
400ml (14fl oz) good-quality vodka

METHOD

1 Ensure that all the dried ingredients are finely chopped, but not powdered.

2 Place all the ingredients except the vodka into a large glass jar with a secure-fitting lid. Pour in the vodka, close the lid tightly, and shake a few times.

3 Label the jar with all the ingredients and the date. Place the jar in a dark cupboard and shake it at least once every day for 3 weeks.

4 Strain the contents of the jar through a muslin bag into a measuring jug and pour the tincture into an appropriately sized (350–400ml/12–14fl oz) sterilized amber glass bottle (p.194). Seal the bottle.

5 Label with all the ingredients and the original starting date. Start by taking a few drops each day and build up to 1 teaspoon 2–3 times a day. Use within 6 months.

NOTE: This tincture is not suitable for use during pregnancy.

Crampbark and valerian tincture

🔲 **RELIEVES MINOR PAIN**　　🔘 **RELIEVES PERIOD PAINS**

Makes 300–350ml (10–12fl oz)

This blend relieves broad-spectrum spasmodic pain due to stress, including discomfort associated with irritability, disturbed sleep, and nervous indigestion. Crampbark helps relieve smooth muscle spasms, valerian and passionflower provide a mild sedative effect and relieve irritability, and chamomile has an anti-inflammatory and antispasmodic effect.

INGREDIENTS

25g (scant 1oz) crampbark
25g (scant 1oz) valerian root
20g (¾oz) passionflower
20g (¾oz) chamomile
400ml (14fl oz) good-quality vodka

METHOD

1 Ensure that all the dried ingredients are finely chopped, but not powdered.
2 Place all the ingredients except the vodka into a large glass jar with a secure-fitting lid. Pour in the vodka, close the lid tightly, and shake a few times.
3 Label the jar with all the ingredients and the date. Place the jar in a dark cupboard and shake it at least once every day for 3 weeks.
4 Strain the contents of the jar through a muslin bag into a measuring jug and pour the tincture into an appropriately sized (350–400ml/12–14fl oz) sterilized amber glass bottle (p.194). Seal the bottle.
5 Label with all the ingredients and the original starting date. Start by taking a few drops each day and build up to 1 teaspoon 2–3 times a day. Use within 6 months.

NOTE: This tincture is not suitable for use during pregnancy.

Black cohosh and sage tincture

 RELIEVES MENOPAUSAL SYMPTOMS

Makes 300–350ml (10–12fl oz)

Herbs can be a great help for perimenopausal and menopausal women. Chaste berry regulates hormonal levels, black cohosh is known as a uterine tonic and a relaxant, and sage and schisandra fruit alleviate perspiration. Skullcap is a relaxant and, together with motherwort, lifts the spirits, and motherwort may also lessen the heart palpitations that often accompany hot flushes.

INGREDIENTS
20g (¾oz) black cohosh root
15g (½oz) chaste berry
10g (¼oz) sage
20g (¾oz) schisandra berries
15g (½oz) motherwort
20g (¾oz) skullcap
400ml (14fl oz) good-quality vodka

METHOD
1 Ensure that all the dried ingredients are finely chopped, but not powdered.
2 Place all the ingredients except the vodka into a large glass jar with a secure-fitting lid. Pour in the vodka, close the lid tightly, and shake a few times.
3 Label the jar with all the ingredients and the date. Place the jar in a dark cupboard and shake it at least once every day for 3 weeks.
4 Strain the contents of the jar through a muslin bag into a measuring jug and pour the tincture into an appropriately sized (350–400ml/12–14fl oz) sterilized amber glass bottle (p.194). Seal the bottle.
5 Label with all the ingredients and the original starting date. Start by taking a few drops each day and build up to 1 teaspoon 2–3 times a day. Use within 6 months.

NOTE: This tincture is not suitable for use during pregnancy.

Sage (Salvia officinalis) (p.102) Sage enhances the strength and vitality of the nervous system and has a reputation for helping to improve the memory.

Birch leaf and nettle root tincture

 **RELIEVES URINARY TRACT INFECTIONS**    **RELIEVES URINARY TRACT INFECTIONS**

Makes 300–350ml (10–12fl oz)

This tincture addresses urinary dysfunctions, water congestion, fluid retention, and uric acid accumulation. It relieves the body of metabolic waste, enhances urine flow, invigorates the urinary bladder, and strengthens the urinary tract. However, care must be taken not to use it without the supervision of a medical professional if you have stones in the urinary tract.

INGREDIENTS

25g (scant 1oz) nettle root
15g (½oz) birch leaves
25g (scant 1oz) pellitory-of-the-wall
   (*Parietaria officinalis*)
15g (½oz) blackcurrant leaves
20g (¾oz) white poplar, or poplar bark
   (*Populus tremuloides*)
400ml (14fl oz) good-quality vodka

METHOD

1 Ensure that all the dried ingredients are finely chopped, but not powdered.
2 Place all the ingredients except the vodka into a large glass jar with a secure-fitting lid. Pour in the vodka, close the lid tightly, and shake a few times.
3 Label the jar with all the ingredients and the date. Place the jar in a dark cupboard and shake it at least once every day for 3 weeks.
4 Strain the contents of the jar through a muslin bag into a measuring jug and pour the tincture into an appropriately sized (350–400ml/12–14fl oz) sterilized amber glass bottle (p.194). Seal the bottle.
5 Label with all the ingredients and the original starting date. Start by taking a few drops each day and build up to 1 teaspoon 2–3 times a day. Use within 6 months.

NOTE: Consult your doctor if your symptoms are severe or if they worsen. This tincture is not suitable for use during pregnancy.

MAKING SOUPS

Soups have a history of being used as a healing aid, especially for anyone recovering from an illness. These recipes have been specially devised to include essential, life-generating plant ingredients; they all taste delicious as well as doing you good.

Onion squash and ginger soup

 WARMS AND NOURISHES

Makes 4–6 servings

This is a great warming winter soup with a hint of the Orient. Ginger is famous for its healing qualities, and fresh ginger is traditionally used to ward off winter ailments: it acts as a diaphoretic, warms up the body, and helps in the elimination of cold. It also improves the digestion and assimilation of nutrients.

INGREDIENTS

2 tbsp olive oil

1kg (2¼lb) onion squash (or butternut squash), peeled, deseeded, and cut into small chunks

1 medium-sized leek, sliced

4 cloves of garlic, crushed

2 tbsp fresh ginger root, grated

1.5 litres (2¾ pints) vegetable stock

lime juice and zest to taste

salt and freshly ground black pepper

METHOD

1 Heat the olive oil in a saucepan, add the squash and leek, and sauté for few minutes. Add the garlic and ginger and a splash of the stock and continue to sauté the ingredients until the leek is soft. Add rest of the stock and bring to the boil. Simmer for approximately 10 minutes or until the squash is cooked through, but still retains some shape.

2 Remove from the heat, add the lime juice and a sprinkle of the lime zest, and season to taste. The soup can be served as it is, or blended until smooth.

Garlic (*Allium sativum*)
(p.19) Garlic is a popular culinary herb that can ward off bacterial infection. It keeps its flavour well when cooked.

Green bean and coriander soup

 CLEANSES

Makes 4 servings

This soup helps to balance blood-sugar levels: research has shown that bean pods contain a substance (arginine) that acts like insulin by regulating blood-sugar levels in the body, although it is weaker and acts more slowly over a prolonged period of time. Bean pods are also known to have a diuretic affect.

INGREDIENTS

2 large potatoes, peeled and diced
2 tbsp olive oil
1 onion, finely chopped
2 carrots, scrubbed and finely sliced
1kg (2¼lb) green beans (preferably yellow), topped, tailed, and sliced
3 garlic cloves, chopped
1 chilli pepper, deseeded and finely chopped
1–2 tsp picante pimenton (hot smoked paprika)
salt and freshly ground black pepper to taste
4 tbsp fresh coriander leaves, finely chopped
4 tbsp half-fat crème fraiche to serve (1 tbsp per serving)

METHOD

1 Place the potatoes in a pot, cover with water, and bring to the boil.

2 In the meantime, warm the oil in a frying pan, add the onion, and sauté until soft. Add the carrots to the frying pan, stir, and continue to sauté for few minutes. Add the beans, stir, cover the pan, turn the heat down low, and allow to sweat. Then add the chopped garlic, chilli pepper, and the smoked paprika.

3 Check that the vegetables are giving off enough juices to prevent the bottom of the pan burning; if necessary add a spoonful or two of water (the idea is that the vegetables cook in their own juices).

4 When the beans are nearly ready (soft, but chewy), add the cooked potatoes to the frying pan and add just a small amount of the water in which the potatoes were cooked.

5 Cook all the vegetables together for a few more minutes so that they combine well. Season to taste.

6 Serve the soup in bowls garnished with fresh coriander leaves and a spoonful of crème fraiche.

Chilli/cayenne pepper (Capsicum frutescens) (p.387) Warming red chillies and dried cayenne pepper stimulate circulation and aid digestion.

Burdock root and carrot soup

 CLEANSING

Makes 4 servings

This is a gentle, cleansing soup for the body. Burdock root is often used in the treatment of skin conditions and eczema, as well as rheumatic complaints, and is also famous as a blood purifier. It is grown commercially as a root vegetable and can be found most readily in Asian, especially Japanese, greengrocers.

INGREDIENTS

3 shallots, finely chopped
100g (3½oz) fresh burdock root, washed and finely chopped
3 large carrots, washed and finely chopped
2 small garlic cloves, finely chopped
salt and freshly ground black pepper
1 tbsp fresh lovage leaves, finely shredded, to garnish
a drizzle of pumpkin seed oil

METHOD

1 Place 2 tablespoons of water into a saucepan, add the shallots, and sauté for 1–2 minutes, stirring occasionally. When the shallots are soft, stir in the burdock root and carrots, keeping the pot covered and the heat turned down low so the vegetables steam in their own juices.
2 Check and stir the ingredients every few minutes and, if necessary, add a little more water. When they are sufficiently soft, add the garlic and cook for another minute. Add 500ml (16fl oz) of boiling water and simmer for 5 minutes.
3 Pour the soup into a blender or food processor and blend until smooth and silky. Season with salt and pepper to taste and serve in individual bowls. Garnish each with shredded lovage leaves and a little pumpkin seed oil.

Lovage (Levisticum officinale) (p.77)
Lovage contains quercetin, a flavonoid reputed to have numerous health benefits including anti-inflammatory properties.

Goji berry and mint soup

 REJUVENATES SKIN

Makes 4 servings

Goji has become famous through the centuries as a food that protects the body from premature ageing. It is now recognized as a "superfood", being a rich source of antioxidants and a tonic that alleviates anxiety and stress, promotes a lighter, more cheerful mood, improves sleep, and increases energy and strength.

INGREDIENTS

100g (3½oz) dried goji berries
1 tbsp olive oil
3 shallots, peeled and finely chopped
2 beef tomatoes, skinned and
    finely chopped
600ml (1 pint) vegetable stock
1 tbsp fresh mint leaves, chopped,
    plus extra to garnish

METHOD

1 Wash the berries and soak them in water for a few minutes to rehydrate them. Heat the oil in a saucepan, sauté the shallots for a few minutes, then add the tomatoes and goji berries. Stir for few minutes before adding the stock. Stir and simmer for a further 20 minutes.

2 Add the mint leaves and remove from the heat. Pour the mixture into a blender or food processor and pulse until smooth. Serve garnished with the extra mint leaves.

NOTE: To skin the tomatoes, cut a cross incision through the skin at the base of the tomato and place in a heatproof bowl. Pour over boiling water to cover and leave to stand for a few minutes. Remove the tomatoes from the water with a slotted spoon. The skin should now peel away easily.

Nettle and sweet potato soup

 PURIFIES SKIN

ACTS AS A SPRINGTIME TONIC

Makes 4 servings

Nettle soup is a classic spring cleanser that has been used as a health tonic for generations in Europe; nettles are full of vitamins and minerals and purify the blood, clear toxins, lower blood pressure, and improve the quality of skin and hair. Sweet potato, which is rich in vitamin A, also helps to improve digestion, remove toxins from the body, and relieve inflammation and dryness.

INGREDIENTS

1 tbsp olive oil
1 medium-sized onion, or
    4 shallots, chopped
1 medium-sized sweet potato,
    chopped into small pieces
2 garlic cloves, squeezed
1 litre (1¾ pints) vegetable stock
250g (9oz) young nettle leaves,
    washed and chopped
salt and freshly ground black pepper
2–3 tbsp barley miso paste
4 tsp half-fat crème fraîche, or
    plain yoghurt

METHOD

1 Heat the oil in a saucepan and sauté the onions or shallots and sweet potato for 2–3 minutes. Add the garlic and stock and bring to the boil. Simmer for 20 minutes, then add the nettles and turn off the heat.

2 Pour the soup into a blender or food processor and blend until smooth.

3 Season to taste with salt and pepper and the miso paste. Serve in individual bowls, each with a swirl (1 teaspoon) of crème fraiche or yoghurt.

Ginseng and astragalus longevity soup

 ENERGIZING   **ENHANCES DIGESTION**

Makes 4 servings

The energizing ingredients in this soup include ginseng, which enhances energy levels and restores strength after a prolonged illness, and astragalus root, which is well known for its beneficial effect on the immune system. It strengthens the lungs, helps to prevent colds, and alleviates any shortness of breath. Chinese black fungus is rich in amino acids, phosphorus, iron, and calcium.

INGREDIENTS

15g (½oz) Chinese black fungus (hei mu er/*Auricularia auricula*)

15g (½oz) fresh or dried astragalus root

15g (½oz) fresh or dried ginseng root

6 shallots, topped and tailed with the skins left on

3 garlic cloves, topped and tailed with the skins left on

1 large carrot, scrubbed

2.5cm (1in) cube fresh ginger root, thinly sliced

150g (5½oz) fresh shiitake mushrooms

150g (5½oz) fresh oyster mushrooms

1 large piece wakame seaweed, cut into small pieces, or 1 tbsp dried

15g (½oz) goji berries, pre-soaked if dried

200g (7oz) buckwheat or soba, noodles

2–3 tbsp barley miso paste

1 handful of flat-leaf parsley, chopped

freshly ground black pepper

METHOD

1 Put the fungus, astragalus root, ginseng root, shallots, garlic, whole carrot, and ginger into a large saucepan, cover with 1.5 litres (2¾ pints) of water and bring to the boil. Simmer on a very low heat for half an hour with the lid on tightly.

2 Take the pan off the heat, strain the liquid through a colander or sieve, and return it to the pan. Discard the astragalus root and ginseng. Squeeze the garlic and shallots from their skins and return them to the soup. Slice the fungus and carrot into small pieces and return them to the soup. Add the mushrooms and wakame seaweed and bring the soup back to simmering point. Add the goji berries. After 10 minutes, add the buckwheat noodles and let them cook through for 5–7 minutes.

3 Serve in individual bowls. Allow each person to add enough barley miso paste to their liking and garnish with the parsley and a grinding of black pepper.

Raw carrot and almond soup

 STRENGTHENS LUNGS

Makes 4 servings

This is a cooling soup, perfect for a hot sunny summer lunch. Fennel is a cooling and cleansing herb with antispasmodic properties, excellent for expelling wind, gently stimulating the digestion and kidneys, and brightening the eyes. This is balanced by the addition of almonds, which are warming by nature as well as extremely nutritious.

INGREDIENTS

200g (7oz) whole almonds
150g (5½oz) carrots, peeled
    and chopped
2 cloves fresh garlic
500ml (16fl oz) mineral water
½ tsp fennel seeds
¼ tsp black peppercorns
pinch of sea salt
1 tbsp fresh fennel leaves,
    finely chopped

METHOD

1 To sprout the almonds, soak them in cold water for half an hour, then rinse them in a colander under running water. Place them in a large bowl, cover with water, and leave overnight to soak. The following day, pop the skins off the almonds and place the almonds in another clean bowl, pour over the filtered or bottled mineral water, and refrigerate. Allow the almonds to continue soaking for up to 24 hours.
2 Strain the almonds and keep the almond-soaked mineral water. Put the carrots into a blender or food processor with the garlic, the strained, soaked almonds, and 1 tablespoon of the almond-soaked mineral water. Blend, adding the rest of the water gradually until the mixture is smooth and silky. Place in the fridge and leave to chill for a few hours until cool.
3 Put the fennel seeds, peppercorns, and salt into a pestle and mortar and grind to a fine powder. Then add the fern-like fennel leaves to the spices. Serve the soup in bowls, with a teaspoon of the seasoning on top.

Courgette and sea greens soup

 ASSISTS WEIGHT CONTROL   **ASSISTS WEIGHT CONTROL**

Makes 4 servings

This soup is healthy yet nourishing, and beneficial to the body. Courgettes are cooling by nature, as they help to build body fluids and relieve dryness, while seaweed is an excellent source of minerals. Seaweed is also known for its ability to help remove toxic waste from the body, improve kidney function, alkalize the blood, assist in weight control, and lower cholesterol.

INGREDIENTS

1 handful dried wakame seaweed, or any other colourful soft-leaf seaweed such as dulse
4 shallots, chopped
1 medium-sized fennel bulb, chopped
5 medium-sized courgettes, sliced
1 tbsp fresh parsley, finely chopped
salt and freshly ground black pepper to taste
a drizzle of pumpkin seed oil

METHOD

1 Soak the seaweed in at least 600ml (1 pint) of clean water.
2 Place a tablespoon of water in a saucepan and heat. Add the chopped shallots and cook over a low heat with the lid on, stirring occasionally.
3 When soft, add the fennel and courgettes. Continue to cook the vegetables with the lid on until they are tender.
4 Drain the seaweed. Place the cooked vegetables in a blender or food processor, add the chopped parsley and 500–600ml (16fl oz–1 pint) of water, and blend until smooth. Add salt and black pepper to taste.
5 Divide the rehydrated seaweed leaves into 4 piles, pour the soup into individual bowls, and scatter the seaweed over the top of each serving. Sprinkle over the fresh parlsey and a little of the pumpkin seed oil and serve.

Dulse (Palmaria palmata)
A mineral-rich seaweed, dulse grows on the northern coasts of the Atlantic and Pacific oceans.

Sprouted puy lentil and turmeric soup

 ENHANCES DIGESTION   **PROMOTES TISSUE REPAIR**

Makes 4 servings

The sprouted lentils in this warming autumn soup are easier to digest than dried lentils and have an enhanced nutritional value, while turmeric helps to improve the digestion and liver conditions such as jaundice. The soup also has anti-inflammatory properties, helping to relieve swelling and pain, including rheumatic and arthritic pain.

INGREDIENTS

1 tbsp olive oil
4 shallots, chopped
1 tsp turmeric powder
2 garlic cloves
100g (3½oz) fresh shiitake
  mushrooms, sliced
200g (7oz) sprouted Puy lentils
  (see note)
1 litre (1¾ pints) home-made
  vegetable stock or cold water
juice of ½ lemon
salt and freshly ground black pepper
1 tbsp coriander leaves, chopped

METHOD

1 Heat the oil in a saucepan, add the chopped shallots, and sauté for 1 minute. Add the turmeric, garlic, and mushrooms and stir. Add the lentils and stock or water and bring to the boil. Simmer for 10 minutes.
2 Switch the heat off and add the lemon juice and salt and pepper to taste. Pour the soup into individual bowls and serve garnished with the chopped coriander leaves.

NOTE: To sprout lentils, place 150g (5½oz) of dried Puy lentils in a glass jar large enough (usually three times the volume of the lentils) for the lentils to expand while sprouting. Fasten a piece of muslin cloth over the opening of the jar, fill it with water, and leave overnight. In the morning pour out the water, rinse the jar and lentils with clean water, and leave the jar of lentils upside down at an angle to drip-dry through the muslin. In the evening, rinse the lentils again and leave to drip-dry overnight. Repeat the process twice daily until the young shoots show (2–4 days). The lentils are ready to use when the shoots are the length or more of a dried Puy lentil.

Turmeric (Curcuma longa) *(p.45)*
A staple of Asian and Middle Eastern cooking and Ayurveda, the turmeric plant belongs to the ginger (Zingiber) *family.*

Roasted barley and chestnut soup

 STRENGTHEN LOWER LIMBS   **ENERGIZES**

Makes 4 servings

This tonic soup makes a great nourishing lunch on a cold winter's day, as it primarily supports kidney energy. It will help to warm up the whole system, and eating it once a week during the winter season is most useful for individuals suffering from aches and pains aggravated by the cold weather.

INGREDIENTS

6 shallots, topped and tailed, with skin left on
4 cloves garlic with skin left on
2 large carrots, washed
200g (7oz) celeriac, peeled and cubed
2½cm (1in) fresh ginger root, washed
150g (5½oz) sweet chestnuts, fresh or precooked
200g (7oz) shiitake mushrooms, stalks removed and sliced
2 long blades wakame seaweed, chopped into small pieces, or 2 tbsp wakame flakes
100g (3½oz) roasted barley (see note below)
1 tbsp barley miso
flat-leaf parsley, to garnish (optional)

METHOD

1 If using fresh chestnuts, roast them first (see note below).
2 Put the whole shallots, garlic, carrots, celeriac, and ginger into a large saucepan, cover with 500ml (16fl oz) of water, and bring to a simmer. Cook, covered, over a low heat for at least 1 hour, occasionally adding some more water if necessary.
3 Take the saucepan off the heat and strain the liquid through a colander into a clean saucepan. Pick out the garlic and shallots from the cooked vegetables and squeeze them out of their skins directly into the liquid.
4 Add the chestnuts to the soup and bring to the boil. Add the mushrooms, wakame seaweed, and roasted barley, and simmer for 15–20 minutes. Then stir in the barley miso until dissolved, remove from the heat, and serve in bowls with the parsley garnish (if using).

NOTE: To roast barley, soak it overnight in lukewarm water, drain, and leave to dry on a tray covered with a clean cloth. When the barley is still damp, heat a large frying pan over a high heat. Turn the heat down to medium, and add a quarter of the barley, stirring constantly. When the grain is golden brown and makes a gravelly noise as you stir it, tip it out of the pan and allow to cool completely on a plate. Repeat with the remaining 3 batches. Store in an airtight jar if you prepare the barley a few days before making the soup.

NOTE: To roast fresh chestnuts, chip into the apex, or tip, of each nut with a sharp knife and place them on a baking tray. Bake in the oven at 180°C (350°F/ Gas 4) for 20–25 minutes. Take them out of the oven. Wrap each chestnut in a cloth and squeeze hard to crush the shell, then peel it all off.

MAKING SALADS

Raw vegetables and herbs are the essence of nourishment, providing nutrients, fluids, and fibre and enhancing the elimination of wastes. These salads combine the healing qualities of fresh vegetables with phytonutrients from herbs, and bring health awareness to the eating experience.

Nasturtium and sprouted seed salad

 DETOXES

Makes 2 servings

Sprouted seeds are a great source of fresh nutrients. Sprouts in general are a mineral-rich food; they often have diuretic and bowel-regulating properties, and are therefore important foods in a detox regime. Nasturtiums flowers impart a delicately peppery taste to this salad. As a medicine, they are thought to have a beneficial influence on the lungs and kidneys.

INGREDIENTS
75g (2½oz) alfalfa sprouts
1 avocado, chopped
1 large tomato, chopped
8 nasturtium flowers

FOR THE DRESSING
1 tbsp olive oil
juice of ½ lemon
¼ tsp mustard
salt and freshly ground black
   pepper, to taste

METHOD
1 Rinse the alfalfa sprouts thoroughly in a colander under running water, then dry them well in a salad spinner or with a clean tea cloth.
2 Mix all the dressing ingredients together and blend well to create a smooth vinaigrette.
3 Place the alfalfa sprouts in a serving bowl and add the avocado and tomato. Pour over the dressing and mix thoroughly. Top the salad with the nasturtium flowers, and serve.

Courgette spaghetti with coriander and pine nut pesto

 PURIFIES SKIN    **EASES CONSTIPATION**

Makes 2 servings

Strands of courgette take the place of pasta in this summer lunch dish. Courgettes have a gently laxative effect and, when combined with essential fatty acids from hemp and pumpkin seed oils, will help to nourish and clear the skin of impurities. Pine nuts add a source of protein to turn this dish into a light, but complete, meal.

INGREDIENTS

2 courgettes (1 green, 1 yellow,
  if possible)
2 tbsp fresh coriander leaves,
  finely chopped
50g (1¾oz) pine nuts, coarsely ground
2 tsp hemp oil
2 tsp pumpkin seed oil
juice ½ lemon
salt and feshly ground pepper
  to taste

METHOD

1 Put the courgettes through a vegetable spiralizer (a turning vegetable slicer) to slice them into long threads, or "spaghetti"; if you don't have a spiralizer, slice the courgettes lengthways as thinly as you can.
2 Put the coriander leaves in a bowl, add the pine nuts, hemp, and pumpkin seed oils, and mix well to make a pesto.
3 Place the courgettes in a serving bowl, add the coriander pesto, and toss the ingredients well. Add some lemon juice and salt and pepper to taste, and serve.

Coriander (Coriandrum sativum)
A member of the carrot and parsley family, coriander has soft stems and small pink-white flowers.

Red clover sprouts and lemon balm salad

 **RELIEVES MENOPAUSAL
SYMPTOMS**

Makes 2 servings

Red clover is often used in the treatment of premenstrual syndrome, and the flowers are a popular ingredient in natural products that help to alleviate hot flushes, prevent loss of bone density, and balance hormones in menopausal women. These sprouts have the same healing properties as the mature flowers.

INGREDIENTS

1 large carrot, scrubbed
100g (3½oz) red clover sprouts
50g (1¾oz) broccoli sprouts
½ mango
1 clove of garlic, peeled
3 tbsp olive oil
juice of 1 lime
salt and freshly ground black pepper,
   to season
8 fresh lemon balm leaves, finely
   chopped, to garnish

METHOD

1 Put the carrot through a vegetable spiralizer (a turning vegetable slicer) to slice it into long threads, or "spaghetti"; if you don't have a spiralizer, slice the carrot into thin sticks or use a vegetable peeler. Put the sprouts and carrot in a large serving bowl.
2 To make the dressing, cut the mango in half, remove the stone, scoop out the flesh into a blender or food processor, add the garlic, olive oil, and lime juice and blend until smooth. Season with salt and pepper, pour the dressing over the vegetables, mix well, add the lemon balm leaves, and serve.

NOTE: You can sprout red clover and broccoli by placing 2 tbsp of each of the seeds into a large glass jar, pour in spring or filtered water, fasten a muslin cloth on the opening of the jar, and leave overnight. Rinse the seeds the following morning by pouring out the old water, adding fresh water, then emptying that out, too. Leave the jars at an angle of 45 degrees and repeat the rinsing process every morning and evening until the sprouts are ready to eat (when they develop small green leaves, after 4–5 days). Once the seeds have sprouted, store in a glass jar with a tight-fitting lid, refrigerate, and eat within a day or two.

Dandelion and primrose leaf salad

 DETOXES

Makes 2 servings

This is an early spring-forager detox salad. Dandelion and chicory are a gentle stimulant for the liver and bladder. Some of the fresh ingredients can be found growing in gardens or small woodland areas, others you may need to buy, such as rocket, chives, and chicory. Rocket can also be grown from seed.

INGREDIENTS

30g (1oz) dandelion leaves
1 tsp wild chives
10g (¹/₄oz) daisy leaves
 (*Bellis perennis*)
10g (¹/₄oz) yarrow leaves
20g (³/₄oz) primrose leaves
10g (¹/₄oz) rocket leaves
1 head of chicory
1¹/₂ tbsp linseed oil
1¹/₂ tbsp lemon juice
white pepper to taste
sesame salt to taste (see note)

METHOD

1 Rinse all the salad leaves and dry them in a salad spinner.
2 To make the dressing, mix the linseed oil, lemon juice, white pepper, and sesame salt in a small bowl. When the salad leaves are dry, place them in a serving bowl, toss with sesame salt, and add the dressing.

NOTE: To prepare the sesame salt, soak 1 tablespoon of golden, or shelled, sesame seeds and 1 tablespoon of black sesame seeds in a bowl of water overnight. The following day, discard the water, tie up the sesame seeds in a muslin bag, and allow them to drip-dry. When dry, lightly pan-roast the seeds, adding 3 good pinches of sea salt as you go, and toss them. Then grind the seeds in a pestle and mortar or food processor and store in a sealed container until needed.

NOTE: Omit the yarrow leaves from this salad if you are pregnant.

Chives (*Allium schoenoprasum*)
The leaves are cyclindrical and hollow with a delicate oniony flavour, and are ideal as a garnish on savoury dishes.

Edible flower salad

 STIMULATES THE SENSES

Makes 4 servings

This summer salad is designed to excite the senses with its abundance of summer colours and unusual tastes. It is worth noting that fresh calendula, nasturtium, viola, and rose flower petals all have unique flavours, so it is best to become accustomed to these different tastes before deciding to incorporate them into your version of this salad.

INGREDIENTS

50g (1¾oz) sunflower greens
   (young sunflower plants)
50g (1¾oz) buckwheat greens
   (young buckwheat plants)
50g (1¾oz) broccoli sprouts (p.229)
1 yellow pepper, cut into sticks
1 red pepper, cut into sticks
1 small cucumber, cut into
   thin rounds
2 ripe tomatoes, cut into wedges
1 tbsp calendula petals
12 nasturtium flowers,
   stalks removed
1 tbsp viola flowers, stalks removed
1 tbsp fragrant rose petals

FOR THE DRESSING

2 tbsp fresh basil leaves
2 tbsp sesame oil
½ clove garlic, peeled
1 tbsp mirin rice wine
1 tbsp lemon or lime juice
salt and freshly ground black pepper
   to taste

METHOD

1 Harvest the sunflower and buckwheat greens, rinse them in clean water, and dry them in a salad spinner before placing them in a salad bowl. Rinse the broccoli sprouts under running water and allow to dry off before adding them to the greens. Add the peppers, cucumber, and tomatoes to the other ingredients.
2 Add the flowers and flower petals to the salad, reserving a few of each for a garnish.
3 Blend all the ingredients for the dressing in a blender or a food processor, pour the dressing over the salad, and gently toss. Just before serving, sprinkle the remaining flowers over the top of the salad.

Nasturtium (Tropaeolum majus)
(p.120) The edible leaves, flowers, and seedpods make a peppery and colourful addition to salads and sandwiches.

Broccoli and rosemary salad

 STIMULATES DIGESTION

Makes 2 servings

Broccoli is an excellent source of sulphur, iron, and B vitamins; it has been credited with enhancing the body's resistance to many diseases, due in part to the important antioxidant sulforaphane. It is essential not to overcook it in order to preserve its healthy chlorophyll. Rosemary stimulates blood circulation, relieves abdominal discomfort due to weak digestion, and improves the memory.

INGREDIENTS

1 large head of broccoli, chopped into florets
1 small avocado, stoned and peeled
2 garlic cloves, peeled
Juice of ½ lemon
Salt and freshly ground black pepper to taste
1 sprig fresh rosemary, leaves stripped and finely chopped (or 1 tsp dried rosemary)
16 olives, pitted

METHOD

1 Make sure that the broccoli florets are cut to a similar size, then place them in a steamer until they are warmed through, but still firm and green.
2 Put the avocado flesh in a blender or food processor with the garlic, lemon juice, salt, and pepper, and blend until smooth. Thoroughly combine all the ingredients, making sure the broccoli is well dressed.
3 Transfer into a serving dish, scatter the chopped rosemary over the top, and garnish with the olives.

Rosemary (*Rosmarinus officinalis*)
(p.98) is a wonderfully aromatic herb with needle-like leaves and a sweet, resinous scent.

Sauerkraut and avocado salad

 REPLENISHES GUT FLORA

Makes 2 servings

Fermented foods such as sauerkraut play an important role in enhancing intestinal health by promoting the growth of organisms that increase nutrient absorption. Cabbage also contains compounds that support colon and breast health, and has antioxidant, antibacterial, and antiviral properties. Once prepared, sauerkraut actually contains more vitamin C than fresh cabbage.

FOR THE SAUERKRAUT
2 medium white cabbages
2 tbsp salt

FOR THE SALAD
50g (1¾oz) alfalfa sprouts, washed
1 avocado, stoned, peeled, and sliced
1 tbsp pumpkin oil
freshly ground black pepper to taste

METHOD

1 To make the sauerkraut (fermented cabbage), shred the cabbage finely in a food processor, pack into a bowl, sprinkle with salt, mix thoroughly, and leave for half an hour.

2 Pound the cabbage with the end of a rolling pin until the juices start flowing. Fill a sterilized glass jar (p.194) with the salted cabbage, adding a handful at the time and pounding it down in the jar with the end of a rolling pin each time so that no air is left between the added layers ("beating in" is essential to the success of this process). Firmly compress the layers of cabbage, leaving some space at the top of the jar for the cabbage to expand (the juices may also overflow).

3 Place the jar on a plate, cover with a saucer as wide as the neck of the jar, and store in a well-ventilated cool, but not cold, place (see note below). Check the jar and remove any scum from the top regularly. After 1 week the cabbage will have fermented sufficiently to be eaten, and should keep for at least 2 weeks if refrigerated.

4 To make the salad, combine 125g (4½oz) of the sauerkraut with the rest of the ingredients in a salad bowl and season to taste.

NOTE: You can also buy ready-made sauerkraut, but it is often sterilized and your homemade version will taste much better. The ideal temperature for fermentation is 20–22°C (68–72°F). Fermentation will stop and the cabbage will spoil above 24°C (76°F) or below 13°C (55°F). If your sauerkraut develops a pinkish hue on its surface, goes dark, or is very soft and mushy, it has not fermented properly and should not be eaten.

Alfalfa (Medicago sativa) *A flowering plant of the pea family, alfalfa was originally cultivated in the Middle East and is now grown throughout the world.*

Nori rolls

 DETOXES

Makes 3–4 servings

Sheets of nutritious toasted nori seaweed are delicious as part of a healthy snack, and are ideal to use as a wrap filled with fresh vegetables. These rolls make an excellent light, detoxing meal to eat on the go – a true raw food "sandwich". In this recipe the rolls are served as a salad with a tasty dressing.

INGREDIENTS

2 heaped tbsp sesame seeds
5 square sheets toasted nori seaweed
1 small or 1/2 a large papaya, peeled, deseeded, and cut into thin strips
1 red pepper, deseeded and cut into thin strips
1 chilli, deseeded and cut into thin strips
10cm (4in) inner white part of a leek, sliced thinly lengthways
1 avocado, stoned, peeled, and cut into thin strips

FOR THE DRESSING

juice of 1 lime
1 clove of garlic, crushed
1/2 tsp fresh ginger root, finely grated
1 tbsp fresh coriander leaves, finely chopped
1 tsp light barley miso paste
1/2 tsp lime zest
1 tsp maple syrup
3 tbsp mineral water

METHOD

1 Firstly, toast the sesame seeds in a small pan over a low heat for 3–4 minutes, stirring frequently, until they turn lightly golden and begin to release a nutty aroma.

2 To make the dressing, put all the dressing ingredients into a blender or food processor with 1 tablespoon of toasted sesame seeds and blend until smooth.

3 Have a small bowl of water ready. Place a sheet of nori on a sushi mat or a square of greaseproof paper a little longer and wider than the sheet of nori.

4 Put a small amount of each ingredient heaped on top of one another in a line 2–3cm (3/4–1 1/4in) from the edge of the bottom of the nori sheet.

5 Drizzle a little of the dressing over the vegetables and scatter over some of the remaining toasted sesame seeds.

6 Lift the bottom edge of the sushi mat (or paper) and roll up the nori with the ingredients inside. To seal the nori roll, wet your fingers in the small bowl of water, dampen the top edge of the nori sheet, and finish rolling the nori. Repeat with the remaining nori sheets, vegetables, and dressing.

7 When ready to serve, slice the nori rolls into three sections, and stand each one upright on a serving plate. Sprinkle each nori roll with toasted sesame seeds, and use any remaining dressing as a dip.

Sesame (Sesamum indicum) *The seeds are exceptionally rich in nutrients and vitamins, including iron, calcium, magnesium, and vitamins B1 and E.*

Mint and cucumber side salad with cashew nut cream

 **COOLS THE DIGESTIVE SYSTEM**

Makes 4 servings

You can happily share this fresh-tasting, minty raita with friends who do not eat milk or milk-related products. Cucumbers are cooling, so this dish is ideal for summer dining; if you serve it in winter, add some finely chopped fresh chilli. Use young cucumbers, which have small, compact seeds, or scoop out the larger seeds from a mature cucumber with a spoon.

INGREDIENTS

1 medium cucumber, peeled
a few fresh mint leaves, finely
   chopped, to garnish

FOR THE CASHEW NUT CREAM

75g (2¹/₂ oz) raw cashew nuts,
   pre-soaked
2 garlic cloves, crushed
2 tsp white miso
2 tbsp freshly squeezed lemon juice
1 tbsp fresh mint leaves,
   finely chopped
1 tbsp fresh coriander leaves,
   finely chopped

METHOD

1 Cut the cucumber in half lengthways and scoop out any large seeds with a spoon. Dice the cucumber finely and place in a serving bowl.

2 Put all the ingredients for the cashew nut cream in a blender or food processor, and blend thoroughly. Add 150ml (5fl oz) of water or more to adjust the consistency to that of a pouring cream.

3 Pour the cashew nut cream over the cucumber and stir together well. Sprinkle with finely chopped mint leaves.

Cucumber (Cucumis sativas) *Although often considered vegetables, cucumbers are actually fruits, as they have enclosed seeds and develop from a flower.*

Cayenne-toasted almonds and kale salad

 STIMULATES DIGESTION

Makes 3–4 servings

Kale is the perfect winter green for this warming salad, as it contains sulphur and its juice is an age-old medicine for stomach and duodenal ulcers. This recipe also contains cayenne pepper to add warmth on cold winter days (although do not include it if you have either of the above-mentioned conditions).

INGREDIENTS

2 tbsp chopped almonds
pinch of cayenne pepper
$\frac{1}{2}$ tsp sweet paprika
pinch of salt
a little lemon juice
250g (9oz) kale, washed, and cut
  into thin strips
1 tbsp olive oil

METHOD

1 Toast the almonds first: heat a thick-bottomed frying pan over a medium heat, add the almonds, and toast for a couple of minutes. Then add the cayenne pepper, paprika, and salt, and toss the almonds in the spices. Add the lemon juice, remove the pan from the heat before the juice begins to burn, and set aside.
2 Heat a saucepan over a medium heat, add 2 tablespoons of water, let the water heat up, add the kale, and close the lid tightly. Lower the heat and allow the kale to sweat for 2–3 minutes only so that it wilts, rather than cooks.
3 Put the kale in a serving dish, toss with the olive oil and another dash of lemon, and garnish with the spicy almonds.

Almonds (Prunus dulcis) *These nuts are an excellent source of vitamin E and are rich in monounsaturated fats, which may help to lower cholesterol.*

MAKING FRUIT BARS

These recipes will help you to incorporate more wild fruits, nuts, and grains into your diet. The variations on these basic ingredients are endless, and depend mainly on the way the grains are prepared, as well as your choice of dried fruits, nuts, and seeds.

Four fruits power bar

 NOURISHES BLOOD

INGREDIENTS
150g (5½oz) wheat grains
150g (5½oz) dry apricots
50g (1¾oz) raisins
50g (1¾oz) blackcurrants
50g (1¾oz) sour cherries
50g (1¾oz) walnuts, soaked for 4
  hours, dried, and lightly pan-toasted
50g (1¾oz) sesame seeds, pan-toasted

Makes 16 bars

Sour cherries bring a sharp, lively flavor to these power bars. Add a combination of other dried berries, fruits, or nuts if you like, to complement the flavour of the sour cherries. These bars are best eaten the day you make them, not only to keep them from spoiling, but to get the maximum goodness from the freshly sprouted grains.

1 To sprout the wheat grains, soak for 12 hours or overnight. Rinse the grains thoroughly and put in a large glass jar (grains expand to two to three times their initial volume). Cover the opening and neck of the jar with muslin cloth and attach it with string or a strong rubber band. Place at a 45° angle in a well-lit spot but not in direct sunlight. Rinse the grains each morning and evening by pouring water through the muslin and emptying it out.

2 The sprouts are ready when seedlings approximately 0.5–1cm (¼in) in length appear. Rinse the seedlings thoroughly in clean water, strain, and spread on a clean cloth to dry. The sprouted grains are ready to use when they are dry to the touch. Place the apricots and raisins in a blender and blend to a paste. Add half of the sprouted grains and blackcurrants and blend until crushed (but not blended to a purée).

3 Transfer to a mixing bowl and add the rest of the grains, berries, and the cherries. Mix well with a wooden spoon. Chop the walnuts into small chunks and add them to the mix. Sprinkle the sesame seeds on a flat surface. Roll out the mixture, or press it with clean hands, over the seeds into a rectangle 1cm (½in) thick. Use a sharp knife to cut the mixture into small rectangular bars. Place the bars on a rack and leave to dry out for a few hours.

Cranberry and apricot power bars

 ENERGIZES

Makes 12–16 bars

Barley has long had a reputation as a highly nutritious cereal; it was eaten by Ancient Greek athletes and Roman gladiators, who were known as *hordearii* ("barley eaters"). Cranberries are packed with antioxidants, and apricots are an excellent source of iron, so these power bars make a highly nutritious and sustaining snack to keep your energy levels up.

INGREDIENTS

150g (5½oz) lightly toasted barley, ground to a powder
100g (3½oz) dried cranberries (presoaked and dried on a cloth or tea towel)
200g (7oz) dried apricots (washed and dried on a cloth or tea towel)
60g (2oz) pistachios, coarsely chopped
40g (1¼oz) pistachios, finely ground

METHOD

1 Prepare the barley first (see below). Put the fruit and coarsely chopped pistachios in a blender or food processor and blend into a thick purée. Then add just enough of the toasted barley powder to make a pliable dough.

2 Sprinkle half the finely ground pistachios onto a flat surface, place the fruit dough on top, and roll it out into a rectangular shape about 6–8mm (¼–½in) thick. Sprinkle the top of the dough with the remaining finely ground pistachios and press them by hand into the mixture.

3 Cut into 3 x10cm (1¼ x 4in) rectangles and place on a baking tray. Bake in a preheated oven at 50°C (122°F/Gas¼) for 2–3 hours until the bars have dried out.

4 Carefully lift the bars off the tray, allow to cool on a wire rack, then wrap them individually in cling film or greaseproof paper. If wrapped and stored in a tin in a cool place, the bars can last for more than a week.

NOTE: To roast barley, soak it overnight in lukewarm water, drain, and leave to dry on a tray covered with a clean cloth. When the barley is still damp, heat a large frying pan over a high heat. Turn the heat down to medium, and add a quarter of the barley, stirring constantly. When the grain is golden brown and makes a gravelly noise as you stir it, tip it out of the pan and allow to cool completely on a plate. Repeat with the remaining 3 batches. Allow the grain to cool completely and store in an airtight container. Grind the toasted grains in a pestle and mortar to make a barley powder.

Linseed and chilli crackers

 PROVIDES OMEGA-3 FATTY ACIDS

Makes approx 12

These healthy crackers can be enjoyed by everyone. Linseed is a valuable food in a balanced diet owing to its high levels of omega-3 fatty acids, which play an essential role in strengthening immunity and maintaining good blood vessel health. The addition of seaweeds, chilli, and fresh parsley make these crackers taste very moreish.

INGREDIENTS

250g (9oz) linseeds
juice of 5 medium-sized carrots
   and 2 celery stems
1 small or medium chilli (according
   to taste), chopped
4 tbsp fresh parsley, finely chopped
4 tbsp dulse or wakame flakes
a large pinch of salt
a sprinkle of chilli powder (optional)

METHOD

1 Add the linseeds to the freshly made carrot and celery juice, then stir in the chilli, parsley, seaweed flakes, salt to taste, and chilli powder (if using). Leave for up to 2 hours to allow the linseeds to soak up the juices.
2 Spread the soaked linseeds in a thin layer on a piece of baking parchment on a baking tray. Bake in a very low oven (50°C/122°F/Gas¼) for 3–4 hours.
3 Use a knife to cut the crackers into squares. Thicker pieces can be served instead of bread with soup.

Blackcurrant and walnut bars

 ENERGIZES

Makes 8 or more bars

If barley grain is soaked in warm water, it cooks very slowly, allowing for little loss of nutrients. Toasted grain is very crunchy and can be partially cracked or milled by laying it in a thin layer on a wooden chopping board and rolling over it with a rolling pin, before using to roll out the bars. Eat the bars within 1–2 days while still fresh.

INGREDIENTS
250g (9oz) barley grains
50g (1¾oz) walnut pieces
100g (3½oz) pitted dates
100g (3½oz) dried blackcurrants
  (or blueberries)

METHOD

1 Wash the barley grains, then soak them in warm water overnight. In the morning, drain the grains, and allow them to dry out for few minutes in a colander. Set aside 150g (5½oz) of the grain and spread the rest in a thin layer over a clean, dry cloth to dry until the next day.

2 The 150g (5½oz) of grain you set aside should still be damp, but no longer wet, and will be ready to toast. Heat a large frying pan over a high heat, then turn the heat down and add the barley in small batches to toast. Make sure that the pan is not too crowded, and that the size of the pan allows for an equal toasting of all the barley grains. Stir constantly until the grain is a golden tan colour and makes a gravelly sound as you stir it.

3 Allow the grain to cool completely, then move it in batches into a pestle and mortar and grind until lightly milled.

4 Toast the walnuts in the same way as the barley, toasting it lightly until golden with a nutty scent.

5 Once the barley grain and walnuts are ready to use, place the untoasted batch of barley grains in a blender or food processor with the dates and whizz to a paste. Turn out into a mixing bowl and stir in the blackcurrants and walnuts. Spread the toasted barley grains over a work surface and place the paste mixture on top, rolling it out into a rectangle or pressing it into shape with clean hands. Cut into bars and place on a rack to dry out.

Heal from the outside

Creams, soaps, bath soaks, and hair treatments

MAKING FACE AND BODY CREAMS

Most of us use a moisturizer every day; you can perfect yours by choosing plant oils and extracts that are exactly suited to your skin type. If you have very sensitive skin, test any skin product on a small area of skin first to check that it does not provoke a reaction.

Rose and avocado body moisturizer

 MOISTURIZES SKIN

INGREDIENTS
½ tsp cocoa butter and shea nut butter mix
1 tsp avocado oil
2 tbsp rose petal infusion
2 tbsp emulsifying wax
2 drops rose essential oil
3 drops geranium essential oil

Makes 40g (1¼oz)

Moisturizing cocoa butter and shea nut butters are combined here with vitamin-rich avocado oil to give skin a nourishing, enriching treat to boost suppleness, banish dry patches, and leave a feeling of velvety smoothness. The beautiful rose fragrance adds a touch of luxury to delight the senses.

1 Melt the cocoa butter and shea nut butter with the avocado oil in a bowl set over a saucepan of boiling water (bain-marie).

2 Gently heat the rose petal infusion (p.342) and emulsifying wax in a small saucepan until the wax has completely dissolved in the infusion. Slowly add the infusion to the oil mixture, whisking it together for about 10 seconds.

3 When the mixture has cooled down, add the oils. Store in a sterilized glass jar (p.194) with a tight-fitting lid, and use within three months.

Gotu kola and ginger body toning cream

 MOISTURIZES SKIN

Makes 40g (1½oz)

This is a nourishing cream with stimulating herbal extracts to restore suppleness and tone. Gotu kola has anti-inflammatory properties and encourages the formation of collagen, which firms and boosts the suppleness of the skin, while ginger, black pepper, and lemon essential oils encourage circulation and help to tone the skin.

INGREDIENTS
1 tbsp apricot oil
2 tbsp gotu kola infusion
2 tsp emulsifying wax
2 drops black pepper essential oil
3 drops ginger essential oil
2 drops lemon essential oil

METHOD
1 Heat the apricot oil in a bowl set over a saucepan of boiling water (bain-marie).
2 Heat the gotu kola infusion and emulsifying wax gently in a saucepan until the emulsifier has dissolved in the infusion.
3 Slowly add the infusion to the apricot oil, stirring constantly. When the mixture has cooled, stir in the essential oils.
4 Store in a sterilized dark glass jar (p.194) with a tight-fitting lid in the refrigerator, and use within 2 months.

Viola and evening primrose skin cream

 MOISTURIZES SENSITIVE SKIN

Makes 40g (1½oz)

A gently soothing and moisturizing skin cream such as this is ideal for sensitive skin. Viola, also known as heartsease, calms and soothes irritated skin and is traditionally used to ease conditions such as eczema. Here it is combined with essential fatty acid-rich avocado and evening primrose oils and gentle chamomile to soothe and nurture delicate skin.

INGREDIENTS
1 tsp lanolin
1 tsp avocado oil
1 tsp evening primrose oil
2 tbsp viola and chamomile infusion (50:50 mix)
10g (¼oz) emulsifying wax

METHOD
1 Melt the lanolin, avocado oil, and evening primrose oil in a bowl set over a saucepan of boiling water (bain-marie).
2 Put the viola and chamomile infusion and emulsifying wax into a saucepan and heat gently until the emulsifier has dissolved.
3 Slowly add the infusion to the lanolin and oil mixture, whisking it together for about 10 seconds.
4 Pour into a sterilized dark glass jar (p.194) with a tight-fitting lid, store in the refrigerator, and use within 2 months.

Frankincense and wild rose skin cream

 MOISTURIZES SKIN

Makes 40g (1½oz)

Keep skin smooth and radiant with this luxurious facial cream. Frankincense is renowned for its toning, restorative, and anti-ageing properties while rosehip oil helps to improve skin elasticity and prevent moisture loss. Neroli oil, the precious essential oil from the blossom of the bitter orange tree, helps to treat fine lines and encourages a bright, radiant complexion.

INGREDIENTS
½ tsp cocoa butter
1 tsp calendula oil
1 tsp rosehip seed oil
10g (¼oz) emulsifying wax
2 drops frankincense essential oil
1 drop neroli essential oil

METHOD
1 Heat the cocoa butter, calendula oil, and rosehip oil in a bowl set over a saucepan of boiling water (bain-marie).
2 Gently heat the emulsifier and 30ml (2 tbsp) water in a saucepan until the emulsifier has dissolved. Slowly add this to the cocoa butter and oil mixture, whisking it together for about 10 seconds.
3 When the mixture has cooled, stir in the essential oils.
4 Store in a sterilized dark glass jar (p.194) with a tight-fitting lid in the refrigerator, and use within 2 months.

Cocoa butter and rose body lotion

 MOISTURIZES SKIN

Makes 100ml (3½fl oz)

Antioxidant-rich cocoa butter is deeply nourishing and easily absorbed by the skin. This enriching lotion includes moisturizing, soothing honey and cooling, balancing rose blended with vitamin E rich wheatgerm oil to smooth and soften skin. It has a subtle yet exotic fragrance created by the blend of ylang ylang, benzoin, geranium, and vetiver essential oils.

INGREDIENTS
15g (½oz) cocoa butter
1 tsp lanolin
5 tbsp wheatgerm oil
3 tbsp rose infusion (p.342)
1 tsp honey
25g (scant 1oz) emulsifying wax
5 drops benzoin tincture
5 drops vanilla extract
5 drops ylang ylang essential oil
2 drops rose absolute essential oil
2 drops geranium essential oil
1 drop vetiver essential oil

METHOD
1 Melt the cocoa butter, lanolin, and wheatgerm oil in a bowl set over a pan of boiling water (bain-marie).
2 Make the rose infusion (p.342) and while it is still hot, dissolve the honey and emulsifying wax in it.
3 Add this infusion mixture to the cocoa butter and oil mixture 1 tablespoon at a time, whisking all the while. Then add the benzoin tincture, vanilla extract, and essential oils.
4 Store in a sterilized glass bottle (p.194) with a tight-fitting lid in the refrigerator for up to 3 weeks. Shake before use.

Geranium and orange body butter

 MOISTURIZES SKIN   **HARMONIZES EMOTIONS**

Makes 100g (3½oz)

A rich and deeply nourishing body butter like this is ideal for dry skin. The essential fatty acid combination of grapeseed and almond oils act to enrich and nourish the skin by strengthening and improving its suppleness. Geranium and orange essential oils also help to tone the skin, and impart a bright, sunny scent.

INGREDIENTS
1 tbsp beeswax
3 tbsp calendula macerated oil
4 tsp grapeseed oil
4 tsp almond oil
20 drops geranium essential oil
20 drops orange essential oil

METHOD
1 Heat the beeswax, calendula, grapeseed and almond oils in a bowl set over a saucepan of boiling water (bain-marie). As the mixture cools, stir in the essential oils.
2 Pour into a sterilized dark glass jar (p.194) with a tight-fitting lid, and leave to set. Use within 3 months.

Rose body butter

 MOISTURIZES SKIN   **REVITALIZES**

Makes 100g (3½oz)

If you want a luxurious and gorgeously scented body butter for nurturing the skin, this is the best choice. This aromatic balm features a triple dose of roses – macerated petal oil, rose absolute, and wild rose hip seed oil – to create a nurturing blend that softens, smoothes, and scents the skin. Geranium and patchouli give depth to the fragrance, making it truly special.

INGREDIENTS
1 tbsp beeswax
3 tbsp rose macerated oil
2 tbsp almond oil
2 tsp rosehip oil
10 drops rose absolute essential oil
10 drops geranium essential oil
5 drops patchouli essential oil

METHOD
1 Heat the beeswax, rose, almond, and rosehip oils in a bowl set over a saucepan of boiling water (bain-marie). As the mixture cools, stir in the essential oils.
2 Pour into a sterilized dark glass jar (p.194) with a tight-fitting lid, and leave to set. Use within 3 months.

Lavender body balm

 MOISTURIZES SKIN   **RELAXES**

Makes 100g (3½oz)

In this creamy and rich body balm with a deeply relaxing fragrance, skin-softening coconut oil is blended with gently moisturizing and soothing almond oil to nourish and nurture the skin. Lavender, and its richly scented cousin, lavandin, are both healing and soothing on the skin and are combined here to give a relaxing fragrance.

INGREDIENTS
55g (2oz) coconut oil
2 tbsp almond oil
1 tbsp beeswax
30 drops lavender essential oil
10 drops lavandin essential oil

METHOD
1 Heat the coconut and almond oils with the beeswax in a bowl set over a saucepan of boiling water (bain-marie). As the mixture cools, stir in the essential oils.
2 Pour into a sterilized dark glass jar (p.194) with a tight-fitting lid, and leave to set. Use within 3 months.

Soothing herbal balm

 TREATS BRUISES, GRAZES, AND STINGS

Makes 40g (1½oz)

An all-purpose emergency salve for bumps, bruises, bites, and grazes, this is an essential first aid remedy to keep at home. The therapeutic blend of herbal extracts, including St John's wort, calendula, and gotu kola, are combined with antiseptic myrrh and niaouli oils to help ease all manner of skin irritations and soothe grazes.

INGREDIENTS
4½ tsp calendula
   macerated oil
2 tsp St John's wort (hypericum)
   macerated oil
8g (1½ tsp) beeswax
12 drops myrrh essential oil
12 drops lavender essential oil
4 drops niaouli essential oil
4 drops echinacea tincture
4 drops gotu kola tincture

METHOD
1 Heat the calandula oil and St John's wort oil with the beeswax in a bowl set over a saucepan of boiling water (bain-marie). As the mixture cools, stir in the essential oils and tinctures.
2 Pour into a sterilized dark glass jar (p.194) with a tight-fitting lid, and leave to set. Use within 3 months.

Balancing lemon moisturizer

 MOISTURIZES OILY AND PROBLEM SKIN

Makes 40g (1½oz)

Mineral-rich, anti-inflammatory nettle and cleansing lavender infusions make this light cream an ideal moisturizer for oily or problem skin. The addition of lemon essential oil, which is machine-pressed from the peel of the ripe, fresh fruit and then distilled, has a toning, tightening effect on the pores and helps to regulate the oiliness of the skin.

INGREDIENTS

1 tsp beeswax
1 tsp cocoa butter
3 tbsp grapeseed oil
2 tsp emulsifying wax
2 tbsp lavender and nettle (50:50 mix) infusion (p.342)
10 drops lemon essential oil

METHOD

1 Heat the beeswax, cocoa butter, and grapeseed oil in a bowl set over a saucepan of boiling water (bain-marie).
2 Dissolve the emulsifying wax in the freshly made, and still warm, lavender and nettle infusion.
3 Slowly add the infusion to the oil mixture, using a fast whisking action for about 10 seconds. When the mixture has cooled, stir in the lemon essential oil.
4 Store in a sterilized dark glass jar (p.194) with a tight-fitting lid in the refrigerator, and use within 2 months.

Marshmallow moisturizer

 MOISTURIZES DRY SKIN

Makes 40g (1½oz)

A deeply enriching, nourishing moisturizer suitable for dry skin, this rich blend of cocoa butter and avocado and almond oils ensures that skin will remain supple and well protected from any moisture loss. Marshmallow has a soothing, softening effect, and geranium and bergamot essential oils are toning and refreshing.

INGREDIENTS

1 tsp beeswax
1 tsp cocoa butter
1 tbsp avocado oil
2 tbsp almond oil
2 tsp emulsifying wax
2 tbsp marshmallow infusion (p.342)
4 drops geranium essential oil
5 drops bergamot essential oil

METHOD

1 Heat the beeswax, cocoa butter, avocado, and almond oils in a bowl set over a saucepan of boiling water (bain-marie).
2 Dissolve the emulsifying wax in the freshly made, and still warm, infusion.
3 Slowly add the infusion to the oil mixture, using a fast whisking action for about 10 seconds. When the mixture has cooled, stir in the essential oils.
4 Store in a sterilized dark glass jar (p.194) with a tight-fitting lid in the refrigerator, and use within 2 months.

Rose and geranium moisturizer

 **MOISTURIZES SKIN**

Makes 40g (1½oz)

This is a light moisturizer for normal skin, with a fresh, floral scent. Apricot is a wonderful skin-conditioning oil, and here it is combined with light, easily absorbed grapeseed oil and nourishing cocoa butter to enrich and smooth. Soothing rose and balancing geranium are also included to regulate moisture levels for soft, dewy skin.

INGREDIENTS

1 tsp beeswax
1 tsp cocoa butter
1 tbsp apricot kernel oil
2 tbsp grapeseed oil
2 tsp emulsifying wax
2 tbsp rose petal infusion
10 drops geranium essential oil

METHOD

1 Heat the beeswax, cocoa butter, apricot, and grapeseed oils in a bowl set over a saucepan of boiling water (bain-marie).
2 Dissolve the emulsifying wax in the freshly made, and still warm, infusion.
3 Slowly add the infusion to the oil mixture, using a fast whisking action for about 10 seconds. When the mixture has cooled, stir in the geranium essential oil.
4 Store in a sterilized dark glass jar (p.194) with a tight-fitting lid in the refrigerator, and use within 2 months.

Chamomile and evening primrose moisturizer

 SOOTHES ECZEMA

Makes 100ml (3½fl oz)

A soothing, unscented cream to nurture delicate skin. Starflower and evening primrose seed oils are nature's best sources of gamma-linolenic acid (GLA) and are renowned for helping to soothe dry, itchy, or inflamed skin. Almond and cocoa butter gently moisturize, and chamomile soothes.

INGREDIENTS

1 tsp beeswax
1 tsp cocoa butter
2 tbsp almond oil
1 tsp borage seed oil
2 tsp evening primrose oil
2 tsp emulsifying wax
2 tbsp chamomile infusion (p.342)

METHOD

1 Heat the beeswax and cocoa butter with the almond, borage, and evening primrose oils in a bowl set over a saucepan of boiling water (bain-marie).
2 Dissolve the emulsifying wax in the freshly made, and still warm, chamomile infusion.
3 Slowly add the infusion to the oil mixture, using a fast whisking action for about 10 seconds. Allow to cool.
4 Store in a sterilized dark glass jar (p.194) with a tight-fitting lid in the refrigerator, and use within 2 months.

Minty fresh foot cream

 MOISTURIZES SKIN   **ENERGIZES**

Makes 100g (3½oz)

Tired, aching feet will benefit from this cooling, refreshing foot cream, which includes both peppermint and spearmint (also known as garden mint) for maximum effect. Its soothing effects will alleviate any discomfort after a long day on the move, and also help to keep skin smooth and in good condition. It will keep for at least 2 months.

INGREDIENTS

2 tsp cocoa butter
2 tsp beeswax
2 tbsp almond oil
1 tbsp wheatgerm oil
2 tbsp spearmint infusion (p.342)
2 tsp emulsifying wax
10 drops peppermint essential oil

METHOD

1 Heat the cocoa butter, beeswax, and almond and wheatgerm oils together in a bowl set over a saucepan of boiling water (bain-marie) until the ingredients have melted.
2 Warm the spearmint infusion gently in a saucepan, but do not allow to boil. Dissolve the emulsifying wax in it. Take the oily mixture off the heat, slowly add the infusion, and stir until cool.
3 Add the peppermint essential oil, decant into a sterilized (p.194) glass jar (such as a screw-cap or kilner jar) with a tight-fitting lid and store in the refrigerator.

"This cooling, soothing cream, which includes both peppermint and spearmint for maximum effect, will bring relief to hot, aching feet after a long day"

Rose hand cream

MOISTURIZES SKIN

Makes 85g (3oz)

Fragrant, smoothing, and nourishing, this hand cream is a perfect treat for hard-working hands. It combines restorative cold-pressed seed oil from wild roses (*Rosa canina*) with soothing flower extracts from damask roses (*Rosa* x *damascena*) to revive dry, irritated, or weather-worn skin. It also includes almond oil and cocoa butter for added moisturization.

INGREDIENTS

1½ tsp cocoa butter
1 tsp beeswax
1 tbsp almond oil
1 tbsp rosehip oil
3 tbsp rosewater
2 tsp emulsifying wax
10 drops rose absolute essential oil

METHOD

1 Melt the cocoa butter, beeswax, and almond oil in a bowl set over a saucepan of boiling water (bain marie).
2 Warm the rosewater gently in a saucepan and dissolve the emulsifying wax into it.
3 Stir the rosewater and emulsifying wax into the oily mixture very slowly and continue stirring until the cream cools.
4 Add the rose absolute essential oil and stir.
5 Store in a sterilized glass jar (p.194) with a tight-fitting lid in the refrigerator, and use within 2 months.

Rose (*Rosa x damascena*) *(p.96) It takes around 250 rose heads to produce just 1ml (20 drops) of rose absolute so the essential oil is expensive to buy.*

Frankincense and orange flower hand cream

 **HELPS REDUCE SCARRING**

Makes 85g (3oz)

Nurturing calendula oil is combined with moisturizing cocoa butter and a toning aromatherapy blend of frankincense and orange essential oils in this smoothing, revitalizing cream. A little precious orange flower water added to the blend imparts a beautiful scent and helps to make a wonderfully restorative treatment for dry skin.

INGREDIENTS

1½ tsp cocoa butter
1 tsp beeswax
2 tsp calendula macerated oil
3 tbsp orange flower water
2 tsp emulsifying wax
10 drops orange essential oil
5 drops frankincense essential oil

METHOD

1 Melt the cocoa butter, beeswax, and calendula oil in a bowl set over a saucepan of boiling water (bain-marie).
2 Warm the orange flower water gently and dissolve the emulsifying wax into it.
3 Stir the orange flower water and emulsifying wax into the oily mixture very slowly and continue to stir until the cream cools.
4 Add the orange and frankincense essential oils and stir.
5 Store in a sterilized glass jar (p.194) with a tight-fitting lid in the refrigerator, and use within 2 months.

MAKING BODY SCRUBS

Scrubs boost circulation and smooth the skin, leaving it feeling radiant with a healthy glow. If you have sensitive skin or eczema, this may be exacerbated by scrubbing; the best treatment is a moisturizer or anti-inflammatory cream such as chamomile and evening primrose moisturiser (p.253).

Aloe and elderflower body scrub

 EXFOLIATES

Makes enough for 1 application

Aloe vera is an extremely soothing and cooling plant extract, and is rich in nourishing vitamins, amino acids, enzymes, and proteins. This body scrub combines fresh, thick, mucilaginous aloe vera juice with elderflowers, which have anti-inflammatory qualities, and ground rice to create an exfoliating paste that refreshes and smoothes the skin.

INGREDIENTS
20g (¾oz) dried elderflowers
2 tbsp aloe vera juice
25g (scant 1oz) ground rice
3 drops benzoin tincture
4 tsp organic, plain yoghurt
4 drops lavender essential oil

METHOD
1 Cover the elderflowers with the aloe vera juice and leave for 15 minutes.
2 Add the ground rice and mix thoroughly.
3 Add the benzoin, yoghurt, and lavender essential oil. Apply to the skin using firm, circular hand movements.

Honey and avocado body scrub

 EXFOLIATES

Makes enough for 1 treatment

Excellent for softening areas of dry, rough skin (but not eczema patches), this exfoliating paste can be quickly whipped up for skin-smoothing emergencies. Honey is a natural treat for the skin, with cleansing, soothing properties; when combined with softening avocado, nourishing olive oil, and exfoliating pumice powder, this simple recipe transforms dull, dry skin.

INGREDIENTS

25g (scant 1oz) crushed pumice stone
1 ripe avocado
1 tbsp honey
1 tbsp olive oil
2 drops lemon balm essential oil
  (optional)

METHOD

1 Grind the pumice stone to a fine powder in a pestle and mortar.
2 Mash the avocado in a bowl with a fork.
3 Slightly warm the honey, then add it to the bowl followed by the olive oil (and lemon balm essential oil if using).
4 Stir the mixture well before gradually adding the pumice.
5 Blend carefully, adding enough pumice to enable the mixture to stick together. Use immediately.

Lavender salt scrub

EXFOLIATES

Makes enough for 1 treatment

For the simplest of scrubs, mix salt and oil into a paste for immediate use. By adjusting the texture and amount of salt, you can tailor the texture to suit your preference. Including powdered herbs and essential oils can add a fragrance that suits your mood; this scrub contains lavender, which is both refreshing and relaxing.

INGREDIENTS

2 tbsp sea salt
1 tsp dried lavender flowers
2 tbsp almond oil
2 drops lavender essential oil

METHOD

1 Use a pestle and mortar to grind the sea salt if you want a finer scrub.
2 Grind the lavender flowers to a rough powder in the pestle and mortar.
3 Mix all the ingredients into a paste and use immediately.

Calendula and oat body scrub

 EXFOLIATES

Makes enough for 1 treatment

A simple recipe like this gently cleanses, soothes, and enriches the skin. Oats have long been used for their skin soothing properties, and they create a nurturing wash for dry skin; they are rich in natural polysaccharides, which become gelatinous in water. Here they are combined with soothing calendula and exfoliating bran to cleanse and smooth the skin.

INGREDIENTS
45g (1½oz) oats
20g (¾oz) bran
15g (½oz) calendula flowers

METHOD
1 Place the oats, bran, and flowers in a muslin bag, tie firmly at the top with string, and use the ends of the string to hang it from the tap so the bath water runs through it.
2 When you are in the bath, rub your skin with the bag, especially on any areas of dry skin.

Honey and orange body scrub

 EXFOLIATES

Makes approx 50g (1¾oz)

Suitable for all skin types, this is an enriching scrub to effectively exfoliate and cleanse the skin. Ground rice provides the exfoliating action, clay is included to draw impurities from the skin, and honey moisturizes and smoothes. Geranium and orange essential oils have a toning effect and also impart a bright, sunny fragrance.

INGREDIENTS
1 tbsp kaolin powder
2 tbsp ground rice
1 tsp orange flower water
1 tbsp clear honey
5 drops calendula tincture
2 drops orange essential oil
1 drop geranium essential oil

METHOD
1 Grind the kaolin and ground rice together in a pestle and mortar to create a fine powder.
2 Add the orange flower water and slightly warmed honey (warming makes the honey easier to blend) to the powder mixture and mix thoroughly with the tincture and essential oils. Decant into a sterilized glass jar (p.194) with a tight-fitting lid.
3 To use, mix the scrub with a little warm water to form a paste and apply to damp skin with a circular motion. Rinse with warm water. Use within 2 months.

Cleansing chamomile hand scrub

 EXFOLIATES

Makes 1 x 40g (1½oz) jar

Use this gentle hand cleanser as an alternative to soap. With its gently exfoliating action, enriching oats to soften and smooth, and glycerin to reduce moisture loss from the skin it both cleans and cares for hard-working hands. Chamomile flower water, which is naturally nurturing, has also been included to bring extra relief and soothe the skin.

INGREDIENTS
2 tbsp vegetable glycerin
15g (½oz) cornflour
1 tsp chamomile flower water
  (or infusion)
2 tsp ground rice
2 tsp finely ground oats

METHOD
1 Warm the vegetable glycerin in a bowl set over a saucepan of hot or boiling water (bain marie).
2 Slowly add the cornflour, stirring constantly to make a paste.
3 Take off the heat and gradually add the chamomile water, still stirring. Mix in the ground rice and oats.
4 Store in a sterilized glass jar (p.194) with a tight-fitting lid and use in the same way as liquid soap. Use within 2 months.

Mandarin and myrrh foot scrub

 EXFOLIATES

Makes 1 x 40g (1½oz) jar

Foot scrubs effectively smooth away hard skin and cleanse and nourish feet to leave them feeling soft and fresh. In this scrub pumice powder effectively removes rough skin and boosts circulation, while a blend of skin-softening marshmallow herb, deeply moisturising cocoa butter, enriching apricot kernel oil, and cleansing mandarin and myrrh essential oils nourish the skin.

INGREDIENTS

15g (½oz) crushed pumice stone
10g (¼oz) cocoa butter
10g (¼oz) beeswax
3 tbsp apricot kernel oil
10g (¼oz) emulsifying wax
2 tbsp marshmallow
  infusion (p.342)
12 drops myrrh essential oil
8 drops mandarin essential oil

METHOD

1 Grind the pumice stone in a pestle and mortar to a fine powder.
2 Warm the cocoa butter, beeswax, and apricot kernel oil together in a bowl set over a saucepan of boiling water (bain-marie) until all the ingredients have melted. Then remove from the heat.
3 Dissolve the emulsifying wax in the freshly made, and still warm, marshmallow infusion. Slowly add the infusion to the oily mixture and stir until cool.
4 Add the pumice stone and essential oils and mix thoroughly.
5 Store in a sterilized dark glass jar (p.194) with a tight-fitting lid in the refrigerator, and use within 3 months.

Marshmallow (Althaea officinalis)
(p.23) The leaves of the marshmallow plant are typically used dried for infusions, ointments, and liquid extracts.

MAKING BODY OILS

Whether used for massages or to condition the skin, enriching, nourishing, and moisturizing body oils are a real treat. If you have very sensitive skin, test any skincare product on a small area of skin first to check that it does not provoke a reaction.

Lavender and bergamot soothing skin oil

 MOISTURIZES SKIN   **RELAXES**

Makes 100ml (3½fl oz)

A relaxing aromatherapy mix of floral geranium, soothing lavender, calming cypress, and fresh, uplifting bergamot is blended into a skin-nourishing base of different vegetable oils to help restore your skin's suppleness and give it maximum protection from moisture loss. This skin oil will keep for up to 6 months.

INGREDIENTS

4 tsp almond oil
4 tsp sunflower oil
4 tsp coconut oil
4 tsp grapeseed oil
2 tsp avocado oil
2 tsp wheatgerm oil
10 drops geranium essential oil
10 drops bergamot essential oil
10 drops lavender essential oil
10 drops cypress essential oil

METHOD

Blend the base oils with the essential oils. Store in a sterilized dark glass bottle (p.194) with a tight-fitting lid away from sunlight.

Stimulating body oil

 MOISTURIZES SKIN   **ENERGIZES**

Makes approx 100ml (3½fl oz)

The wonderfully enriching base of plant oils in this body oil is rich in natural essential fatty acids, minerals, and vitamins to restore suppleness and elasticity to the skin. A stimulating aromatherapy blend of peppermint, juniper, lavender, and rosemary also boosts the circulation and invigorates the senses.

INGREDIENTS

4 tsp almond oil
4 tsp sunflower oil
4 tsp coconut oil
4 tsp grapeseed oil
2 tsp avocado oil
2 tsp wheatgerm oil
10 drops lavender essential oil
10 drops peppermint essential oil
10 drops juniper essential oil
10 drops rosemary essential oil

METHOD

1 Blend all the ingredients together.
2 Store in a sterilized dark glass bottle (p.194) with a tight-fitting lid and use within 3 months.

Geranium and orange body oil

 MOISTURIZES SKIN   **REVITALIZES**

Makes approx 100ml (3½fl oz)

This enriching body oil treats both body and mind to bring a deep sense of well-being. It is an excellent all-purpose skin-conditioning or massage oil, with a bright, sunny scent. Geranium essential oil has a balancing effect on the skin and is used by aromatherapists to help treat anxiety and tension, while orange essential oil is toning and refreshing.

INGREDIENTS

2½ tbsp almond oil
2½ tbsp sunflower oil
4 tsp calendula macerated oil
20 drops geranium essential oil
20 drops orange essential oil

METHOD

1 Blend all the ingredients together.
2 Store in a sterilized dark glass bottle (p.194) with a tight-fitting lid and use within 3 months.

Detox body oil

 MOISTURIZES SKIN　　 **STIMULATES CIRCULATION**

Makes approx 100ml (3½fl oz)

A stimulating and detoxifying blend of oils like this can help to boost the circulation and strengthen and tone the skin for a smoother appearance. For the best results, try dry-skin brushing your body with a natural bristle brush before having a warm bath or shower, then massage the body oil into your skin.

INGREDIENTS

2½ tbsp soya oil
2½ tbsp almond oil
4 tsp wheatgerm oil
5 drops lemon essential oil
5 drops frankincense essential oil
5 drops orange essential oil
2 drops juniper essential oil
2 drops black pepper essential oil
2 drops vetiver essential oil
2 drops eucalyptus essential oil

METHOD

1 Blend all the ingredients together.
2 Store in a sterilized dark glass bottle (p.194) with a tight-fitting lid and use within 3 months.

Calendula and St John's wort soothing oil

 SOOTHES SUNBURN AND SHINGLES

Makes enough for 1 treatment

Always try to protect your skin from overexposure to the sun, but if you do accidentally get sunburnt, use this soothing oil to ease the discomfort. Do not apply before any exposure to the sun, as St John's wort is known to be photosensitizing. This oil blend can also be applied to relieve the pain of shingles.

INGREDIENTS

1 tsp calendula oil
1 tsp St John's wort oil
2 drops lavender essential oil

METHOD

Blend the ingredients together and gently apply to the skin.

Lemon (Citrus limon)
As well as cleansing and toning the skin, lemon essential oil also encourages mental focus.

Sesame and soya skin oil

 NOURISHES SKIN

Makes approx 100ml (3½fl oz)

If you are going on holiday, take this deeply nourishing skin oil to restore suppleness to your skin if it becomes dehydrated by the sun and sea. Sesame is rich in antioxidant vitamin E, coconut replenishes moisture, and grapeseed and soya feed the skin with nourishing essential fatty acids. Toning petitgrain essential oil has a clean, refreshing scent.

INGREDIENTS

2½ tbsp soya oil
2½ tbsp sesame oil
2½ tbsp coconut oil
4 tsp grapeseed oil
40 drops petitgrain essential oil
5 drops lavender essential oil

METHOD

1 Blend all the ingredients together.
2 Store in a sterilized dark glass bottle (p.194) with a tight-fitting lid and use within 3 months.

Coconut and lime skin oil

 NOURISHES SKIN

Makes approx 60ml (2fl oz)

Easily absorbed, skin-softening coconut oil is combined with deeply moisturizing cocoa butter and nourishing vitamin E-rich wheatgerm oil in this blend to restore radiance to dull, dry skin. A few drops of lime essential oil give the oil a refreshing, uplifting aroma. Apply in the evening to nourish the skin overnight.

INGREDIENTS

2 tsp wheatgerm oil
20g (¾oz) cocoa butter
3½ tbsp coconut oil
10 drops lime essential oil
5 drops benzoin tincture

METHOD

1 Blend all the ingredients together in a bowl (if necessary, gently warm the cocoa butter and coconut oil over a bain-marie first to liquify and aid blending).
2 Store in a sterilized dark glass bottle (p.194) with a tight-fitting lid and use within 3 months.

Baby massage oil

 **SUITABLE FOR BABY'S SKIN**   **RELAXES**

Makes approx 100ml (3½fl oz)

Suitable for use from 3 months, this is a gentle, soothing oil for delicate skin. Rose absolute, lavender, and Roman chamomile essential oils, which are renowned for their soothing and skin-conditioning properties, are combined with a base of gentle sunflower and calendula oils to give a mild and soothing skin oil that is excellent for babies or anyone with sensitive skin.

INGREDIENTS
5½ tbsp sunflower oil
4 tsp calendula macerated oil
8 drops lavender essential oil
6 drops Roman chamomile
   essential oil
6 drops rose absolute essential oil

METHOD
1 Combine all the ingredients and massage into a baby's skin.
2 Store in a sterilized dark glass bottle (p.194) with a tight-fitting lid and use within 3 months.

Baby bath oil

SUITABLE FOR BABY'S SKIN   **RELAXES**

Makes approx 100ml (3½fl oz)

Gently nourishing sunflower and calendula oils form a soothing base for this simple bath oil that moisturizes dry or delicate skin with a calming, comforting scent. Mandarin oil, which is expressed from the peel of the fruit, is excellent for children, as its sweet, citrus fragrance is calming and has a soothing effect. Suitable for use from 3 months.

INGREDIENTS
5½ tbsp sunflower oil
4 tsp calendula macerated oil
10 drops mandarin essential oil

METHOD
1 Combine the sunflower, calendula, and mandarin oils together. Use 2 tsp of blend per bath.
2 Store in a sterilized dark glass bottle (p.194) with a tight-fitting lid and use within 3 months.

MAKING BODY SPRITZES

Creating your own fragrant body splashes with essential oils and herbal blends is a simple way of keeping your skin fresh and enhancing your sense of well-being. If you have very sensitive skin, test any skin product on a small area of skin first to check that it does not provoke a reaction.

Spicy witch hazel deodorant

 **DEODORIZES**

Makes 100ml (3½fl oz)

This fresh, fragrant-smelling underarm spray is ideal if you wish to avoid products containing aluminium derivatives. Witch hazel is gently astringent and acts as a perfect base for an antibacterial blend of essential oils. Spray the deodorant on to clean, dry skin after bathing and reapply as often as required. It can also be used to freshen feet. Use within 6 months.

INGREDIENTS
90ml (3fl oz) witch hazel
2 tsp vegetable glycerin
2 drops clove essential oil
2 drops coriander essential oil
5 drops grapefruit essential oil
2 drops lavender essential oil
10 drops lemon essential oil
5 drops lime essential oil
5 drops palmarosa essential oil

METHOD
1 Mix the witch hazel and vegetable glycerin together.
2 Add the essential oils, and mix well.
3 Store in a sterilized dark glass bottle (p.194), preferably with an atomizer spray. Shake well before use to ensure the ingredients are well blended.

Witch hazel (Hamamelis virginiana)
(p.63) The "witch" in witch hazel is derived from the Old English word wice, meaning "pliant" or "bendable".

Bergamot and mint deodorant

 DEODORIZES

Makes approx 85ml (2¾fl oz)

A refreshing combination of witch hazel and lavender water are the main ingredients for this fragrant underarm body spray, which keeps skin fresh. It also contains a cleansing, antibacterial blend of essential oils that includes citrussy bergamot, grapefruit, and lemon and invigorating peppermint and woody cypress. Spray on clean, dry skin. May also be used on the feet.

INGREDIENTS

1 tsp vegetable glycerin
2½ tbsp witch hazel
2½ tbsp lavender water
10 drops bergamot essential oil
8 drops grapefruit essential oil
7 drops lemon essential oil
4 drops peppermint essential oil
1 drop cypress essential oil

METHOD

1 Combine the vegetable glycerin with the witch hazel.
2 Stir in the essential oils.
3 Store in a sterilized dark glass bottle (p.194) with a fine mist atomizer. Shake well before use to ensure the ingredients are well blended. Use within 6 months.

Geranium and orange body splash

 REVITALIZES

Makes approx 95ml (3¼fl oz)

With its bright, sunny fragrance, this body spray refreshes the skin, lifts the spirits, and leaves the skin lightly scented. Aloe vera, which makes a cooling, soothing base, is combined with earthy vetiver and brightly scented geranium oils and delicately scented orange flower water, made from the blossom of the bitter orange tree.

INGREDIENTS

80ml (2¾fl oz) distilled water
2 tsp aloe vera juice
1 tsp orange flower water
2 drops patchouli essential oil
1 drop geranium essential oil

METHOD

1 Combine all the ingredients.
2 Store in a sterilized dark glass bottle (p.194) with a fine mist atomizer. Shake well before use to ensure the ingredients are well blended. Use within 2 months.

Geranium (Pelargonium graveolens)
*Geranium is used in aromatherapy
to treat the skin, and as a remedy to
alleviate tiredness and fatigue.*

Citronella spray

 PROTECTS AGAINST INSECT BITES

Makes approx 25ml (5 tsp)

The two essential oils in this insect repellent spray are distilled from citronella grass and the leaves of *Eucalyptus citriodora*, the Australian lemon-scented gum tree. Both oils have a sharp, citrus scent and are scientifically proven to keep mosquitoes at bay. Apply this fragrant mist every two hours on exposed skin.

INGREDIENTS
5 tsp lavender flower water
3 drops *Eucalyptus citriodora* essential oil
2 drops citronella essential oil

METHOD
1 Combine the lavender water and essential oils.
2 Store in a sterilized dark glass bottle (p.194) with a fine mist atomizer. Shake before use to ensure the ingredients are well blended. Use within 6 months.

After-bite soother

SOOTHES

Makes approx 30ml (2 tbsp)

Witch hazel, yarrow, and plantain all have anti-inflammatory and styptic properties; when combined with soothing calendula, cooling aloe vera, and a cleansing blend of lavender and tea tree essential oils, they become a handy herbal extract spray that will bring immediate relief from the irritation and pain of bites and stings.

INGREDIENTS
4 tsp with hazel
1 tsp aloe vera juice
1.5ml (30 drops) plantain tincture
1.5ml (30 drops) calendula tincture
1.5ml (30 drops) yarrow tincture
24 drops lavender essential oil
6 drops tea tree essential oil

METHOD
1 Combine all the ingredients.
2 Store in a sterilized dark glass bottle (p.194) with a fine mist atomizer. Shake before use to ensure the ingredients are well blended. Use within 6 months.

Rose body splash

 STIMULATES THE SENSES

Makes approx 95ml (3¼fl oz)

This subtle, floral body splash features a luxurious blend of damask rose flower water and earthy patchouli and bright geranium essential oils. Aloe vera and rose water are both gentle, soothing, and cooling – a perfect combination to pep up tired skin. For extra refreshment in hot weather, store the bottle in the refrigerator in between each use.

INGREDIENTS
75ml (2½fl oz) distilled water
2 tsp aloe vera juice
2 tsp rose flower water
3 drops rose absolute essential oil
3 drops geranium essential oil
1 drop patchouli essential oil

METHOD
1 Combine all the ingredients.
2 Store in a sterilized dark glass bottle (p.194) with a fine mist atomizer. Shake before use to ensure the ingredients are well blended. Use within 2 months.

Frankincense body splash

 ENERGIZES

Makes approx 95ml (3¼fl oz)

Frankincense essential oil, which is distilled from the resin of the tree, is gently astringent and has a toning effect on the skin. Combined with fresh citrus oils of mandarin and bergamot orange, it creates a subtly scented blend that has cleansing and revitalising properties and will refresh all skin types.

INGREDIENTS
5½ tbsp distilled water
2 tsp aloe vera juice
1 tsp lavender flower water
4 drops frankincense essential oil
2 drops mandarin essential oil
2 drops bergamot essential oil

METHOD
1 Combine all the ingredients.
2 Store in a sterilized dark glass bottle (p.194) with a fine mist atomizer. Shake before use. Use within 2 months.

Aloe vera (Aloe barbadensis)
(p.20) The gel from this plant is extremely soothing and is rich in vitamins, enzymes, amino acids, and proteins.

MAKING BODY POWDERS

Body powders help to keep the skin soft, smooth, and silky. Essential oils can be added to the powder base to give a subtle fragrance to the skin. If you have very sensitive skin, test any skin product on a small area of skin first to check that it does not provoke a reaction.

Calendula body powder

 SOOTHES SKIN

Makes 20g (¾oz)

A soothing talc-free body powder such as this is perfect for delicate or sensitive skin, for keeping skin dry in hot or humid weather, or for soothing and protecting areas of skin that are prone to chafing or rubbing. Apply to clean, dry skin after bathing using cotton wool balls, or just sprinkle the powder on your body and lightly smooth it over the skin. It will keep for up to 6 months.

INGREDIENTS
20g (¾oz) kaolin powder
5 drops calendula tincture
5 drops lemon essential oil

METHOD
1 Sift the kaolin evenly on to a plate. Mix the tincture and essential oil and spray them on to the kaolin using an atomizer pump. Allow the powder to dry.
2 Store in an old, clean body powder dispenser or clean pepper shaker.

"Try one of these fragrant home-made body powder recipes as a treat after a relaxing aromatherapy bath"

Lavender and tea tree powder

 **SOOTHES SKIN**

Makes approx 20g (¾oz)

A cleansing, talc-free, lightly scented body powder such as this is ideal for use before and after sports or strenuous activity to keep skin fresh and to protect against chafing. Apply after bathing to freshly dried skin. Use cotton balls to apply the powder, or just sprinkle it on your body and lightly smooth it over the skin.

INGREDIENTS
20g (¾oz) cornflour
1ml (20 drops) propolis tincture
5 drops lavender essential oil
5 drops tea tree essential oil

METHOD
1 Sift the cornflour evenly onto a wide, flat plate.
2 Mix the propolis tincture and essential oils together and decant into a clean container with a fine mist atomizer.
3 Spray this mix onto the cornflour, taking care to spray evenly and not to saturate the powder, which may cause lumps. Allow the powder to dry.
4 Store the dry powder in an old, clean body powder dispenser or clean pepper shaker. Use within 6 months.

Rose body powder

 **SOOTHES SKIN**

Makes approx 20g (¾oz)

This fragrant, talc-free, floral body powder includes soothing, cooling rose to smooth the skin. Geranium complements and strengthens the scent of rose, while earthy patchouli gives lasting depth. Apply after bathing to freshly dried skin. Use cotton balls to apply the powder, or just sprinkle it on your body and lightly smooth it over the skin.

INGREDIENTS

20g (¾oz) cornflour
5 drops rose absolute essential oil
4 drops geranium essential oil
1 drop patchouli essential oil

METHOD

1 Sift the cornflour evenly onto a wide flat plate.
2 Mix the essential oils together and decant into a clean container with a fine mist atomizer.
3 Spray this mix onto the cornflour, taking care to spray evenly and not to saturate the powder, which may cause lumps.
4 Allow the powder to dry and store in an old, clean body powder dispenser or clean pepper shaker. Use within 6 months.

Blackcurrant and sage foot powder

 DEODORIZES

Makes approx 15g (½oz)

This is a cleansing powder to help keep feet dry and fresh. Sage is known for its cool, drying character and blackcurrant for its astringent properties. Lightly dust the powder over the feet after cleaning and drying them, then rub the powder gently into the skin. It can also be sprinkled into your footwear for added protection.

INGREDIENTS
1 tbsp dried sage
2 tbsp dried blackcurrant leaves
10g (¼oz) kaolin powder
5 drops lemon essential oil

METHOD
1 Grind the dried herbs together in a pestle and mortar to a fine powder.
2 Add the kaolin and mix thoroughly, then add the lemon essential oil and mix again. Allow the powder to dry.
3 Store the powder in an old (clean) body powder dispenser or (clean) pepper shaker. Use within 2 months.

Blackcurrant (Ribes nigrum) (p.94)
The leaves of the blackcurrant bush have useful cleansing properties, and were traditionally used in gargle recipes.

Baby powder

**SUITABLE FOR
BABY'S SKIN**

Makes approx 20g (¾oz)

A light, fine powder such as this is designed to soothe and dry a baby's delicate skin. It is so mild and gentle that it is suitable for even newborn babies: Roman chamomile, which has soothing and anti-inflammatory properties, and propolis, a natural antiseptic, are mixed into a base of smoothing cornflour. Always keep powder away from a baby's mouth and nose.

INGREDIENTS

3 tsp cornflour
5 drops propolis tincture
2 drops Roman chamomile
  essential oil

METHOD

1 Sift the cornflour evenly onto a wide flat plate.
2 Mix the propolis tincture and Roman chamomile essential oil together and decant into a clean container with a fine mist atomiser.
3 Spray this mix onto the cornflour, taking care to spray evenly and not to saturate the powder, which may cause lumps.
4 Allow to dry and then store in an old (clean) body powder dispenser or (clean) pepper shaker. Use within 6 months.

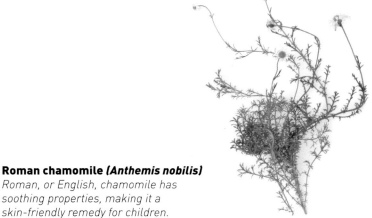

Roman chamomile (Anthemis nobilis)
Roman, or English, chamomile has soothing properties, making it a skin-friendly remedy for children.

MAKING SOAPS

Soap-making is fun, and soaps make lovely gifts. With careful preparation you can make your own soaps, but read the safety information on page 343 first and follow the instructions closely. It is worth noting that the cheapest olive oil makes better soap. Store the soaps in an airtight container.

Rosemary gardener's soap

 **CLEANSES SKIN**   **REVITALIZES**

INGREDIENTS

300ml (½ pint) cheap olive oil
175ml (6½fl oz) coconut oil
120ml (4fl oz) cooled, boiled,
  or distilled water
60g (2oz) caustic soda (lye crystals)
1 tbsp green clay
4 crushed spirulina tablets
1 tbsp bran or oatmeal
30 drops rosemary essential oil

Makes 16 bars

Fresh, scented rosemary adds to the cleansing properties of this soap, which also contains gently exfoliating oatmeal to smooth roughened hands. Spirulina and green clay lend colour. Sprinkle a few dried rosemary flowers on top of the soap when it is semi-set as a decoration, if you wish.

1 Mix the olive and coconut oils in a saucepan with a whisk over a low heat until the temperature reaches 60°C (140°F). To make the lye mix, pour the water into a stainless steel or glass bowl placed in a sink in case the contents froth over when you add the caustic soda. Wearing protective goggles, gloves, and an apron, add the soda to the water and mix with a wooden spoon until the crystals have dissolved. Leave to cool.

2 Add the cooled lye mix to the hot oils in the saucepan and stir with a wooden spoon until well mixed. Then beat with a metal whisk for about 20 seconds. The consistency should now be similar to that of thick custard so that a line is visible if drawn on its surface. Stir in the green clay, crushed spirulina tablets, bran or oatmeal, and rosemary essential oil.

3 Pour the mix into a 23cm (9in) square stainless steel dish 5cm (2in) deep and greased with olive oil. Cover with a cloth and leave for 24 hours. While still soft, remove the soap wearing plastic gloves, and cut into bars using a cheese wire or knife. Arrange on trays and leave to dry out fully and harden; this will take several weeks. Check the pH of the finished soap before using (it should be around 10–10.5).

Calendula and chamomile soap

 **CLEANSES SKIN**

Makes 16 bars

Soothing calendula (marigold) and chamomile are combined with gentle evening primrose oil in this mild soap bar for delicate skin. Try adding a few flowers to the top of the soap when it is semi-set, if you wish, for a decorative touch. Read the safety information on page 343 carefully before you start, and follow the instructions closely.

INGREDIENTS

300ml (½ pint) cheap olive oil
175ml (6½fl oz) coconut oil
120ml (4fl oz) cooled, boiled, or
  distilled water
60g (2oz) caustic soda (lye crystals)
2 tsp calendula macerated oil
1 tsp evening primrose oil
25 drops chamomile essential oil
10 drops lavender essential oil

METHOD

1 Measure out the olive and coconut oils into a saucepan and place the pan over a low heat. Heat the mix, stirring with a whisk, until the temperature reaches 60°C (140°F).

2 To make the lye mixture, pour the water into a glass or stainless steel bowl, then place the bowl in a sink in case the contents froth over when the caustic soda is added. Wearing protective goggles, gloves, and an apron, add the caustic soda to the water and mix with a wooden spoon until the crystals have dissolved (always add the caustic soda to the water rather than the other way round). Leave to cool.

3 Add the cooled lye mixture to the hot oils in the saucepan and stir with a wooden spoon until well mixed. Then beat with a metal whisk for about 20 seconds. The consistency should now be similar to that of thick custard so that a line is visible if drawn on its surface. Stir in the essential oils to fragrance the soap. Pour the mixture into a 23cm (9in) square stainless steel dish at least 5cm (2in) deep and greased with olive oil, cover with a cloth, and leave to set for 24 hours.

4 While still soft enough to cut, remove the soap wearing plastic gloves and cut into bars using a cheese wire or knife. Arrange the bars on trays and leave to dry out fully and harden; this will take several weeks. During this time the pH value of the soap will drop, becoming more neutral and therefore milder. You may find that a whitish residue appears on the surface; this can be scraped off if you prefer. The soap will continue to dry out for several months depending on the weather, but the reduction of the pH value will slow and remain stable after a few weeks. Check the pH of the finished soap before using (it should be around 10–10.5).

Neem cleansing soap

 **CLEANSES SKIN**

Makes 16 bars

Neem has a long history of use in India and Africa for its cleansing properties. Here, antiseptic propolis, which is used by bees to protect their hives, has been added, as well as cleansing lavender and tea tree essential oils. Try adding a few lavender flowers to the soap when it is semi-set, if you wish. Read the safety information on page 343 carefully before you start.

INGREDIENTS

300ml (½ pint) cheap olive oil
175ml (6½fl oz) coconut oil
120ml (4½fl oz) cooled, boiled, or
    distilled water
60g (2oz) caustic soda (lye crystals)
1 tsp neem oil
5 drops propolis tincture
40 drops lavender essential oil
30 drops tea tree essential oil

METHOD

1 Measure out the olive and coconut oils into a saucepan and place the pan over a low heat. Heat the mix, stirring with a whisk, until the temperature reaches 60°C (140°F).

2 To make the lye mixture, pour the water into a glass or stainless steel bowl, then place the bowl in a sink in case the contents froth over when the caustic soda is added. Wearing protective goggles, gloves, and an apron, add the caustic soda to the water and mix with a wooden spoon until the crystals have dissolved (always add the caustic soda to the water rather than the other way round). Leave to cool.

3 Add the cooled lye mixture to the oils in the saucepan and stir with a wooden spoon until well mixed. Then beat with a metal whisk for about 20 seconds. The consistency should now be similar to that of thick custard so that a line is visible if drawn on its surface. Stir in the neem oil, propolis tincture, and essential oils to fragrance the soap. Pour the mixture into a 23cm (9in) square stainless steel dish at least 5cm (2in) deep and greased with olive oil, cover with a cloth, and leave to set for 24 hours.

4 While still soft enough to cut, remove the soap wearing plastic gloves and cut into bars using a cheese wire or knife. Arrange the bars on trays and leave to dry out fully and harden; this will take several weeks. During this time the pH value of the soap will drop, becoming more neutral and therefore milder. You may find that a whitish residue appears on the surface; this can be scraped off if you prefer. The soap will continue to dry out for several months depending on the weather, but the reduction of the pH value will slow and remain stable after a few weeks. Check the pH of the finished soap before using (it should be around 10–10.5).

Relaxation soap

 CLEANSES SKIN　　 **RELAXES**

Makes 16 bars

This delightful soap has a fragrant, aromatherapeutic combination of essential oils to help ease the cares of the day. Rose creates a relaxed sense of well-being, marjoram is warming and comforting, and lavender helps the mind to unwind and restores a sense of balance. Read the safety information on page 343 carefully before you start.

INGREDIENTS

300ml (½ pint) cheap olive oil
175ml (6½fl oz) coconut oil
120ml (4fl oz) cooled, boiled, or
  distilled water
60g (2oz) caustic soda (lye crystals)
2 tsp almond oil
10 drops lavender essential oil
10 drops rose absolute essential oil
5 drops marjoram essential oil

METHOD

1 Measure out the olive and coconut oils into a saucepan and place the pan over a low heat. Heat the mix, stirring with a whisk, until the temperature reaches 60°C (140°F).

2 To make the lye mixture, pour the water into a glass or stainless steel bowl, then place the bowl in a sink in case the contents froth over when the caustic soda is added. Wearing protective goggles, gloves, and an apron, add the caustic soda to the water and mix with a wooden spoon until the crystals have dissolved (always add the caustic soda to the water rather than the other way round). Leave to cool.

3 Add the cooled lye mixture to the hot oils in the saucepan and stir with a wooden spoon until well mixed. Then beat with a metal whisk for about 20 seconds. The consistency should now be similar to that of thick custard so that a line is visible if drawn on its surface. Stir in the essential oils to fragrance the soap. Pour the mixture into a 23cm (9in) square stainless steel dish at least 5cm (2in) deep and greased with olive oil, cover with a cloth, and leave to set for 24 hours.

4 While still soft enough to cut, remove the soap wearing plastic gloves and cut into bars using a cheese wire or knife. Arrange the bars on trays and leave to dry out fully and harden; this will take several weeks. During this time the pH value of the soap will drop, becoming more neutral and therefore milder. You may find that a whitish residue appears on the surface; this can be scraped off if you prefer. The soap will continue to dry out for several months depending on the weather, but the reduction of the pH value will slow and remain stable after a few weeks. Check the pH of the finished soap before using (it should be around 10–10.5).

Exotic soap

 **CLEANSES SKIN**　　　**STIMULATES THE SENSES**

Makes 16 bars

Ylang ylang essential oil is distilled from the flowers of the cananga tree (*Cananga odorata*), a member of the custard apple family native to the Philippines and Indonesia. The fragrant oil is combined here with rose, geranium, and clary sage to make a delicately aromatic and skin-smoothing soap. Read the safety information on page 343 carefully before you start.

INGREDIENTS

300ml (½ pint) cheap olive oil
175ml (6½fl oz) coconut oil
120ml (4½fl oz) cooled, boiled, or
　distilled water
60g (2oz) caustic soda (lye crystals)
2 tsp avocado oil
12 drops ylang-ylang essential oil
12 drops geranium essential oil
12 drops clary sage essential oil
5 drops rose absolute essential oil
1 tsp vanilla extract

METHOD

1 Measure out the olive and coconut oils into a saucepan and place the pan over a low heat. Heat the mix, stirring with a whisk, until the temperature reaches 60°C (140°F).

2 To make the lye mixture, pour the water into a glass or stainless steel bowl, then place the bowl in a sink in case the contents froth over when the caustic soda is added. Wearing protective goggles, gloves, and an apron, add the caustic soda to the water and mix with a wooden spoon until the crystals have dissolved (always add the caustic soda to the water rather than the other way round). Leave to cool.

3 Add the cooled lye mixture to the hot oils in the saucepan and stir with a wooden spoon until well mixed. Then beat with a metal whisk for about 20 seconds. The consistency should now be similar to that of thick custard so that a line is visible if drawn on its surface. Stir in the essential oils to fragrance the soap. Pour the mixture into a 23cm (9in) square stainless steel dish at least 5cm (2in) deep and greased with olive oil, cover with a cloth, and leave to set for 24 hours.

4 While still soft enough to cut, remove the soap wearing plastic gloves and cut into bars using a cheese wire or knife. Arrange the bars on trays and leave to dry out fully and harden; this will take several weeks. During this time the pH value of the soap will drop, becoming more neutral and therefore milder. You may find that a whitish residue appears on the surface; this can be scraped off if you prefer. The soap will continue to dry out for several months depending on the weather, but the reduction of the pH value will slow and remain stable after a few weeks. Check the pH of the finished soap before using (it should be around 10–10.5).

MAKING CLEANSERS

A cleansing routine is essential to support and maintain healthy skin, especially if you live or work in an urban environment with higher levels of pollution. If you have very sensitive skin, test any skin product on a small area of skin first to check that it does not provoke a reaction.

Soothing lavender cleanser

 CLEANSES SKIN

Makes 60ml (2fl oz)

This is a simple cleanser for sensitive or dry skin. Oats have long been used for their skin-soothing properties, as they are rich in natural polysaccharides that become glutinous in water to create a nurturing wash for delicate skin. Almond oil also soothes and enriches skin, helping to prevent moisture loss, while lavender soothes the skin and adds a gentle fragrance.

INGREDIENTS
25g (scant 1oz) organic oats
a little mineral water
1 egg yolk
3½ tbsp almond oil
5 drops lavender essential oil

METHOD
1 Put the oats in a bowl, pour on enough mineral water to cover, and leave to soak for at least 1 hour.
2 Whisk the egg yolk in a blender or food processor, adding a drop of almond oil at a time. The mixture should be a thick emulsion when all the oil has been added. Add the lavender essential oil, adding a drop at a time so it blends in well.
3 Strain the oats, squeezing all the liquid (oatmilk) into a bowl. Reserve the oatmilk, but discard the oats. Add the oatmilk slowly to the egg mixture, stirring or blending it in gently so that it thins to the consistency of a lotion.
4 Store in a sterilized glass bottle (p.194) with a tight-fitting lid. Refrigerate and use within 3 days.

Honey and rose petal face scrub

 EXFOLIATES

Makes enough for 1 application

Honey is one of nature's best skin treatments. It softens, soothes, and protects the skin from moisture loss, as well as acting as a lubricant. Rose oil, with its cooling and tonifying properties, and lavender oil, which freshens, and purifies, are also added to this gently exfoliating scrub to help condition and balance the skin and give you a feeling of relaxed well-being.

INGREDIENTS

25g (scant 1oz) dried
  rose petals
2 tbsp dried lavender flowers
1 drop lavender essential oil
1 drop rose essential oil
2 tsp clear honey

METHOD

1 Make an infusion (p.342) using half the rose petals and a cupful of boiling water. Cover and leave to one side.
2 Using a pestle and mortar, grind the remaining rose petals and the lavender flowers until they are of a powdery consistency. Combine the powdered herbs with the essential oils and honey, and add enough rose infusion for the mixture to form a soft paste.
3 To use, apply to the face and gently rub in a circular motion to cleanse the skin.

Elderflower and aloe vera facial polish

 EXFOLIATES

Makes enough for 1 treatment

Elderflower is mildly astringent and its anti-inflammatory and emollient properties mean that it has long been beneficial for skin. Combined with cooling aloe vera and soothing chamomile, this gentle, refreshing facial polish is suitable for all skin types. As it contains fresh dairy ingredients, this polish is for immediate use.

INGREDIENTS

25g (scant 1oz) elderflower or
  10 elderflower teabags
25g (scant 1oz) chamomile
  or 10 chamomile teabags
2 tsp aloe vera juice
2 tbsp plain yoghurt

METHOD

1 Make an infusion using 240ml (8fl oz) of boiling water and half the herbs. Cover and leave to one side.

2 Grind the rest of the herbs to a fine powder using a pestle and mortar. If using tea bags, the herbs will already be chopped to a fine powder so they are ready to use.

3 Mix the herbs, aloe vera, and yoghurt, then add the infusion a teaspoon at a time, stirring as you go, until it makes a thin paste (but thick enough not to run off your skin).

4 Apply to the face after cleansing; be sure to avoid the area directly around the eyes and mouth. To exfoliate, gently massage the paste onto your skin with your fingertips in small circular movements.

5 Use the remaining infusion (with extra water as necessary) to rinse off the paste and tone the skin.

MAKING TONERS

Toners are used after cleansing to help refine the skin and maintain its pH balance; they also remove any last traces of cleanser before moisturizing. If you have very sensitive skin, test any skin product on a small area of skin first to check that it does not provoke a reaction.

Lavender and aloe vera toner

 TONES SKIN

Makes 100ml (3½fl oz)

This refreshing toner is suitable for all skin types, especially problem skin, and contains a stimulating aromatherapy blend to cleanse the skin and regulate oiliness: witch hazel and lavender waters create a gently astringent and purifying base to tone the pores of the skin and promote a clear complexion. Use within 6 months.

INGREDIENTS

80ml (2¾fl oz) lavender
  flower water
2 tsp witch hazel
1 tsp aloe vera juice
14 drops bergamot essential oil
4 drops lemon essential oil
4 drops petitgrain essential oil
4 drops lavender essential oil
2 drops rosemary essential oil
2 drops black pepper essential oil

METHOD

1 Combine all the ingredients thoroughly.
2 Store in a sterilized glass bottle (p.194), preferably with an atomizer spray, out of direct sunlight, and shake well before use.

Lemon (Citrus limon) *The ripe peel of fresh lemons contains an essential oil that is refreshing, cleansing, and tonifying.*

Rose toner

 TONES SKIN

Makes 100ml (3½fl oz)

This simple toner refreshes and balances the skin. Rose soothes while vinegar, which has a tonic action, stimulates circulation and helps to regulate the skin's natural pH. Apple cider vinegar – produced by a simple fermentation process that retains all the apples' nutritional goodness – is fortified with extra enzymes produced during fermentation.

INGREDIENTS

85ml (2¾fl oz) mineral water
2 heaped tsp dried, or 4 heaped tsp fresh rose petals
1 tsp dried, or 2 tsp fresh elderflower
1 tbsp apple cider vinegar

METHOD

1 Make an infusion (p.342) with the water, rose petals, and elderflower. Once cooled, add the cider vinegar and pour into a sterilized glass bottle (p.194) with a tight-fitting lid.
2 Shake well before each use to blend. Apply after cleansing on cotton wool or with a muslin cloth. Gently wipe over the skin. Refrigerate and use within 3 months.

Herbal toner

 TONES SKIN

Makes 100ml (3½fl oz)

Witch hazel extract is a useful remedy that helps to calm and refresh tired skin. Its astringent properties also help regulate the production of sebum and minimize pores for a more even skin tone. Combined with anti-inflammatory chamomile, balancing rose, and stimulating rosemary, this gentle toner is suitable for all skin types

INGREDIENTS

75 ml (2½fl oz) distilled water
1 tbsp witch hazel
2 tsp aloe vera
3 drops chamomile blue essential oil
3 drops rosemary essential oil
3 drops rose absolute essential oil

METHOD

1 Combine all the ingredients and decant into a sterilized glass bottle (p.194) with a tight-fitting lid.
2 Shake well before each use to blend. Apply after cleansing on cotton wool or with a muslin cloth. Gently wipe over the skin. Refrigerate and use within 3 months.

Herbal face and body spritz

 REVITALIZES SKIN

Makes 100ml (3½fl oz)

Revitalizing fresh mint is the essential ingredient of this refreshing fragrant herbal spritz, which is ideal for hot summer days and nights to help cool your skin. Spray it in a fine mist over exposed skin on the face and body as often as required. Store in the refrigerator when not in use so the spritz stays fresh and cool, and use within 2 days.

INGREDIENTS
3 heaped tsp fresh mint
1 heaped tsp fresh dill
1 heaped tsp fresh parsley
85ml (2¾fl oz) mineral water

METHOD
Make an infusion (p.342) with the herbs (using just enough boiling water to cover the herbs). Once brewed, add the mineral water and pour into a sterilized glass bottle (p.194) with an atomizer spray.

Refreshing facial spritz

 REVITALIZES SKIN   **ENERGIZES**

Makes 100ml (3½fl oz)

Orange flower water is a wonderfully restorative remedy for the skin, and aromatherapists use its delicate scent to help treat stress. This refreshing spritz is ideal to use when travelling to refresh the skin and ease the mind. Store in the refrigerator when not in use so the spritz stays fresh and cool, and use within 2 days.

INGREDIENTS
85ml (2¾fl oz) distilled water
2 tsp aloe vera juice
1 tsp orange flower water
1 drop propolis tincture
1 drop lemon essential oil
1 drop rosemary essential oil

METHOD
Combine all the ingredients and decant into a sterilized glass bottle (p.194) with an atomizer spray. Shake well before each use.

Dill (Anethum graveolens)
A popular culinary herb due to its fragrant, lacy, frond-like leaves, dill is best used fresh.

MAKING FACE MASKS

Taking some quiet time to relax with a soothing face pack can be one of life's indulgent pleasures. For extra purification, try a clay mask for a real home spa treat. If you have very sensitive skin, test any skincare product on a small area of skin first to check that it does not provoke a reaction.

Witch hazel and lavender face mask

 CONDITIONS SKIN

Makes enough for 1 treatment

Green clay is the common name for montmorillonite, a naturally occurring mineral-rich clay with highly absorbent properties. As it dries, it draws impurities from the skin and cleanses pores. At the same time, gently astringent witch hazel and soothing lavender tighten the pores and help to promote a clear complexion.

INGREDIENTS
2 tsp green clay powder
2 tsp witch hazel
1 egg, lightly beaten
2 drops lavender essential oil

METHOD
1 Mix the green clay with the witch hazel to make a paste. Add the beaten egg and mix in the lavender essential oil.
2 Apply the pack to your face and leave on for 10 minutes. Gently remove with cool water, then pat dry with a clean towel.

"Spend 10 minutes relaxing with a natural home-made face pack as an indulgent, fragrant treat for your skin and your mind"

Strawberries and cream exfoliating facial mask

 CONDITIONS SKIN

Makes enough for 1 treatment

This fruity mask refreshes and brightens skin. Strawberries, which are rich in natural fruit acids that help to exfoliate the skin, are combined with ground oats to give texture and extra polish, unclog pores, and smooth the skin. As it uses fresh fruit and dairy ingredients, this recipe is for immediate use.

INGREDIENTS
2 tbsp ground oats
3 large ripe strawberries
1 tsp single cream

METHOD
1 Using a pestle and mortar, grind the oats to a fine powder. Mash the strawberries with a fork and combine with the oats. Add the cream and mix to a thick paste (add a little more cream if needed to create the right consistency).
2 Apply the paste to freshly cleansed skin (avoiding the area directly around the eyes and mouth) and leave for 10 minutes.
3 Remove the paste by applying a little water in the palms of your hands to loosen it, then gently rub it away in gentle circular movements. Rinse with cool water and pat dry with a towel.

Strawberry (Fragaria x ananassa)
These fresh berries are highly nutritious and full of vitamins. Antioxidant anthocyanins give them their red colour.

Lavender clay mask

 **CONDITIONS SKIN**

Makes enough for 1–2 treatments

Natural clay minerals draw impurities from the skin and deeply cleanse it. With moisturizing honey and antioxidant-rich aloe vera, and reviving, balancing lavender water and essential oil, this soothing, purifying mask leaves skin feeling fresh and smooth. Store in a sterilized dark glass jar (p.194) with a tight-fitting lid and use within 2 months.

INGREDIENTS
2 tbsp aloe vera juice
1 tsp lavender water
1 tsp clear honey
½ tbsp kaolin powder
1 tbsp bentonite powder
1 drop lavender essential oil

METHOD
1 Combine the aloe vera, lavender water, and honey. Add the clay powders by sprinkling them gradually over the mixed liquids while stirring continually. Press the mixture through a sieve. Add the essential oil and stir again to mix well.
2 Apply to freshly cleansed skin (avoiding the area directly around the eyes and mouth). Leave for 10 minutes. Rinse with warm water and pat dry with a towel.

Grapefruit clay mask

 **CONDITIONS SKIN**

Makes approx 50ml (1¾fl oz)

This variation on a clay mask is more suited to oilier skin types. Grapefruit is naturally rich in fruit acids, and combined with cleansing clay minerals, mildly astringent and toning witch hazel, and soothing, nutrient-rich aloe vera, it leaves skin cleansed, refreshed, and revitalized. Store in a sterilized dark glass jar (p.194) with a tight-fitting lid and use within 2 months.

INGREDIENTS
2 tbsp aloe vera juice
1 tsp witch hazel
1 tsp fresh grapefruit juice
1½ tsp kaolin powder
½ tbsp bentonite powder
1 drop lemon essential oil

METHOD
1 Combine the aloe vera juice, witch hazel, and grapefruit juice. Add the clay powders by sprinkling them gradually over the mixed liquids while stirring continually. Press the mixture through a sieve. Add the essential oil and stir again to mix well.
2 Apply to freshly cleansed skin (avoiding the area directly around the eyes and mouth). Leave for 10 minutes. Rinse with warm water and pat dry with a towel.

Rose clay mask

 CONDITIONS SKIN

Makes enough for 1–2 treatments

This nourishing mask purifies and smoothes the skin. Rose, used for its cooling and balancing properties, is combined with aloe vera – an extremely soothing plant extract that is rich in vitamins, amino acids, enzymes, and proteins, and has excellent moisturizing properties. Store in a sterilized dark glass jar (p.194) with a tight-fitting lid and use within 2 months

INGREDIENTS
2 tbsp aloe vera juice
1 tsp rose water
1 tsp clear honey
½ tbsp kaolin powder
1 tbsp bentonite powder
1 drop rose absolute essential oil

METHOD
1 Combine the aloe vera, rose water, and honey. Add the clay powders by sprinkling them gradually over the mixed liquids while stirring continually. Press the mixture through a sieve. Add the essential oil and stir again to mix well.
2 Apply to freshly cleansed skin (avoiding the area directly around the eyes and mouth). Leave for 10 minutes. Rinse with warm water and pat dry with a towel.

Golden banana facial mask

 CONDITIONS SKIN

Makes enough for 1 treatment

This rich, nourishing treatment revitalizes dry skin. Fresh banana is richly moisturizing and smoothing, while golden calendula oil contains carotenoids, a precursor to skin-nurturing vitamin A. The oil also has excellent healing and anti-inflammatory properties. As it uses fresh fruit ingredients, this recipe is for immediate use.

INGREDIENTS
1 ripe banana
1 egg yolk
2 tsp calendula macerated oil

METHOD
1 Peel the banana, place in a bowl, and mash with a fork. Add the egg yolk and calendula oil and mix all the ingredients together.
2 Apply to freshly cleansed skin (avoiding the area directly around the eyes and mouth). Leave for 10 minutes. Rinse with cool water and pat dry with a towel.

Avocado and aloe vera facial mask

 CONDITIONS SKIN

Makes enough for 1 treatment

A deeply nourishing and soothing facial mask suitable for all skin types. Avocado is vitamin- and mineral-rich, as well as being high in fatty acids, lecithin, and phytosterols, which makes it an excellent moisturizer for dry skin. As it uses fresh fruit and dairy ingredients, this recipe is for immediate use.

INGREDIENTS

1 ripe avocado
1 tsp clear honey
1 tsp lemon juice
1 tsp natural yoghurt
1 tsp aloe vera juice

METHOD

1 Split the avocado in two and scoop the flesh out into a bowl. Mash with a fork to make a paste, then add the other ingredients and mix.
2 Apply to freshly cleansed skin (avoiding the area directly around the eyes and mouth). Leave for 10 minutes. Rinse with cool water and pat dry with a towel.

Apple and cinnamon facial mask

 NOURISHES SKIN

Makes enough for 1 treatment

This cleansing mask is ideally suited to oily or problem skin, as it gently regulates and cleanses the skin. Apples contain natural fruit acids, which help to gently exfoliate the skin, while moisturizing honey and ground oats help to smooth and polish it. As it uses fresh fruit and dairy ingredients, this recipe is for immediate use.

INGREDIENTS

1 ripe apple, peeled and grated
½ tsp single cream
1 tsp clear honey
1 tbsp ground oats
½ tsp ground cinnamon

METHOD

1 Mix all the ingredients together well in a bowl with a fork to form a paste.
2 Apply to freshly cleansed skin (avoiding the area directly around the eyes and mouth). Leave for 10 minutes. Rinse with cool water and pat dry with a towel.

MAKING BALMS

Balms are a simple way to nourish skin and protect it from moisture loss. Make sure that the containers you use to store your home-made balms are sterilized (p.194). If you have very sensitive skin, test any skincare product on a small area of skin first to check that it does not provoke a reaction.

Calendula and mandarin lip balm

 MOISTURIZES SKIN    HELPS PREVENT COLD SORES

INGREDIENTS
1 tsp beeswax
70g (2¼ oz) cocoa butter
1 tsp coconut oil
5 drops lemon balm tincture
5 drops calendula tincture
10 drops mandarin essential oil

Makes 80g (2¾oz)

Mandarin essential oil, expressed from the fresh peel of the fruit, is gently antiseptic and cleansing. Lemon balm is active against the herpes virus, so this balm will also help to prevent or treat cold sores. Cocoa butter helps to condition, soothe, and protect lips.

1 *Melt the beeswax*, cocoa butter, and coconut oil over a saucepan of hot water (bain-marie).

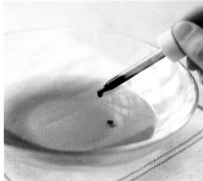

2 *Add the tinctures* and essential oil to the mixture, then stir.

3 *Divide between* two small sterilized jars (p.194) and allow to set. It will keep for about 3 months.

Lavender and myrrh soothing lip balm

 **MOISTURIZES SKIN**

Makes 10g (¼oz)

This very simple blend of ingredients is quick to make, but provides long-lasting relief by effectively smoothing, moisturizing, and protecting lips from drying out. The nourishing combination of therapeutic lavender and myrrh essential oils also helps to condition the lips and soothe any chapped or cracked skin. This balm is best used within 6 months.

INGREDIENTS

2 tsp cocoa butter and shea butter, combined
2 drops lavender essential oil
1 drop myrrh essential oil

METHOD

1 Melt the cocoa butter and shea butter in a bowl set over a saucepan of boiling water (*bain-marie*). Add the essential oils and pour into a small sterilized jar (p.194) with a tight-fitting lid.
2 Allow to cool and set. This may take up to 12 hours (depending on the room temperature).

Mother-to-be balm

 **HELPS PREVENT STRETCH MARKS**    **MOISTURIZES SKIN**

Makes 40g (1½oz)

This nourishing fragrance-free balm will help soothe the discomfort of expanding skin and improve resistance to stretch marks. Deeply moisturizing coconut and apricot kernel oils help to increase the skin's strength and suppleness, while beeswax locks in moisture and has protective properties. Antioxidant-rich calendula has a soothing action. Use within 3 months.

INGREDIENTS

1 tsp beeswax
5 tsp coconut oil
1 tsp apricot oil
1 tsp calendula macerated oil

METHOD

1 Heat the beeswax with the coconut, apricot, and calendula oils in a bowl set over a saucepan of boiling water (bain-marie) until the beeswax has melted.
2 Pour into a sterilized dark glass jar (p.194) with a tight-fitting lid and leave to cool and set. This may take up to 12 hours (depending on the room temperature).

Tea tree and thyme foot balm

TREATS ATHLETE'S FOOT

Makes approx 80g (2¾oz)

A cleansing and soothing balm to help in the treatment of ailments such as athlete's foot or fungal infections. Research on tea tree and thyme essential oils has shown their potent antifungal and antibacterial properties. Combined here with marshmallow and comfrey extracts to soothe, they also promote the regeneration of healthy skin. Will keep for up to 6 months.

INGREDIENTS

2 tsp beeswax
3 tbsp almond oil
1 tbsp wheatgerm oil
1 tsp marshmallow tincture
1 tsp comfrey tincture
5 drops thyme essential oil
5 drops tea tree essential oil

METHOD

1 Combine the beeswax and almond and wheatgerm oils in a bowl set over a saucepan of boiling water (bain-marie). Heat until the beeswax has melted.

2 Take off the heat and, when cooled slightly, add the tinctures and essential oils. Decant into a sterilized jar (p.194) with a tight-fitting lid and allow to cool and set. This may take up to 12 hours (depending on the room temperature).

MAKING BATH BOMBS

Fizzing bath bombs, which are easy to make and require only simple ingredients, are a delight to the senses. They make great presents, too – once you have pressed the mixture into a ball and wrapped it in kitchen foil, simply cover it in colourful tissue paper and decorate it with ribbons.

Citrus bath bombs

 **SOOTHES TIRED MUSCLES**    **REVITALIZES**

Makes 4 small bombs

This citrus bath bomb will always liven up bath time. Grapefruit, lemon, and lime essential oils are combined with fresh-scented rosemary essential oil to release a vibrant fragrance as the ingredients fizz and dissolve in the water. You can add some colour by replacing the almond oil with green avocado oil or orange carrot oil.

INGREDIENTS

80g (2¾ oz) sodium bicarbonate
1 tbsp citric acid
4 drops grapefruit essential oil
4 drops lemon essential oil
1 drop lime essential oil
1 drop rosemary essential oil
a pinch of dried calendula
   petals, chopped
a dash of carrot oil (optional)
a dash of avocado oil (optional)
finely chopped herbs or
   flowers (optional)

METHOD

1 Mix the sodium bicarbonate and citric acid together on a plate. Sprinkle the essential oils onto the sodium bicarbonate mixture and add the calendula petals.
2 If you want to add some colour to your bath bomb, add a dash of carrot oil to give an orange colour, or avocado oil for a green tint. You might also like to add finely chopped herbs such as mint, or flowers including lavender or calendula.
3 Use the mixture as a powder sprinkled directly into the bath, or press firmly into shaped moulds such as old camera film cases, ice-cube trays, and pastry cutters. Add the powder or block to the bath water just before you step into the bath.
4 To make the bath bomb into a present, simply press the mixture into a round ball, wrap it in aluminium foil, cover the foil with tissue paper, and add some ribbons or other decorations.

Exotic bath bombs

 SOOTHES TIRED MUSCLES

 **STIMULATES THE SENSES**

Makes 4 small bombs

Just add this sensually scented fizzing bath bomb to running bath water to make bathtime a special occasion. The powdery mix softens the water, while the aromatherapeutic blend of earthy vetiver, exotic Madagascan ylang ylang flowers, and warm, relaxing citrus brings peace of mind and a deep sense of well-being.

INGREDIENTS

3 tbsp sodium bicarbonate
1 tbsp citric acid
4 drops mandarin essential oil
3 drops vetiver essential oil
2 drops ylang ylang essential oil
1 petitgrain essential oil
2 tsp St John's wort (hypericum) macerated oil
a pinch of rose petals, finely chopped

METHOD

1 Mix the sodium bicarbonate and citric acid together on a flat plate. Add the essential oils by sprinkling them over the powder.
2 Use a spoon to heap the powder into the centre of the plate. Make a small well in the centre of the powder, add the deep red St John's wort oil and the rose petals.
3 Gradually mix the powder, oil, and rose petals together. The hypericum oil helps the ingredients to bind together, as well as add colour.
4 Press the mixture firmly into shaped moulds such as ice-cube trays or pastry cutters, or simply hand-mould the ingredients into balls. Store in a dry place and use within 2 months.

Sunshine bath bombs

 **SOOTHES TIRED MUSCLES**   **REVITALIZES**

Makes 4 small bombs

This gentle yet warmly scented fizzing bath bomb is ideal for children, lifting the spirits but also calming the emotions with its warm, citrus scents of mandarin and orange combined with soothing, relaxing lavender. Golden calendula oil and grated citrus zest give the bomb added colour and texture.

INGREDIENTS

3 tbsp sodium bicarbonate
1 tbsp citric acid
7 drops mandarin essential oil
2 drops orange essential oil
1 drop lavender essential oil
2 tsp calendula oil
a pinch of orange, mandarin, or lemon peel, finely grated

METHOD

1 Mix the sodium bicarbonate and citric acid on a flat plate. Add the essential oils by sprinkling them over the powder, then use a spoon to heap the powder into the centre of the plate.
2 Make a small well in the centre, add the calendula oil, and gradually mix it into the powder to bind the bath bomb together. It will also add a little colour. Add the citrus peel zest whilst mixing.
3 Press the mixture firmly into shaped moulds such as ice-cube trays, pastry cutters or simply hand-mould the ingredients into balls. Store in a dry place, and use within 2 months.

MAKING BATH INFUSIONS

Adding herbs to your bath is one of the easiest and enjoyable ways to benefit from their amazing natural properties. Simply lie back and let the fragrant essences in the infusions lift your spirits, ease any tension headaches, and help you to relax. There's no better way to get a good night's sleep.

Rose and calendula bath infusion

 **SOOTHES TIRED MUSCLES**   **RELAXES**

Makes enough for 1 bath

This gentle bath infusion nurtures and refreshes, making it a wonderful tonic for dry and sensitive skin. The cooling and balancing properties of roses are renowned; this recipe uses extracts from both the flowers and the vitamin- and flavonoid-rich hips. It also includes cider vinegar to soften the skin and calendula to soothe it.

INGREDIENTS
2 tsp dried rose petals/buds
1 tsp dried rosehips
1 tsp salt
1 tsp cider vinegar
5 drops calendula tincture
8 drops rose essential oil
2 drops geranium essential oil

METHOD
1 Make an infusion (p.342) using the rose petals, rosehips, and 500ml (16fl oz) of hot water.
2 Strain the infusion and add the rest of the ingredients.
3 Use immediately by adding to a ready-run warm bath.

Lemon grass and rosemary bath infusion

 RELAXES   **SOOTHES
TIRED MUSCLES**

Makes enough for 1 bath

Lemon grass, bay, and rosemary are all herbs that are well known for their fragrant, culinary use, but they can be just as useful in body care. This stimulating and warming aromatic bath blend eases tired muscles and is ideal for restoring the body after physical activity, sport, or periods of over-exertion.

INGREDIENTS
2 tsp dried bay leaves, chopped
1 tsp dried rosemary
5 drops lemon grass essential oil

METHOD
Make an infusion (p.342) with 500ml (16fl oz) of water, the bay leaves, and the rosemary. When cooled, add the lemon grass essential oil. Use immediately, adding it to a freshly run bath.

Lavender and aloe vera bath infusion

 RELAXES    **SOOTHES
TIRED MUSCLES**

Makes enough for 1 bath

This bath infusion will soothe sensitive skin and encourage a sense of well-being and relaxation. Lavender, which initially has a reviving, restorative effect, has been long used to ease both body and mind. This makes it a perfect remedy in this gentle bath blend, along with soothing aloe vera and nurturing chamomile.

INGREDIENTS
2 tsp lavender
2 tsp chamomile
30ml (2 tbsp) aloe vera juice
10 drops lavender essential oil

METHOD
1 Make an infusion (p.342) with 500ml (16fl oz) of water and the lavender and chamomile flowers. When cooled, add the aloe vera juice and lavender essential oil.
2 Use immediately, adding it to a freshly run bath. Ensure that your bath is not too hot if you have dry or sensitive skin.

Seaweed and arnica bath infusion

 RELAXES

 SOOTHES
TIRED MUSCLES

Makes enough for 1 bath

This revitalizing blend restores the body after a long day. Nutrient-rich bladderwrack seaweed is traditionally used to soothe irritated and inflamed tissues in the body, and here it is partnered with arnica – a famous remedy for bumps, bruises, and strains – and a stimulating blend of essential oils. Add to your bath water, lie back, and relax.

INGREDIENTS
½ tsp bladderwrack
1 tsp comfrey
2 tsp juniper berries
2 heaped tsp sea salt
5 drops arnica tincture
2 drops pine oil
2 drops lavender essential oil
2 drops lemon essential oil
2 drops juniper essential oil

METHOD
1 Make an infusion (p.342) with 500ml (16fl oz) of water and the dried herbs.
2 Add the salt and stir until well dissolved. Mix in the arnica tincture and the essential oils.
3 Use immediately, adding the infusion to a freshly run bath.

Detox bath infusion

 STIMULATES
CIRCULATION

 SOOTHES
TIRED MUSCLES

Makes enough for 1 bath

To encourage the elimination of toxins from the body, nutrient-rich bladderwrack is combined with cleansing sea salt, circulation-boosting juniper, black pepper, and lemon essential oils. For the best results, try dry body brushing with a natural bristle brush or body mitt before your bath to exfoliate the skin and energize the body.

INGREDIENTS
½ tsp bladderwrack
1 tsp celery seeds
2 tsp fennel seeds
2 heaped tsp sea salt
2 drops juniper essential oil
2 drops black pepper essential oil
2 drops lemon essential oil
2 drops eucalyptus essential oil

METHOD
Make an infusion (p.342) with 500ml (16fl oz) of water and the dried herbs. Add the essential oils to the salt, then add the salt to the infusion and stir until well dissolved. Use immediately, adding it to a freshly run bath.

Fennel seed (Foeniculum vulgare) (p.57)
These seeds are actually small, strongly flavoured, aromatic fruits, which make a cleansing, toning infusion for the skin.

Ginger and juniper warming foot soak

WARMS UP THE BODY   **STIMULATES CIRCULATION**

Makes enough for 1 treatment

This aromatic soak boosts the circulation and eliminates the chill from cold feet. Ginger has long been used for its warming action, while juniper is stimulating and cloves have mild pain-relieving properties. The aromatic bay leaves and orange peel in this therapeutic blend also delight the senses as the foot soak takes effect.

INGREDIENTS

1 tbsp dried rosehips
2 tbsp dried hibiscus
1 tsp cloves
1 tsp juniper berries
3 bay leaves, crushed
1 tbsp orange peel, fresh or dried
3 drops ginger essential oil

METHOD

1 Place all the ingredients in a muslin (cheesecloth) bag and gently stir the bag in a large bowl of boiling water.
2 After 10 minutes, add sufficient cold water to make the soak a comfortable temperature, but still hot. Immerse your feet in the liquid for as long as is comfortable, or until the water has cooled.

Juniper berries (*Juniperus communis*) *(p.73) The fruits of this conifer species are in fact fleshy female seed cones and not true berries.*

Relax and restore bath herbs

 RELAXES   **SOOTHES TIRED MUSCLES**

Makes enough for 1 bath treatment

Mildly astringent, tannin-rich raspberry leaves blend well with skin-soothing violet and relaxing lavender to create this fragrant, skin-friendly wash that eases the mind and body. Oatmeal has also been included, as it is known to be an excellent remedy for dry skin: it gently softens and nurtures the skin to leave it feeling smooth and moisturized.

INGREDIENTS
2 tbsp raspberry leaves
2 tbsp violet leaf
2 tbsp lavender
2 tbsp oatmeal, powdered

METHOD
1 Combine the herbs and oatmeal and grind in a pestle and mortar (or a coffee grinder or blender) to make a rough powder.
2 Place the powder in a muslin bag. Hang the bag under the taps while running your bath so that the warm water flows through the herbs, then add the bag to your bath water. Lie back and relax.

Raspberry (Rubus idaeus) *(p.99) Rich in vitamins, minerals, and astringent tannins, raspberry leaf has been used as a folk remedy for centuries.*

Postnatal sitz bath

 ASSISTS WITH POST-BIRTH HEALING

Makes enough for 1 bath treatment

A soothing herbal blend to encourage postnatal recovery. Calendula helps to encourage natural cellular regeneration, while chamomile is gentle and soothing. Yarrow and shepherd's purse have anti-inflammatory properties. Cleansing lavender nurtures the skin and also provides a calming fragrance to aid relaxation.

INGREDIENTS
2 tbsp calendula
2 tbsp chamomile
2 tbsp lavender
1 tbsp yarrow
1 tbsp shepherd's purse
  (*Capsella bursa-pastoris*)

METHOD
1 Boil enough water to make an infusion with the herbs (p.342).
2 When cool, add the blend to a warm shallow bath (the water should only come up to the level of your hips). Allow yourself 10 minutes to soak in the bath. If you have had stitches, limit yourself to one sitz bath per day.

MAKING HAIR AND SCALP TREATMENTS

Beautiful hair depends on a healthy scalp. Keep your scalp in good condition by washing your hair in warm, not hot, water, and using home-made herbal treatments to add extra nutrition. Then rinse through for shiny, revitalized hair with bounce.

Comfrey hair tonic

 TREATS ALL HAIR TYPES

INGREDIENTS
3 tsp dried calendula
3 tsp dried comfrey
1 tsp dried horsetail

Makes 1 treatment

Comfrey has a conditioning effect on the hair and scalp, as it is rich in an extract, allantoin, that helps to encourage natural cellular regeneration. Calendula soothes the scalp and is an excellent rinse for hair alongside shine-enhancing horsetail. This simple tonic nourishes both the hair and scalp to restore your hair's natural vitality.

1 *Infuse the dried herbs* with 100ml (3fl oz) of boiling water in a bowl.

2 *Allow to stand* and cool for 20 minutes, then strain through a sieve into a bowl. Discard the herbs.

3 *Add the strained liquid* to your shampoo up to a maximum ratio of 50 per cent (the more you add, the thinner the shampoo will be). Use any excess infusion as a final rinse for the hair.

Horsetail shampoo for dull hair

 TREATS DULL HAIR

Makes 100ml (3½fl oz)

Silica-rich horsetail is a traditional remedy used to restore vitality to lack-lustre hair. Combined with classic, shine-boosting, growth-encouraging rosemary, cooling, oil-balancing sage, and rich almond oil, it moisturizes and nourishes hair to make it stronger and healthier. It also enhances natural shine and bounce.

INGREDIENTS
3 tbsp ordinary shampoo
3 tbsp infusion of equal parts
  horsetail, rosemary, and sage
scant 1 tsp almond oil
6 drops rosemary essential oil

METHOD
Blend all the ingredients together well. Use within 1 week, or keep refrigerated and use within 2 weeks.

Nettle shampoo for dandruff

 TREATS DANDRUFF

Makes 100ml (3½fl oz)

Borage, also known as starflower oil, is rich in essential fatty acids, including gamma-linolenic acid, and is especially nourishing to dry, irritated skin. Combined with mineral-rich nettle, calming lavender, and cooling sage, this rinse helps to soothe irritated scalps prone to dandruff. Cedarwood and lemon essential oils add to the restorative properties of the herbs.

INGREDIENTS
3 tbsp ordinary shampoo
3 tbsp infusion of equal parts
  lavender, nettle, and sage
scant 1 tsp borage (starflower) oil
6 drops cedarwood essential oil
2 drops lemon essential oil

METHOD
Blend all the ingredients together well. Use within 1 week, or keep refrigerated and use within 2 weeks.

Nourishing conditioner for dry and damaged hair

 **TREATS DRY AND DAMAGED HAIR**

Makes 100ml (3½fl oz)

Softening marshmallow and nourishing comfrey are combined here with a double calendula boost – both the soothing herbal infusion and the nutrient-rich oil - to bring first aid to brittle, fragile hair. Frankincense and Roman chamomile essential oils also lend their soothing, tonifying properties to this herbal conditioner.

INGREDIENTS
3 tbsp ordinary conditioner
3 tbsp infusion of equal parts comfrey, marshmallow, and calendula
scant 1 tsp calendula oil
8 drops frankincense essential oil
2 drops chamomile Roman essential oil

METHOD
Blend all the ingredients together well. Use within 1 week, or keep refrigerated and use within 2 weeks.

Rosemary conditioner for all hair types

 TREATS ALL HAIR TYPES

Makes 100ml (3½fl oz)

Stimulating rosemary is probably the most well-known herb included in treatments to encourage thick, healthy hair. It is sometimes used to darken the hair, so blondes may want to halve the quantity of the rosemary and add a chamomile infusion to make up the correct quantity. Avocado is a rich, nourishing oil that enriches the scalp and deeply moisturizes the hair.

INGREDIENTS
3 tbsp ordinary conditioner
3 tbsp infusion of equal parts rose, rosemary, thyme
scant 1 tsp avocado oil
5 drops cedarwood essential oil
3 drops orange essential oil
3 drops rosemary essential oil

METHOD
Blend all the ingredients together well. Use within 1 week, or keep refrigerated and use within 2 weeks.

Thyme and cider rinse

 TREATS DANDRUFF

Makes 100ml (3½fl oz)

Thyme essential oil is warming and stimulating, has strong antifungal and antibacterial properties, and is traditionally used to give hair added strength. Apple cider vinegar makes a wonderfully cleansing, shine-enhancing hair tonic. This simple combination makes an excellent pre-wash treatment for anyone prone to dandruff.

INGREDIENTS

100ml (3½fl oz) apple cider vinegar
10 drops thyme essential oil

METHOD

Blend the ingredients together and massage into the scalp. Leave for up to 5 minutes. Rinse with warm water and shampoo as usual. Use within 6 months.

Thyme (*Thymus vulgaris*) *(p.116)*
A soothing, warming herb, thyme has antiseptic properties and is regarded as a "tonic".

Enriching coconut conditioner

 **TREATS ALL
HAIR TYPES**

Makes 100g (3½oz)

Coconut makes a wonderful nurturing treatment for all hair types. It is easily absorbed into the scalp, enriches and moisturizes the skin, and softens and smooths hair. A combination of lavender, mandarin, and petitgrain essential oils bring a cleansing, fresh fragrance to this deeply conditioning treatment.

INGREDIENTS

100g (3½ oz) jar coconut oil
8 drops lavender essential oil
7 drops mandarin essential oil
5 drops petitgrain essential oil

METHOD

1 Melt the coconut oil by standing the jar in a bowl of hot water (the water only needs to come half way up the sides of the jar). When the coconut oil is has melted, remove the jar from the bowl. Add the essential oils to the coconut oil, and stir before it sets. Allow to cool.

2 To use, melt a little of the infused oil in the palms of your hands and massage into the hair and scalp. Leave on for at least 2 hours, then shampoo off. Applying your shampoo before wetting your hair makes it easier to remove the coconut treatment. Use within 6 months.

"Coconut oil is one of nature's best treatments for moisturizing the skin and hair. Look for organic or virgin cold-pressed coconut oil for maximum nutritional benefit"

Lavender and rosemary conditioner

 TREATS ALL HAIR TYPES

Makes 100g (3½oz)

Super-enriching coconut is one of the greatest treats for the hair and scalp. It moisturizes the skin while smoothing and softening the hair, and is perfect for conditioning unruly curls or taming flyaway ends. The addition of lavender, rosemary, and geranium essential oils will stimulate hair growth and restore vitality to dull hair.

INGREDIENTS

1 x 100g (3½oz) jar coconut oil
10 drops lavender essential oil
8 drops rosemary essential oil
6 drops geranium essential oil

METHOD

1 Melt the coconut oil by standing the sealed jar in a bowl of hot water so that the water reaches halfway up the side of the jar.
2 Remove the jar, add the essential oils to the melted coconut oil, and mix thoroughly. Allow to cool and set. (In hot weather you may want to keep this blend in the fridge to keep it solid.)
3 To use, warm some of the blend by rubbing it in the palm of your hand to melt it, then work it methodically through the hair, concentrating on massaging the scalp. Then wrap a warm towel around your head and leave for 30 minutes.
4 Remove the oil by applying neat shampoo and working it into the hair before adding water. Rinse the hair and repeat with shampoo if necessary.

Stimulating hair oil

 **TREATS ALL
HAIR TYPES**

Makes enough for 1 treatment

Rich, green avocado oil is pressed from the flesh of the fruit rather than the seed. It is vitamin- and mineral-rich, as well as being high in essential fatty acids, and is extremely moisturizing. Tonifying rosemary and basil essential oils are also added to stimulate hair growth in this intensive conditioning treatment.

INGREDIENTS
2 tsp avocado oil
2 drops rosemary essential oil
2 drops basil essential oil

METHOD

1 Mix the avocado oil and essential oils together and decant into a bottle. Heat the oils by placing the bottle in a bowl of hot water.

2 Massage the oil into the scalp with firm circular movements with the pads of your fingers. Leave the mixture on the hair for 30 minutes, then shampoo as usual. Applying your shampoo before wetting your hair makes it easier to remove the hair oil. Use within 6 months.

Sweet basil (Ocimum basilicum) *In aromatherapy, basil is used to help clear the mind and relieve intellectual fatigue, while giving clarity and mental strength.*

Calendula and banana hair treatment

 **TREATS ALL
HAIR TYPES**

Makes enough for 1 treatment

Bananas are rich in potassium and amino acids, and make a great treatment for smoothing and nourishing dry or damaged hair. Combined with antioxidant calendula macerated oil and exotic ylang ylang, this simple but effective moisturizing hair mask is particularly effective for taming unruly or frizzy curls.

INGREDIENTS

1 ripe banana
2 tsp calendula macerated oil
3 drops ylang ylang essential oil
A dash of lemon juice to add to rinse

METHOD

1 Use a blender to purée the banana to a smooth paste (this will make it easier to rinse from your hair), then combine with the calendula and ylang ylang oils.

2 Wet your hair, squeeze out the excess water with a towel to leave hair damp, comb through, then apply the banana paste by massaging it into the hair.

3 Cover your hair with clingfilm, an old showercap, or a large plastic food bag (this will stop the mixture drying out) and leave for 30 minutes. Wash out the mask using your normal shampoo with a dash of added lemon juice.

Source Herbs

Find out how to grow medicinal herbs for yourself, whether in a garden or in a windowbox, and discover how to forage for herbs in the wild or buy the best fresh or dried herbs to make your own remedies.

Planning your herb garden

Choosing your favourite herb plants and growing them is a great way to start your own herb garden. Select herbs that will flourish in your climate, and take some time to choose which plot – or in what containers – to grow your herbs. Be mindful of how much sun your herbs need and position them appropriately in your garden.

Use your space Position pots against a south-facing wall in a sheltered spot to give them the best of the sun.

Pots

• Most culinary herbs take well to pot culture, and the advantage of planting herbs in different pots is that you can move the plants around the garden for more sun or shade depending on the month, or move any frost-tender herb plants indoors during the winter months.

• Alternatively, window boxes allow you to grow a good selection of herbs in one space, and can be conveniently positioned by a kitchen window to make picking them at the last moment for cooking or garnishing dishes even easier.

• Plant herbs in generous containers with drainage holes in the bottom. Use fine soil mixed in equal quantities with vermiculite for Mediterranean herbs, and 100 per-cent potting soil for delicate herbs.

• Potted herbs require frequent watering, and daily watering in the summer.

Beds and borders

• If you have a vegetable garden or ornamental beds or borders, plant culinary and medicinal herbs in between existing plants. Position sun-loving herbs where they will get lots of light, and tuck shade-lovers around taller ornamentals.

• A small, informal, dedicated herb garden packed with herbs can occupy as little as 1.5 x 3.5m (5 x 11½ft). If possible, position it where you can see it.

• A formal arrangement is possible even in the tiniest of gardens: plant low-growing herbs such as thyme or chamomile between paths made of crushed rocks, bricks, or flagstones.

• Sketch out your dream garden on graph paper before you dig it. Then mark out planting areas in geometric or soft, curving patterns.

• If you add trellises, arbors, arches, pillars, water features, and statues you can give it a formal look. If you have a sloping garden, terraces make a beautiful addition to the design.

Sharing space Many herbs make pretty and practical additions to vegetable beds.

Testing the soil

Try this simple test before you plant herbs. The best soil is loam (a mix of clay and sand). Clay needs sand and compost to improve aeration; sandy soil retains water and nutrients only when you add compost to it.

1 *Remove any grass,* weeds, or plants from the surface and lift out a clod of earth with a spade. Repeat in two other places in your garden patch.

2 *Mix the samples* well, squeeze some mixed soil in your palm, and thump it with a finger. If it falls apart, it is loam; if gritty, it is sandy; if it forms a lump, it is clay.

Making your own compost

Add grass clippings, leaves, uncooked vegetable waste, and dead (but not diseased) plants to a compost bin that is 1.5m (5ft) square and 90cm (3ft) high. Do not add weeds or grasses that have set seed.

1 *Collect your compostable material* in the bin. Keep the heap moist and turn it every two weeks, using a fork or shovel, until the material starts to break down.

2 *You can use* your compost when it has turned dark brown in colour, is crumbling in texture, and looks and smells like soil.

Growing herbs

There are many advantages to growing herbs from seed. Home-sown herbs are cheaper than those bought from a nursery, and home-grown seedlings have healthy, garden-ready root balls when the time comes to plant them out. Some herbs are best propagated in other ways, though (p.334).

Growing from seed

1 *Fill a pot* with fine soil and gently firm down. Water the soil and let it drain. Sow seed in dents or on the soil surface (according to the packet instructions).

2 *Lightly cover* the seed with vermiculite or more potting soil. Water again. Set the tray in a warm place and never let the soil dry out.

Transplanting

As seedlings develop they need more space to grow. Transplant them into individual or bigger pots when they have formed four or more true leaves above the seed leaves.

1 *Remove the seedlings* from their pot, gently pulling them out by their true leaves, not by the stem, and squeezing the base of the pot or tray.

2 *Make a hole in a pot* of soil and lower in the seedling. Fill with more soil, firm down gently, water, and position in a warm, bright spot out of direct sunlight.

Growing young plants

Sometimes it may not be practical to raise plants from seed yourself, especially if you only want to grow a handful of different plants and don't have space to sow lots of seedlings, or if a plant is hard to grow from seed. Garden centres have a good selection of young plants, but nurseries have a broader range.

Potting on

If you want to grow your herb plant in a pot, replant it when you get home from the nursery in a pot one size bigger than the one you bought it in. You will need to repeat the process when your plants outgrow their new pots.

1 Make sure *your new pot has a drainage hole. Place a handful of gravel at the bottom, half-fill with potting compost, and remove the plant from its pot.*

2 Remove the plant *from its old pot. Set the plant into its new pot and fill with potting soil, firming in gently as you go. Water the plant well.*

Planting into the garden

Young plants bought from a nursery should be big enough to plant outdoors in the garden immediately. Plant them out as soon as you can to allow their roots to establish.

1 Prepare the soil *by digging into the top 15–30cm (6–12in) of soil until it becomes loose. Dig a generous hole and place the plant in the hole to the same depth it was in its pot.*

2 Backfill around the plant *and firm it in with the palms of your hands. Water the plant well.*

Propagation

Once your favourite herb plants are well established, you can increase their number, or grow a few insurance plants in case some do not survive a harsh winter, by using various propagation methods. See the individual entries in the A–Z section for the best technique to use for growing each plant.

Stem cuttings

Take softwood cuttings from young stems in spring, semi-ripe cuttings from ripening, stiffening stems in late summer, and hardwood ones from woody stems at the end of the growing season.

1 Select a healthy, *non-flowering stem with mature leaves, cut the stem at an angle just above the leaf attachment, and strip the lower leaves.*

2 Cut the stem *straight across 5cm (2in) below the last leaf. Plant vertically in a pot of soil. Water well. Cover with a clear plastic bag to retain moisture.*

Root cuttings

Make new plants from sections of semi-mature or mature roots of plants such as mint when they are dormant (not growing) in mid- to late winter.

1 Lift the plant *and tease the roots apart. Cut a 5-cm (2-in) piece of root; avoid fibrous or immature roots.*

2 Trim the root *straight across at the top and diagonally at the base. Plant upright in soil. Cover with vermiculite.*

Watering and feeding

Herbs grown in pots and in the ground have different requirements. Check seed packet instructions or ask at your local garden centre or nursery about your chosen plant's specific requirements, although these general guidelines will keep all plants healthy.

Watering

Beds: You cannot always cater for the preferences of individual plants, but they will usually tolerate shared conditions as long as they have moist, well-drained soil. Work lots of compost into the soil to help it retain moisture and water it deeply when the top 5cm (2in) seems dry. The best time to water, if you are using an overhead sprinkler or a watering can, is in the morning, so that the sun has time to dry the leaves.

Pots: Herbs that are planted in pots need to be watered more often than those positioned in the ground, as their roots cannot travel as far to locate moisture. In very warm weather and on hot summer days you should water these potted plants every day, or purchase drip irrigation systems and install them in each pot with set timers to automatically water them. You can help the soil to retain more water using special granules that absorb water and release it as and when needed.

Water early Try to water your herbs in the morning to avoid mildew and rot overnight.

Feeding

Beds: Plants in open ground do not need much feeding because their roots travel to find the nutrition they require. However, you can give them a helping hand by spreading a 5-cm (2-in) layer of compost over the soil surface as a mulch over winter, then digging it into the soil in spring to restore nutrients. Herbs that are harvested frequently during the growing season benefit from the occasional fertilizer feed in midsummer too.

Pots: Potted plants also need more attention when it comes to food. Ideally, feed them with fertilizer in granules or liquid form every six weeks throughout the growing season, especially if they are harvested regularly. Start feeding in spring when new growth appears, and scrape away the top 5cm (2in) of soil in the pot and replace it with good, fresh soil. Stop feeding the plants in late summer, or you will encourage new growth when they should be slowing down before the dormant winter season.

Feed well Feed potted herbs with fertilizer every six weeks during the growing season.

Weeds, pests, and diseases

Weeds compete with plants for water, sunlight, nutrients, and space – the key to defeating them is to remove them as you see them. One of the virtues of many herbs is that the aromatic volatile oils they exude are produced primarily to ward off insects; so many of the plants in your herb garden will naturally protect themselves against pests.

Weeding by hand This is the most effective way of removing all parts of the weeds once established.

Beating weeds

Once weeds start to appear on the surface of the soil in spring, you need to remove them by hand or with the help of a hand-fork for those that have long roots. To help prevent the weeds returning, remove them before they set seed and make sure you get as much of the root out of the soil as possible, particularly with perennial weeds. Check the soil regularly for any new shoots that may be appearing and remove them immediately.

If you want to clear a large area of weeds from the soil before planting in it, try solarizing: clear a patch of soil, water it thoroughly, then cover the area with a piece of clear plastic sheeting and bury it at the edges to prevent any air getting in and out. Over the course of the next six to eight weeks, the sun will create killing heat and steam under the plastic sheet. After that time, remove the plastic and plant your herb plants immediately.

Pests

Caterpillars: Pick off by hand, wearing a glove, and dispose of them. Encourage parasitic wasps to eat them by planting flowering herbs, or spray infested plants with 500ml (16fl oz) water blended with a peeled clove of garlic (strain the liquid before use).

Slugs and snails: Set traps of shallow bowls of beer to drown them, or pick off by hand at night when they are most active. Alternatively, use non-toxic pellets or apply copper tape to containers (right) to give them a mild electric shock as they pass over it.

Aphids: Along with scale, whitefly, mealy bugs, thrips, spittle bugs, and red spider mites, aphids weaken a plant's growth. Spritz them off plants with water from a hose or use an organic, insecticidal soap.

Vine weevils: A major pest, these grubs come out at night and chew notches out of leaf margins and devour roots. They are difficult to control biologically, but you can add nematodes to the soil to kill them.

Short, sharp shock Apply copper tape just below the rim of pots or other containers to deter slugs and snails.

Avoiding diseases and bacteria

Most herbs are remarkably free of plant diseases and many can be prevented by good care and maintenance, but occasionally diseases do develop. Deal with them quickly to avoid lasting damage.

Diseases: Grow resistant varieties and apply good cultural practices and hygiene in the garden. Try not to work in the garden when it is wet as you may inadvertently spread diseases. Examine plants regularly, removing infected leaves as they fall. Dispose of any infected plant material carefully – preferably by burning it.

Bacteria: If bacteria enters a plant through a wound, spray the affected area with a simple home-made organic solution. To make the solution, purée a dozen peeled garlic cloves and then blend the garlic purée with 1.2 litres (2 pints) of water. Strain the liquid, decant it into a bottle with a spray mist nozzle attachment, and apply as necessary. If the plant does not respond within several days, clip off the infected parts and destroy them. Ensure that you sterilize your clippers or secateurs before you use them again on other plants.

Organic spray You can easily blend your own spray and use it to treat any bacterial diseases that may affect your plants.

Fungi

Although fungi is fairly rare amongst herbs, mint is prone to rust and downy and powdery mildews can develop in warm, humid, and wet conditions. Spray with an alkaline solution to prevent fungi taking hold, and use organic controls for fungal diseases.

Powdery mildew A white fungus can develop on the leaves of herbs such as this sage.

Viruses

Mosaic viruses cause white, yellow, or light green dots on leaves. Other viruses cause curled leaves, and ring spot viruses cause pale, yellowed ringed spots on leaves. They do not cause serious damage, but you can pull up affected plants and destroy them.

Curled leaves This can be a sign of a virus that has been transmitted by sucking insects or infected tools.

Foraging for herbs

Harvesting from the wild offers a free source of herbal remedies, and provides the satisfaction of collecting your own herbs. The active constituents of wild plants are often more concentrated, as they are likely to be growing in their preferred environment. A variety of plants can even be found growing on waste ground or in "wild zones" in urban areas.

Harvesting whole plants During the growing season, do not take more than half a plant to allow it to regrow.

Sustainability

Some common plants, such as nettle or plantain, may be gathered readily from the wild. However, many rarer species are under great pressure due to over-harvesting and a decline in natural habitats. In many countries it is illegal to dig up the roots of any wild plant, and certain species may be protected.

In some countries there is a strong tradition of wild harvesting or foraging. The trade in wild plants is monitored by the CITES convention developed by the IUCN (International Union for the Conservation of Nature); any endangered species are added to their "red list" and should never be gathered.

Never pick rare plants from the wild, even if they are plentiful locally. Do not deplete a stock of plants in an area; gather only enough for immediate use. Do not harvest bark in the wild – you may damage the tree.

Safety

Proper identification of wild plants is absolutely essential. Some plants that look similar to useful herbs may be poisonous; this is especially true of plants from the Umbelliferae family, which includes angelica and gotu kola and also some toxic plants such as hemlock. Always use a field guide with clear identification charts, and if you are not absolutely certain, don't risk it.

Avoid plants growing along a main road, whether in the countryside or in the city, because of the high amounts of lead and other pollutants they may contain. Similarly, avoid plants growing at the base of trees in urban areas if they are evidently favoured spots for dogs.

It is also important to check that waste ground has not been used as a dump for toxic waste; ask locally if you are in doubt. Do not collect herb plants close to factories or any other obvious potential source of pollution. Always check that there are no signs of recent weed killer use or crop spraying.

Foraging for berries Be sure to identify herbs and fruit carefully before harvesting them in the wild.

Plants in the wild Nettles are one of the plants that can be found growing in parks and on waste ground.

Where to forage

In urban areas a number of herbs known as "pioneer plants" can be found growing readily on waste ground or in wild zones, which are found in most large parks. The edges of allotments or disused railway lines can also be good places to find relatively uncontaminated plants. Avoid main roads, but if you gather young shoots in the spring and avoid the mature plant and roots, you can minimize the amount of undesired pollutants.

Most of us live in cities, and by gathering plants very close to your home you reduce the carbon footprint associated with their transportation. There is also an argument that plants tough enough to survive city conditions may be particularly appropriate and useful for city dwellers; certainly they are likely to have very concentrated levels of active constituents.

In rural areas, one of the best places to forage for herbs is the land and hedgerows around organic farms, but don't go on to a farmer's property without asking their permission first.

If you are in doubt about whether an area is suitable for foraging from a sustainability point of view, ask your local Wildlife Trust or equivalent for advice on the plants you wish to collect.

When to harvest

Herbs produce their volatile oils at night, so the best time to harvest most plants is in the early morning once the dew has evaporated. Collecting on a dry day means they will keep better and are less likely to grow mould. Pick a plant at the peak of its season and maturity to ensure it will have the highest concentration of active constituents.

Unless otherwise specified in the individual plant's page in the A–Z (pp.10–137), collect the leaves as they unfurl during the spring or early summer months; the flowers as they start to bloom; and fruits and berries just as they become ripe.

Harvest the seeds from plants such as fennel while they are still on the plant, or cut off stems with whole seedheads to dry. Smaller, dry seeds can be gathered by shaking a seedhead into a paper bag.

Most berries are ripe if they come away from the plant easily when gently tugged, or you can snip off complete trusses and separate the berries from the stems at home in your kitchen.

Harvesting seeds Leave seedheads on the plants and gently shake the plant over your hand to harvest the seeds.

Buying and storing herbs

Sometimes it may not be practical to raise fresh herb plants from seed yourself, so buy the plants from a reputable garden centre or nursery. Similarly, some herbs grow better in a different climate, or you may require them out of season, so buying fresh or dried versions of a herb is a better option than attempting to grow them yourself.

Pick a perfect plant

Do not buy plants with any obvious problems or diseases, such as leaves with yellow veins or mildew; all herbs should have bright, sturdy stems and foliage. Knock the plant out of its pot and check the roots, too – they should be healthy and plentiful and not fighting for space. Check each plant for any live insects, as you do not want to bring a potential problem home with you.

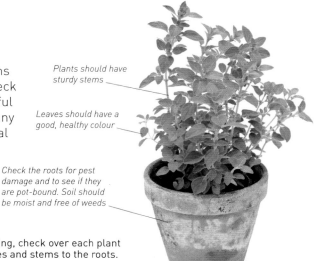

Plants should have sturdy stems

Leaves should have a good, healthy colour

Check the roots for pest damage and to see if they are pot-bound. Soil should be moist and free of weeds

Potted plants Before buying, check over each plant you choose from the leaves and stems to the roots.

Roots

Vigorous leaves and stems do not always mean that a plant is disease-free; sometimes problems lie beneath the surface of the soil. Roots are the lifeline of a plant, so it is important that they are healthy.

1 *A healthy specimen should lift easily out of its pot and its roots should be plentiful, but not overcrowded, with plenty of soil visible.*

2 *If you have a less-than-healthy plant, tease out and thin the overcrowded roots before planting it out in good soil. Remove any root weevils and grubs.*

Fresh herbs

It's worth buying fresh or cut herbs if a herb proves tricky to grow, you don't live in an ideal growing climate, the growing season for a herb is over, or you need a larger amount of a herb than you already have growing in your garden. Most supermarkets now sell a range of fresh herbs in their fresh fruit and vegetable section, or you may be able to get some herbs, such as parsley or watercress, from a farmer's market. Always buy fresh, "juicy-looking" herbs and, if possible, organically grown.

Delicate herbs such as tarragon, parsley, or mint keep well for a few days in a jug or a vase of fresh water if kept in a cool room. Many herbs, such as basil or marjoram, can be kept chilled while still on their stems, but first rinse the herbs, pat them dry with a paper towel, loosely wrap the stems in a piece of damp kitchen roll, and store in the fridge.

Most herbs keep their properties well during freezing; chop the herbs finely, coat them in a little olive oil or water, then spoon the mixture into small freezer bags or an ice-cube tray (right) and keep frozen until needed for up to six months.

Preserving fresh herbs Cover finely chopped fresh herbs with a little water or oil in an ice-cube tray and freeze.

Dried herbs

Most herbs keep their medicinal properties well if dried carefully. It also means they can be harvested at their peak time and stored to use when out of season. Traditionally, herbs are harvested in one season – for example, spring – then grown on for a full year until they are ready to harvest again. Most herbs remain effective for six to 12 months, after which time any remaining stock should be discarded and replaced.

Always dry herbs from organically grown plants only; it is not advisable to ingest concentrated pesticides or synthetic fertilizer residues in addition to the active properties of the herb.

It is essential that you buy dried herbs only from ethical companies that actively pursue a policy of minimal environmental impact by encouraging organic cultivation and ensuring sustainable harvesting by indigenous communities. Such companies will also make sure that their herbs are fresh. Suppliers should ensure that they sell the correct species and there is no infestation present.

Store your bought dried herbs in an airtight – preferably glass – container in a dry, dark cupboard to preserve their therapeutic properties.

Store dried herbs in airtight jars All dried herbs should be stored out of direct light and used within six to 12 months.

HERB BASICS

Infusions

An infusion is the best way to harness the properties of the softer, green, or flowering parts of a plant. A standard therapeutic infusion is 1 heaped tsp of a single dried herb or 2 tsp of a mixture of dried herbs (for fresh herbs use double the amount) to 175ml (6fl oz) boiling water, but see individual herb entries in the A-Z (pp.10–137) for specific dosage instructions.

INGREDIENTS

1 heaped tsp dried herb, or 2 tsp chopped fresh herb
175ml (6fl oz) boiling water

METHOD

1 Place the chopped herbs in a cup or teapot, and pour the boiling water over the herbs.
2 Leave to steep for 10 minutes, preferably covered to avoid the loss of volatile oils in the steam. Strain the infusion before use.

Decoctions

To use the woodier parts of a plant, make a decoction as directed below. A standard decoction is 1 tsp dried herb or 2 tsp fresh herb to 175ml (6fl oz) water, but see individual herb entries for specific dosage instructions. Use a steel or enamelled cast iron pan if possible, as aluminium can react with anything cooked in it and could taint the decoction. This recipe makes three cups.

INGREDIENTS

15g (½oz) dried herb or mixture of herbs, or 30g (1oz) fresh herbs
750ml (1¼ pints) cold water

METHOD

1 Place the chopped herbs in a saucepan, and pour in the water.
2 Cover the pan with a lid and bring to the boil, then simmer gently for 15–20 minutes.
3 Strain the decoction and divide into 3 doses for use that day.

Macerated oils

This is the quickest, most practical method of making a macerated or infused oil, and is known as the "heat" method. Adjust the quantities below to make a larger or smaller amount of oil; there should be enough oil to completely cover the chopped herbs in the bowl.

INGREDIENTS

100g (3½oz) dried herbs or 300g (10oz) finely chopped fresh herbs
500ml (16fl oz) vegetable oil, such as organic sunflower or olive oil

METHOD

1 Place the finely chopped herbs in a heatproof bowl, and add the oil to completely cover the herbs.
2 Place the bowl over a pan of boiling water on the hob, cover the bowl, and heat gently for 2 hours. Top up the water as needed.
3 Strain the mixture and repeat by adding fresh herbs to the oil and warming again for 1 hour.
4 Strain the oil, pour into a sterilized dark glass bottle (p.194), and label with the name and date.
5 If using fresh herbs, let the oil stand for a few hours after straining to allow water from the herbs to sink to the bottom. Pour off the oil into the sterilized bottle and discard any water. Store in a cool place and use within 3 months.

Tinctures

The medicinal properties of herbs can be extracted using a mixture of water and herbs to give a preparation called a tincture. The alcohol acts as a preservative, making this an excellent way to store herbs out of season; a tincture will keep for up to 12 months.

Volume for volume, tinctures are much stronger than infusions, decoctions, or macerates, so should be used in smaller quantities. See individual herb entries in the A–Z (pp.10–137) for specific dosage instructions. Tinctures may vary in strength (eg. 1:3 or 1:5), so always follow the dosage instructions on the bottle when buying. Dosages in the A–Z are based on a 1:5 tincture unless otherwise specified. These quantities makes an approximately 1:5 tincture.

INGREDIENTS

200g (7oz)dried herb (fresh herbs will need to be dried prior to use, in order to reduce the water content of the tincture)

1 litre (1¾ pints) 37.5% proof vodka

METHOD

1 Chop the herbs finely, and place in a large sterilized sealable jar (p.194).

2 Immerse the herbs completely in the alcohol.

3 Seal the jar and store for 2 weeks away from direct sunlight, shaking occasionally.

4 Strain the mixture through a muslin cloth and then filter through an unbleached coffee filter.

5 Pour into a sterilized dark glass bottle (p.194). Label clearly with the name and date, and store in a cool, dark place.

IMPORTANT SAFETY INFORMATION

HERB SAFETY

Herbs and herbal remedies should be treated with respect. Individual herb entries in the A–Z (pp.10–137) give cautionary notes for each herb. Follow the method, dosage, and usage instructions closely.

ESSENTIAL OIL SAFETY

Essential oils contain the active ingredients of a plant in a highly concentrated form, and should be treated with respect and always diluted in vegetable base oil before use. A typical dilution for a massage oil is 2 per cent combined essential oils to 98 per cent base oil. Essential oils must be diluted before adding to a bath, e.g. 5 drops of essential oil in 15ml (1 tbsp) of vegetable oil or milk. They should never be taken internally without professional recommendation, and children under two should not be treated with essential oils. Some essential oils, such as basil and sage, should be avoided during pregnancy; consult an aromatherapist before using any essential oils at this time.

SOAP SAFETY

Soap-making requires accurate measuring and is potentially dangerous. The soap recipes in this book are not to be attempted by children. Buy 100 per cent sodium hydroxide (caustic soda) and always wear protective plastic gloves and goggles. When you first make a soap, it is extremely alkaline because of the caustic soda and has a very high pH value that drops over several weeks as the soap dries out. Test its pH value (pH testing kits are widely available) to see if it is too alkaline to use. It will eventually drop to a pH of 10–10.5, which is normal for soap but can still be an irritant to sensitive skin.

Glossary

ADAPTOGENIC A restorative herb which helps increase the body's resistance to fatigue or stress

ALTERATIVE Normalizes or re-establishes healthy nutritive processes

ANALGESIC Relieves pain

ANAPHRODISIAC Represses sexual desire

ANODYNE Allays pain

ANTACID Helps neutralize stomach acid

ANTHELMINTIC Treats infections by parasitic worms

ANTI-ALLERGENIC Alleviates allergic reactions

ANTIBACTERIAL Kills bacteria or inhibits their growth or replication

ANTIBIOTIC With properties that can destroy or inhibit the growth of microorganisms

ANTICATARRHAL Efficacious against catarrh

ANTICOAGULANT Hinders blood clotting

ANTIDEPRESSANT Helps alleviate depression

ANTIDIARRHOEAL Helps treat diarrhoea

ANTI-EMETIC Helps reduce vomiting

ANTIFUNGAL Destroying or inhibiting the growth of fungi

ANTIHIDROTIC Reduces sweating

ANTIHISTAMINIC Counteracts the effect of histamine or inhibits its production in the body

ANTI-INFLAMMATORY Helps counteract inflammation

ANTIOXIDANT A substance that reduces the damage caused by oxidation, such as the harm caused by free radicals

ANTIPARASITIC Kills or inhibits the growth or reproduction of parasites

ANTIRHEUMATIC Relief of symptoms of rheumatism

ANTISCORBUTIC Helps prevent scurvy (a condition caused by lack of vitamin C)

ANTISPASMODIC Reduces muscle spasm and tension

ANTITHROMBOTIC Preventing or interfering with the formation of a thrombus or blood clotting

ANTITUSSIVE Helps alleviate coughing

ANTIVIRAL With properties that can destroy or inhibit the growth of viruses

ASTRINGENT Causes contraction of tissues and inhibits the flow of blood or other secretions

BITTER A digestive tonic, alterative or appetizer

BRONCHODILATOR Opens up the bronchial tubes (air passages) of the lungs

CARMINATIVE Reduces flatulence and gastric discomfort

CHOLERETIC Increases secretion of bile by the liver

CHOLAGOGUE Stimulates the flow of bile

DEMULCENT Softens and soothes inflamed surfaces

DIAPHORETIC Promotes sweating

DIURETIC Encourages flow of urine

EMMENAGOGUE Stimulates blood flow to the pelvis and uterine area, may stimulate menstruation

EMOLLIENT Softening and soothing, especially to the skin

EXPECTORANT Promotes the discharge of mucus or phlegm from the respiratory system

FEBRIFUGE Helps to reduce a fever

HAEMOSTATIC Capable of stopping haemorrhaging or bleeding

HEPATIC RESTORATIVE Supports the liver

HYPOGLYCAEMIC Lowers the concentration of glucose in the blood

HYPOLIPIDAEMIC Regulates cholesterol levels

HYPOTENSIVE Helps lower blood pressure

LAXATIVE Encourages bowel movements

NERVINE Affects the nervous system (can be either stimulating or relaxing)

NUTRITIVE Beneficially nutritious

OESTROGENIC Promote or mimic the action of female hormones

OXYTOCIC Stimulates the smooth muscle of the uterus to contract, hastening or facilitating childbirth

PERIPHERAL VASODILATOR Improves blood flow, especially to hands and feet, used to treat conditions of poor circulation

PROGESTEROGENIC Having or stimulating a progesterone-like activity

PURGATIVE Strong laxative

RELAXANT Tending to relax or to relieve tension

RUBEFACIENT Stimulates the flow of blood to the skin, causing localized reddening

SEDATIVE Soothing and calming

SOPORIFIC Inducing or tending to induce sleep

STOMACHIC Beneficial to or stimulating digestion in the stomach

STYPTIC Stops external bleeding

VASODILATOR Increases diameter of blood vessels

Index

Useful websites

Neal's Yard Remedies
www.nealsyardremedies.com

For courses in herbal medicine and aromatherapy,
email: courses@nealsyardremedies.com

National Institute of Medical Herbalists
www.nimh.org.uk

British Association for Nutritional Therapy
www.bant.org.uk

Garden Organic
www.gardenorganic.org.uk

Arne Herbs
www.arneherbs.co.uk

G Baldwin & Co
www.baldwins.co.uk

Jekka's Herb Farm
www.jekkasherbfarm.com

Poyntzfield Herb Nursery
www.poyntzfieldherbs.co.uk

Petersham Nurseries
www.petershamnurseries.com

Acknowledgments

Neal's Yard Remedies would like to thank the following for their valuable contribution to making this book happen: Julie Wood, Elly Phillips, Dr Pauline Hili and the NYR technical team past and present, and Dr Merlin Willcox.

Dorling Kindersley would like to thank the team at Neal's Yard Remedies, Peacemarsh, for the use of the organic physic garden in July and August 2010 for many of the herb photographs in this book. We would also like to thank Philip Robbshow at Sheepdrove Organic Farm for his help.

Thanks to the following for supplying plants for photography: Arne Herbs, Jekka's Herb Farm, Petersham Nurseries, Poyntzfield Herb Nursery, and South Devon Chilli Farm.

Illustrations Debbie Maizels
Art direction Luis Peral, Nicky Collings
Food styling Jane Lawrie
Prop styling Wei Tang
Proofreading Jennifer Latham
Index Hilary Bird
Recipe testing Katy Greenwood
Editorial assistance Roxanne Benson-Mackey, Kajal Mistry
Design assistance Danaya Bunnag, Emma Forge
DK Picture Library Lucy Claxton, Romaine Werblow